To Victor Shaltiel,
with my best wishes,

Margalit Bejarano
Edna Aizenberg
September, 2012

D0875425

Contemporary Sephardic Identity in the Americas

Modern Jewish History
Henry Feingold, *Series Editor*

Other titles in Modern Jewish History

The "Bergson Boys" and the Origins of Contemporary Zionist Militancy
Judith Tydor Baumel

Bundist Counterculture in Interwar Poland
Jack Jacobs

*Immigrants in Turmoil: Mass Immigration to Israel
and Its Repercussions in the 1950s and After*
Dvora Hacohen; Gila Brand, *trans.*

Jewish High Society in Old Regime Berlin
Deborah Hertz

Jews, Turks, Ottomans: A Shared History, Fifteenth Through the Twentieth Century
Avigdor Levy, *ed.*

"Silent No More": Saving the Jews of Russia, the American Jewish Effort, 1967–1989
Henry L. Feingold

Torah and Constitution: Essays in American Jewish Thought
Milton R. Konvitz

An Uneasy Relationship: American Jewish Leadership and Israel, 1948–1957
Zvi Ganin

We Are Many: Reflections on American Jewish History and Identity
Edward S. Shapiro

Contemporary Sephardic Identity in the Americas

An Interdisciplinary Approach

Edited by **Margalit Bejarano**
and **Edna Aizenberg**

Syracuse University Press

For a listing of books published and distributed by Syracuse University Press,
visit our Web site at SyracuseUniversityPress.syr.edu.

ISBN: 978-0-8156-3272-6

Library of Congress Cataloging-in-Publication Data

Contemporary Sephardic identity in the Americas : an interdisciplinary approach /
edited by Margalit Bejarano and Edna Aizenberg.
     p. cm. — (Modern Jewish history)
  Includes bibliographical references and index.
  ISBN 978-0-8156-3272-6 (cloth : alk. paper) 1. Sephardim—America.
2. Jews—America.   3. America—Ethnic relations.   I. Bejarano, Margalit.
II. Aizenberg, Edna.
  E29.J5C66 2012
  305.800973—dc23   2012010223

Manufactured in the United States of America

Contents

Part 3

Culture in Transition: Language, Literature, and Music

Tables

Contributors

Edna Aizenberg is professor emeritus of Hispanic studies at Marymount Manhattan College in New York. One of the founders of Latin American Jewish studies in the United States and a world-renowned Borges scholar, she is co-president of the Latin American Jewish Studies Association (LAJSA). She is also the author of pioneering studies on literary Sephardism in Latin America. Her numerous books include *Borges, the Aleph Weaver* (1984); *Borges el tejedor del Aleph y otros ensayos: del hebraísmo al poscolonialismo* (1997); *Borges and His Successors: The Borgesian Impact on Literature and the Arts* (1990); *Parricide on the Pampa? A New Study and Translation of Alberto Gerchunoff's "Los gauchos judíos"* (2000); and *Books and Bombs in Buenos Aires: Borges, Gerchunoff, and Argentine Jewish Writers* (2002).

Monique R. Balbuena is associate professor of literature in the Honors College at the University of Oregon. From 2006 to 2011 she served as the secretary of the Latin American Jewish Studies Association (LAJSA). She was a Starr Fellow at the Center for Jewish Studies at Harvard University and a Frankel Fellow at the Frankel Institute for Advanced Judaic Studies at the University of Michigan. Balbuena sits on the editorial boards of the *Journal for Jewish Identities*, the *Journal for the Study of Sephardic and Mizrahi Jewry*, the *Levantine Review*, and the *Encyclopedia of Jews in the Islamic World*, which she joined as the modern literature editor. Balbuena is also the author of *Poe e Rosa à luz da Cabala* (1994) and *Homeless Tongues: Poetry and Languages of the Sephardic Diaspora* (2012).

Margalit Bejarano teaches history in the Department of Romance and Latin American Studies at Hebrew University and is the academic director of the Divisions of Latin America, Spain, and Portugal and the former director of the

Oral History Division of the Avraham Harman Institute of Contemporary Jewry, and a Fellow of the Liwerant Center, Hebrew University of Jerusalem. Her major fields of research are Sephardic communities in Latin America and the history of the Jews in Cuba and of the Cuban and Latin American Jews in Miami. Her publications include *La comunidad hebrea de Cuba: la memoria y la historia* and *La historia del buque San Luis: La perspectiva cubana*.

Susana Brauner teaches twentieth-century world history and Latin American history in the Universidad Argentina de la Empresa (UADE) and is researcher and teacher of the MA Diversity Culture Studies in the Universidad Nacional Tres de Febrero (UNTRF). Her numerous publications on Syrian Jews and their descendants in Argentina include *Los judíos de Alepo en Argentina* and *Orto-doxia religiosa and pragmatismo político: los judíos de orígen sirio*.

Judith R. Cohen teaches ethnomusicology and medieval music at York University, Toronto, and is the general editor of the Alan Lomax Spanish Recordings and the first recipient of the Alan Lomax Fellowship in Folklife Studies at the Library of Congress's Kluge Center. She is author of many articles on Sephardic music and on Crypto-Jewish traditions in Portugal and is also a singer, with several CDs of traditional Sephardic and related music.

Jane Gerber is professor of history and director of the Institute for Sephardic Studies at the Graduate Center of the City University of New York. Her many publications include *Sephardic Studies in the University* (1995), *The Jews of Spain* (National Jewish Book Award in Sephardic Studies, 1993), *Jewish Society in Fez 1450–1700* (1980), *The Jews in the Caribbean* (2013) and the forthcoming *Cities of Splendor in the Shaping of Sephardic Jewry*. Gerber was formerly the president of the Association for Jewish Studies and co-chair of the Academic Advisory Council of the Center for Jewish History in New York. She heads the advisory board of the American Sephardi Federation.

Henry A. Green is the former director of Judaic and Sephardic studies at the University of Miami, Florida. He has served as a visiting fellow at Oxford University, the Hebrew University of Jerusalem, and the University of Toronto and has published extensively on Israel and American Jewry. Currently, he is professor of religious studies at the University of Miami and director of Sephardic Voices, an international effort dedicated to collecting testimonies of Jewish refugees from Arab and Islamic lands.

Yael Halevi-Wise is an associate professor of English and Jewish studies at McGill University in Montreal. She is the author of *Interactive Fictions: Scenes of Storytelling in the Novel* (2003) and editor of *Sephardism: Spanish Jewish History in the Modern Literary Imagination* (2011), which showcases representations of Sephardic history in different cultures. As an Israeli who grew up in Mexico and studied comparative literature in the United States, Halevi-Wise's work draws upon each of these environments to illuminate how they contribute to the development of the novel as a modern genre.

Liz Hamui Halabe is professor-researcher at the Faculty of Medicine in the UNAM. Her studies are related to the sociology of religions, with particular emphasis on Mexican Jewry and social medicine. Most of her works focus on the qualitative perspective. She is the author of numerous books and articles on the Aleppan community and on the religious transformation of Mexican Jews.

Mollie Lewis Nouwen is assistant professor of history at the University of South Alabama. Her book manuscript, "Oy, My Buenos Aires: Jewish Immigrants and the Creation of Argentine National Identity, 1905–1930," deals with the role of Ashkenazi Jews in ethnic and national identity creation during the mass-migration era in Buenos Aires.

Raanan Rein is professor of Latin American and Spanish history at Tel Aviv University. He is the editor of the journal *Estudios Interdisciplinarios de América Latina y el Caribe*. Rein's many publications include *The Franco-Perón Alliance: Relations Between Spain and Argentina 1946–1955* (1993), *Argentina, Israel, and the Jews: Perón, the Eichmann Capture, and After* (2003), *Rethinking Jewish Latin Americans* (co-edited with Jeffrey Lesser) (2008), and most recently *Argentine Jews or Jewish Argentines? Essays on Ethnicity, Identity, and Diaspora* (2010). Rein is co-president, together with Edna Aizenberg, of LAJSA.

Introduction

A Mosaic of Diverse Identities

MARGALIT BEJARANO *and* EDNA AIZENBERG

The Sephardic population in the Americas is formed by a large number of small groups, divided according to communities of origin in the Iberian Peninsula, the Middle East, and North Africa, and dispersed among English-, Spanish-, Portuguese-, and French-speaking societies. From a local perspective, the presence of the Sephardim in each Jewish community is overshadowed by that of the dominant groups of Ashkenazim from Eastern Europe, creating the Sephardic image as "a minority within a minority." Seen from a global perspective, however, we may view the Sephardic diaspora as a mosaic of identities that together form the largest concentration of Sephardim outside the State of Israel (DellaPergola 2002).[1] The collection of articles in this volume offers a comparative dimension for the study of each Sephardic piece as part of a transnational diaspora.

The idea for the book emerged in a colloquium held at the Hebrew University in July 2005 that analyzed the situation of Sephardic studies in the Americas and presented an agenda for future research. The colloquium was organized by the Division of Latin America, Spain, and Portugal of the Avraham Harman Institute of Contemporary Jewry. It demonstrated the imbalance that exists

---

1. The Sephardic dispersion is divided among North America (with 546,000), the European Union (with 411,000), and Latin America (with 105,000). DellaPergola's figures for Latin America are considerably lower than the 180,000 suggested by FESELA (the Sephardic Federation of Latin America).

in the field of Sephardic studies: there is an abundance of works focusing on Spain in the Middle Ages, Crypto-Jews in Latin America, Jews in the English-speaking colonies, and Jews under Ottoman rule, as compared with the paucity of publications on the Sephardic experience in the American continent—North and South—during the last one hundred years. Studies on Latin American Sephardim are generally limited to monographs on a specific community; they are often written in Spanish or Portuguese and are not accessible to the English-reading public.

An attempt to break the regional boundaries of Jewish history was made by Haim Avni in a comprehensive study that analyzes the Jewish presence in the Americas from the discovery of the New World until 1950 in a comparative context of countries speaking English, Spanish, and Portuguese (1992, 148–49). Following a similar comparative approach, the present collection focuses on the Sephardic communities that have been founded in Latin America, the United States, and Canada during the last one hundred years.

The Young Turks revolution in 1908 marks the beginning of a large wave of emigration from the Ottoman Empire to the American continent. The decree of compulsory military service for non-Muslim minorities (who until 1909 were able to redeem themselves from conscription) was the main cause of migration of the young men who became the pioneers who founded most of the present-day communities.

Recent studies on Arabs and Jews in Latin America show similar patterns of immigration and economic integration between Sephardic Jews from Muslim countries and Syrian-Lebanese immigrants (Klich and Lesser 1998; Kabchi 1997; Klich 2006; Rein 2008). Arabs and Jews spoke Arabic and shared the tastes of food and music; they had similar customs and traditions, as well as social norms.

Immigrants from the Middle East tended to settle in urban centers, and the majority started their trajectory as peddlers, moving gradually into commerce. A few returned to their homelands in search of brides or to retire as rich men; their success motivated chains of migration from their villages or hometowns to specific destinations in the New World. The young men who escaped conscription and tried to improve their miserable economic situations became the pioneers of many of the present-day Sephardic communities in the Americas.

⚿

The use of the term "Sephardim" as a comprehensive definition to all the groups that are not Ashkenazim is subject to scholarly debates. In an essay on the historical roots of the Kol Shearith Israel Congregation in Panama, which was founded by Caribbean Jews of Portuguese descent, Ralph de Lima Valencia argues that the term Sephardim is limited to the descendants of the Jews expelled from Spain and Portugal who maintained the Hispanic tradition. He argues that "it is erroneous to catalogue as Sephardim the Jews that lived in Persia and other Jewish communities in the Middle East . . . who had not had any historic ties with the Iberian Peninsula, but remained in the Near East for long centuries" (Congregation Kol Shearith Israel 1977, 3–4).[2]

Nissim Elnecavé, in his encyclopedic work *Los hijos de Ibero-Franconia* (The children of Ibero-Franconia), presents an opposite approach, according to which all the Jewish communities that do not stem from an Ashkenazic origin are part of the Sephardic world. Emphasizing the common Sephardic background of all the Jewish communities in the Mediterranean Basin, which he defines as a *mare nostrum sephardicum*, he includes among them communities in countries that had no direct contact with the Jews from the Iberian Peninsula, such as Yemen, Iran, and India (1981, 22–23).

Joseph Papo, in his study on Sephardim in the United States, summarizes the divergence between the "purists," who hold an exclusive definition of the term Sephardic as bearing Iberian elements, and the supporters of an inclusive definition, who point out that the Ladino-speaking "quintessential Sephardim . . . frequently succeeded in transmitting significant elements of their cultural heritage to their Jewish neighbors" (1987, 3–4).

In a more recent study Itzhak Bezalel traces the transitions in Jewish historiography in an attempt to categorize the Jewish ethnic groups. He concludes that there are no accepted definitions and that the terms "Sephardic" and "Mizrahi" remain ambiguous (2007). In a symposium that took place in 2008 at the Ben Zvi Institute in Jerusalem entitled "How to Write the History of the Sephardim,"

---

2. This is a bilingual publication, with Spanish and English in opposite columns.

Shmuel Trigano argued that the Jewish people are divided into two branches—
Ashkenazim and Sephardim—according to the different *Halachic* authority (religious law) on which they rest (2006, 1:16).[3] Alisa Meyuhas Gionio disagreed with
this view, claiming that the term Sephardim refers exclusively to the descendants
of Spanish Jewry, and the unique criterion for categorization is of a linguistic
nature (2007).

While conscious of the problematic use of the term Sephardic, the editors of
this volume tend to accept the view presented by Papo, who, regardless of existing
divergences, decided to consider "as Sephardim all those Jews whose religious
rituals, liturgy and Hebrew pronunciation bear the imprint of a common non-
Ashkenazi tradition, and who consider themselves to be part of the Sephardi
world" (1987, 4). We thus use the term Sephardim as a comprehensive definition to all the non-Ashkenazi communities: the Sephardic and Portuguese Jews
who settled in America during the colonial era, the descendants of Iberian Jews
who preserved the Judeo-Spanish language and identity, as well as the Arabic-
speaking Jews from the Middle East and North Africa.

Emigration of Jews from the Ottoman Empire toward the Americas was an integral part of the general waves of emigration from the Middle East that were
caused by the socioeconomic deterioration in the mother communities and the
new opportunities in America. While the United States, and in particular New
York City, was the major destination of the immigrants, small groups arrived in
the remotest corners of Latin America.

The first part of the book traces the broad outlines of community and culture. It follows the Sephardim's paths of immigration to the Americas, their settlement, and the development of an old-new Sephardic culture. The opening
chapter by Margalit Bejarano points out the correlations between the decline of
the Jewish communities during the disintegration of the Ottoman Empire and
the emergence of the Sephardic communities in the New World, analyzing the

---

3. The symposium was organized in honor of the publication of Shmuel Trigano's three volumes: *Le monde sépharade*. The religious laws of the Sephardim are based on Rabbi Yosef Caro,
while the Ashkenazim rely upon Rabbi Moshe Isserles.

South Florida. Raanan Rein and Mollie Lewis's chapter deals with the Zionist identity of the Sephardim and their relations with the Ashkenazim. The essay analyzes the publication *Israel*, the first newspaper in Spanish published by Moroccan Sephardim in Argentina, as a reflection of different and complementary identities. The authors question the link between the Zionism of the Sephardim in Argentina and the imagined motherland of Jewish Palestine, suggesting that Zionism gave Jewish Argentines a mother country, in the same sense that Italy served as the *madre patria* of the Italian immigrants, providing a historical narrative and a complementary identity of being Argentines and Jews. *Israel* was addressed to a Spanish-speaking audience, becoming a bridge between Sephardim and Ashkenazim.

Susana Brauner focuses on Syrian Jews, who are considered as the main Sephardic group that resisted assimilation. She analyzes the religious transitions during the second half of the twentieth century among the Aleppan and Damascene communities in Buenos Aires.

Economic progress in the 1940s brought about the emergence of a young secular leadership that opened the Syrian communities to the influence of the surrounding society. From the mid-1950s, however, the Aleppan community experienced a religious revival, influenced by a charismatic rabbi brought over from the mother community. The religious revival relied on the economic power of the credit cooperatives in the Syrian sector that supported religious, economic, and cultural institutions. It was also manifested in the emergence of radical groups, often under the influence of Ashkenazic rabbis, who joined ultra-Orthodox organizations and strengthened the movement of *teshuvah* (return to religion).

The new religious leadership that emerged in the 1970s was influenced by ultra-Orthodox rabbis from Israel and the United States, as well as by the movement of *Chabad*. Brauner presents the acceptance of the ultra-Orthodox rabbis by economic elites of Syrian Jewry as the legitimate heirs of Jewish culture and the only ones able to prevent assimilation, succeeding in imposing institutional religious standards through subsidies and entering the communal political game, together with Ashkenazic religious circles.

Continuing the discussion on religion, Liz Hamui Halabe analyzes the religious transitions among Mexican Sephardim who affiliate with three different communities: Monte Sinai, which belongs to the Jews from Damascus and Lebanon; the Unión Sefaradí; which unites Jews from Turkey, Greece and the Balkans; and Maguén David, the organization of the Jews from Aleppo.

Facing globalization change and economic turbulence, each group adopted varying strategies. The Aleppans started to configure new forms of identity and a sociocultural space in order to protect their children from external influences that might lead to assimilation. The Damascene community was less rigid in its religious observance and more open to Zionist influence. The Sephardic Union was more culturally oriented. The rabbis of this sector respected the secular and modern lifestyle of most of the members. They also held strong pro-Zionist positions and were concerned about events in Israel.

According to Hamui Halabe, the period between 1970 and 2002 was marked by growing confrontations between sectors aiming to open the community and the ultra-Orthodox who wanted to close the community in order to "preserve Judaism." The ultra-Orthodox groups are anti-Zionist, and their relationship with Israel is aimed primarily at the Sephardic religious sector, without considering the rest of Israeli society.

Henry A. Green analyzes the demographic profile of the Sephardic population in Miami, providing updated statistics on communities that are in constant transition. Although many of the Sephardim were born in Muslim countries, their settlement in South Florida is a second or third migration, and they adopted the language of their previous country of residence—Spanish, French, Hebrew or English—reflecting the complex encounter of different transnational Sephardic groups in the context of the growing predominance of the Hispanic population around Miami. The result is an ever-shifting blend of Hispanism, Sephardism, and Judaism.

One case of such dynamism is presented by Margalit Bejarano, who details the four identities of the Cuban Sephardim in Miami—as Jews, Sephardim, Cubans, and Americans. The collective identity of this group combines memories from the Sepharad that shaped their language and culture; from the Turkey that consolidated their social patterns, and from the Cuba whose language and way of life they adopted. Sitting at the crossroad between north and south, this small community was transformed into a bridge between Hispanics and Anglos, Ladino-speaking Sephardim and Jews from Latin America.

⚓

The third part of the book addresses the questions of culture in transition: language, literature, and music. How do the old and the new interact? Can frameworks other than "nostalgia" be fruitful for the study of contemporary Sephardic cultural production? How is Sephardic-marked creativity inserted within the landscape of the broader Latin American cultural landscape?

Monique R. Balbuena develops the issue of today's Sephardic creativity in Latin America, delving into the renewed interest in Ladino, or Judeo-Spanish. The essay analyzes this interest and situates it within a trend in the world at large. Balbuena studies how recent treatments of multiculturalism have prompted an inner look at intra-Jewish difference and an acceptance and even an enthusiastic claim of Sephardic heritage and Jewish multilingualism. While there is a tendency to limit Ladino poetry to folklore and medieval traditions, she highlights the modern appropriations of Ladino in pop culture and in verse that establish formal and intertextual connections to modern/ist lyric poetry, seeking to take the authors out of a context of Sephardic nostalgia and to place them in a theoretical discussion on minor literatures and issues of nationalism.

Among other creators, Argentine poet Beatriz Mazliah takes part in a contemporary resurgence of Ladino poetic creation. Singer Fortuna, from Brazil, has catapulted this endangered language to the realm of Brazilian pop culture in her recordings. Brazilian novelist Moacyr Scliar incorporates Ladino as a mark of a dormant memory. Argentine Juan Gelman uses it to detach himself from a national identity and reaffirm his diasporic positioning. And Mexican writer Rosa Nissán includes long sections in Ladino in her novel in Spanish, *Novia que te vea*, which interrogates Jewish Sephardic identity in Mexico.

Nissán's novel receives special attention in the essay by Yael Halevi-Wise. Situating Rosa Nissán's autobiographical novels in the context of contemporary Mexican literature, her chapter emphasizes Nissán's singular insertion of Ladino expressions within the modern Spanish of her texts. Nissán's use of Ladino is more than a quaint spice that generated a great popular appeal for her novels.

Within each text, Ladino ostensibly distinguishes the generation of the parents (particularly the mother), who immigrated to Mexico from Asia, from a new brand of Sephardic Jews born in Mexico. But the overall effect of Nissán's Ladino is to create a vital historical link that unites contemporary Mexicans (who speak a modern Spanish) with those Jews who were expelled from Spain five hundred years ago (and kept alive a medieval Spanish dialect) and that now blends into mainstream modern Hispanic society in the Americas. Nissán continues the dialectic of participation/enclosure that marks Mexican Sephardic life, injecting a woman's perspective into the blend.

The final chapter travels up north—as far north as this book will go—and takes up the important musical heritage of the Sephardim. Judith Cohen presents a short historical survey of Sephardim in Canada, but she focuses on the French-speaking Moroccan Jews concentrated in Quebec, mostly in Montreal. This Sephardic community occupies a unique position: it is a French, Judeo-Spanish, and Arabic-speaking Jewish group within primarily francophone and at least nominally Catholic Quebec, and, at the same time, it has had to fit into a predominantly English and Yiddish-speaking, long-established Ashkenazic community. Sephardim were perceived as Jews by the French majority but were not accepted by the English-speaking Jews.

The essay examines the material culture of music and its social organization. It analyzes the repertoire of liturgical music based on the cultural tradition brought over from Morocco, as well as the music performed by different groups and in different organizations, such as the ensemble Gerineldo or the activities of the Senior Citizens' clubs. Using personal interviews and recordings of informants from Morocco and from the former Ottoman Empire, Cohen presents some key singers and explains the role of specific genres, such as wedding songs, romances, *coplas*, and life-cycle songs. She concludes with a comparison of the music of Moroccan and Mediterranean Jews and the impact of their new surroundings on their music.

Taken together, the essays in this book form an account of an impressive, dynamic, multicultural, and multilingual Sephardic presence in the Americas. The emigration from the Ottoman Empire that started one hundred years ago resulted in the atomization of the Sephardic communities, as they became divided among countries of origin and dispersed in remote places. But their dynamism allowed them to adapt and survive, striving to retain the old, yet gesturing continually to the new. On the threshold of the twenty-first century these communities became subject to transnational migrations and globalization that call for a new definition of the boundaries between the different Sephardic groups and new interpretations of their culture. Their contribution to the texture of contemporary Jewish life deserves to be better known and better studied.

Part 1   Sephardim in the Americas

Community and Culture

1

The Sephardic Communities of Latin America

A Puzzle of Subethnic Fragments

MARGALIT BEJARANO

The disintegration of the Ottoman Empire was followed by the reemergence of small enclaves of the old Sephardic world in different corners of Latin America. Emigrants from the Middle East and the Balkan countries, fleeing misery, war, and political transitions, were able to transplant to the remote corners of the continent their traditional way of life and to reconstruct ethnically based communal frameworks. The entities that they created were shaped by the social structure in the countries of provenance more than by the legal requirements of the host societies.

Coming from a Muslim world, in which the status of the ethno-religious minorities was defined by law, the Sephardic immigrants had to adapt themselves to the secular Catholic environment of the Latin American republics, where religious organization was on a voluntary basis, owing to the separation between church and state.

Daniel Elazar points out the affinity between the Muslim environment of the Middle East and the pre-modern Iberian societies of Latin America as a factor that determined the course of immigration (Elazar and Medding 1983, 9; see also Mörner and Sims 1977, 73). Ladino-speaking Jews had the advantage of using a similar language to that of the host societies with whom they shared common cultural roots. Their arrival in Ibero-America was a symbolic reencounter between the descendants of the Jews that preserved the nostalgic memory of

3

Sepharad as the essence of their identity and the new nations that were formed as a consequence of the discovery and conquest of America.

In their countries of origin, in the Middle East and North Africa, the Sephardim constituted the dominant Jewish element. In Latin America they were exposed to the predominance of the Ashkenazim and to an encounter with other Sephardic groups. They were compelled to redefine the boundaries that separated them not only from the ethnic groups that constituted the majority societies, but also from other Jewish groups—Yiddish-speaking Ashkenazim, as well as Sephardim coming from different communities of origin. In a circular letter distributed in 1917 among Ladino-speaking Jews in Buenos Aires, the board of the Society Chesed Shel Emet complained about not being able to purchase a cemetery because of "the lack of union among the Sephardic Jews, because not all of us come from the same country, and even when we come from the same country, because we don't come from the same town or village, and even between those you may find antagonisms."[1]

Immigration to Latin America was a process of atomization and dispersion: The Sephardim were scattered throughout the continent and divided into small nuclei that identified with their communities of origin. The history of each individual community was shaped by the confrontation between its cultural and social heritage and the conditions in the respective country. The objective of this chapter is to reconstruct the history of these communities both horizontally (according to their geographical divisions) and vertically (according to their communal origin), combining the fragments of a metaphorical jigsaw puzzle.

Early Sephardic Settlement

The Jews from the Middle East and North Africa were not the first Sephardim who reached Latin America. They were preceded by converted Jews who immigrated to Hispanic America and Brazil and returned clandestinely to the religion of their ancestors, as well as by members of the Spanish Portuguese Jewish nation who settled in the Protestant colonies. Although most of them were gradually

---

1. Minutes Sociedad *Israelita Sefaradi Hesed Chel Emet*, hm2/1422A, Central Archives of the Jewish People, Jerusalem.

assimilated, they left the imprint of the Sephardic presence among the first settlers on the historical memory of the Latin American and Caribbean nations.

Crypto-Jews in Ibero America

The legal status of the Jews in the colonies of Spain and Portugal was identical
to that in the mother countries. Following expulsion or forced conversion (from
Spain in 1492 and from Portugal in 1497), the presence of Jews was absolutely
forbidden and persons found to be secretly practicing Judaism were treated as
Catholic heretics and handed over to the Inquisition. The converted Jews and
their descendants were marked as *conversos* or New Christians and remained a
socially separate group, subject to legal discrimination that included restrictions
on their admission into the colonies of the New World.

Nevertheless, a large number of New Christians, especially from Portugal,
found their way to Hispanic America and Brazil. Many of them returned secretly
to Judaism, risking their lives as heretics who were liable to be burned at the stake.
The Crypto-Jews were not able to leave written documents, and their history,
studied amply by various scholars, rests mainly on the records of the Inquisition.[2]

The Inquisition was active in Hispanic America since its discovery in 1492,
and throughout the colonial period, which lasted until the 1820s.[3] Clergymen
encouraged believers to spy on persons suspected as Judaizers and to hand them
over to the Inquisition. The first Holy Office in the Americas was erected in
Mexico City in 1570, the second in Lima (Peru) in 1571, and the third in Carta-
gena (Colombia) in 1607. In Brazil visiting messengers of the Inquisition sent
their victims for trial in Lisbon.

The Crypto-Jews were integrated into the colonial societies, achieving
wealth and status similar to other Spaniards or Portuguese. Disconnected from
the Jewish world they developed their own version of the Jewish religion that was
influenced by the Catholic environment. Periodical campaigns by the Inquisition

2. See, for example, the comprehensive studies of Martin Cohen (1971) and Avni (1992). For
bibliographical data consult Sable (1978) and Elkin and Sater (1990).

3. Independence was gained in most Spanish colonies between 1810 and 1820, apart from
Cuba and Puerto Rico, who remained under Spanish rule until 1898. Brazil was a Portuguese
colony from its discovery in 1500 until its independence in 1822.

and lay authorities uncovered the secret identities of the Judaizers, especially during the union between the crowns of Spain and Portugal (1580–1640) and in eighteenth-century Brazil.

Religious persecutions decimated the fragile nuclei of Crypto-Jews, but their assimilation was also caused by the abrogation of the discriminatory laws that distinguished between Old and New Christians (Martin Cohen 1971, ix). The remnants of the Crypto-Jews gradually disappeared, but several aristocratic families preserved the tradition of their Sephardic ancestry well into the twentieth century.

The Jewish Community in Dutch Brazil

The Dutch conquered Pernambuco in Northeastern Brazil and established a prosperous colony that existed between 1630 and 1654—when they were defeated by Portugal. This historical episode, which had a profound impact on the history of the plantation economy in the Caribbean (Goslinga 1971), played an important role in the history of the Jews in America. Sephardim from Amsterdam settled in Recife (capital of Pernambuco) and founded the first Jewish community in the Western hemisphere, shielded by the religious tolerance of the Dutch authorities.

The Jews from Amsterdam who found their way to Dutch Brazil, and later to the colonies in the Caribbean, were part of the "Spanish-Portuguese Jewish Nation" (*La Nación*). They were descendants of the Jews who remained in the Iberian Peninsula and shared its culture and values. All members of "The Nation" belonged to the same ethnic group, but their religious identification varied with their countries of residence (Arbell 2002, 10). Their immigration to Western Europe facilitated their economic integration in the mercantilistic system of the emerging colonial powers, and at the same time confronted them with the traditional Jewish world. Their early modernization was combined with a Jewish revival, which turned them—in the words of historian Yosef Kaplan— "From New Christians to New Jews" (2003).

The "New Jews" who reached Brazil were active in the sugar plantations and in colonial commerce. They founded two Jewish communities, Zur Israel and Magen Avraham, which were structured according to the model of the mother community in Amsterdam, and their presence encouraged New Christians who lived as Catholics in Brazil to join the Jewish community.[4]

When the Dutch capitulated to the Portuguese forces, the Jews were compelled to leave the colony. Some of them returned to Holland, while others dispersed in the Dutch, English, and French colonies in the Caribbean. A small group of refugees from Brazil found its way to New Amsterdam, becoming the founders of the Jewish community in the United States.

Jewish Communities in the Colonies of the Caribbean

During the second half of the seventeenth century, Spanish-Portuguese Jews settled in the new colonies that were founded along the Wild Coast (the Guianas) and in the Caribbean Islands. They came from Dutch Brazil, as well as from Amsterdam, London, Bordeaux, and Hamburg. They engaged in the plantation economy, producing sugar, cocoa, vanilla, and other staples, and took an active part in commerce, shipping, maritime insurance, and public services.

In the Protestant colonies of Holland, England, and Denmark the Jews were free to practice their own religion. Jews were officially expelled from the French Catholic colonies in 1685, but their presence was generally tolerated by the local authorities (Loker 1991, 33–42). They founded well-organized communities that preserved the Portuguese language and their customs and traditions, including synagogues with sand-covered floors.

The history of the Jews in the Caribbean has been studied by various scholars (Arbell 2002; Loker 1991; R. Cohen 1982; Emmanuel and Emmanuel 1970; see also Arbell 1999) and, the history before the independence of the Latin American republics is beyond the scope of this study. It presents, however, similar patterns of fragmentation and dispersion that are relevant to the understanding of the twentieth-century Sephardic communities in Latin America.

The Spanish-Portuguese Jews in the Caribbean maintained ethnic and family ties as the basis of economic and social networks and preserved with zeal their unique traditions. To overcome their small numbers and constant mobility

---

4. For the history of the Jews in Dutch Brazil, see Wiznitzer (1960).

between the islands, they developed chains of communications for the preservation of endogamic marriages, social assistance, and religious services.

Curaçao, the "Mother of the Jewish Communities in the New World," was a source of inspiration and assistance to other Sephardic communities in the Western hemisphere. With its economic decline, early in the nineteenth century, several Curaçaoan Jews immigrated to the independent Latin American republics in the Circum-Caribbean.

Sephardic Immigration to Latin America after Independence

The first Jewish communities were established along the coasts of Venezuela and Colombia by Sephardic Jews from Curaçao. These Jews favored the rebellion against Spain, and some of them assisted its leader, Simon Bolívar, who became the president of Greater Colombia (1819–1830), which later broke into three states—Venezuela, Colombia, and Ecuador. The new government abolished the Tribunal of the Inquisition in 1821, and in 1829 it granted religious freedom to immigrants (Arbell 2002, 159–61, 300–302; Mirelman 1992, 235–36).

One of the oldest Sephardic communities was established in the port town of Coro, Venezuela, sixty miles distant from Curaçao. The Jews prospered economically and filled an important role in the commercial development of Coro, a few of them achieving prominence in politics or in letters. Religious life, however, was quite limited, with no spiritual leadership. A Jewish cemetery was erected in 1830, but the gravestones did not include Hebrew inscriptions, evidence of the quick assimilation of the Curaçaoan Jews in Coro.[5] According to Lily Blank: "the confluence of religious isolation, the lack of rabbinical authorities and the high rate of intermarriage hastened the assimilation and ultimately the disappearance of this small Jewish community" (1993, 211–13).

Similar small communities were established in other port towns, such as Barcelona (Venezuela) Baranquilla (Colombia), and Panama. The Sephardic Jews from the Caribbean were integrated into the upper classes, serving in the

---

5. The cemetery in Coro was declared a National Monument in 1970 by the minister of public works, Joseph Curiel, grandson of the founder of the cemetery, Joseph Curiel (see Arbell 2002, 302–6).

highest political posts. Their success, however, resulted in what Mordechai Arbell calls "Comfortable Disappearance" (1998). Social acceptance and intermarriage caused their religious assimilation, but at the same time they continued to identify themselves with their ethnic group—considering themselves descendants of the Jewish Nation.

The only Spanish-Portuguese community that is still active today is Kol Shearith Israel in Panama, which was founded in 1876 by Sephardim from Curaçao, St. Thomas, and other Caribbean islands (Congregation Kol Shearith Israel 1977). The economic development that followed the construction of the Panama Canal attracted immigration. On the eve of World War I and during the 1920s new waves of Sephardic Jews from the Middle East, the Balkan countries, and North Africa settled in Panama, creating their separate communal organizations in 1933 (Dayán de Mizrachi and Arjona 1986, 21–22). The members of Kol Shearith Israel, well integrated among the local bourgeoisie, felt socially distant from their poor brethren. For religious purposes they preferred to adopt Reform Judaism, which seemed more adequate to their social milieu. At the same time they continued to preserve their Sephardic identity, stressing their Hispanic tradition and distinguishing themselves from the new arrivals (3–4).

In the long run, however, the presence of larger traditional Jewish groups strengthened the trends of survival of the Spanish-Portuguese, offering communal services, Jewish spouses, and a multiethnic community that sheltered their separate identity.

Emigration from Muslim Countries

Emigration from Muslim countries coincided with the period of mass migration to Latin America. The major country of immigration was Argentina, with a vast unpopulated territory and an economy based on cattle ranches. In the 1870s Argentina started to grow wheat and became an exporter of cereals to the European market. In order to meet the growing demand for a labor force, the landowning oligarchy encouraged immigration, particularly of agricultural workers, with a policy that was formulated in the slogan "To govern is to populate." Of the eleven million immigrants who entered Latin America between 1851 and 1924, 46 percent went to Argentina, 33 percent to Brazil, 14 percent to Cuba, 4 percent to Uruguay, and 3 percent to Mexico (Mörner and Sims 1977, 40–41). Although the majority of the immigrants came from Italy, Spain, and Portugal, the Jews formed part of two non-Latin minorities, coming from Eastern Europe and from Muslim countries; the former were Ashkenazim and the latter Sephardim.

From Morocco to Brazil

The Jewish migration from Muslim countries to Latin America started in the 1820s with a thin stream that flowed from Morocco to Brazil and, since the end of the nineteenth century, also to Argentina and Venezuela. These countries continued to be the three major destinations of Jews from the Maghreb until after the independence of Morocco (in 1956). Immigrants to Latin America came generally from "Spanish Morocco"—a small area in the northwestern coast of Morocco that between 1912 and 1956 was under Spanish protection.

Dom Pedro, the son of the King of Portugal, declared the independence of Brazil in 1822 and placed himself as its emperor. The official religion of the empire continued to be Roman Catholic, but the constitution granted other faiths the permission to worship in private. This limited religious tolerance opened the door for the legal admission of Jews. Two small congregations were established in Belém (capital of the state Pará), in northeastern Brazil: Eshel Abraham in 1826 and Shaar Hashamaim in 1828 (Avni 1992, 102–3).

The communities of origin of the Moroccan immigrants to Latin America were Tetuan, Tangier, and a few other towns in the northwestern coast of Morocco that were open to European influence and to foreign trade. The geographical proximity of Spain and Portugal strengthened the Iberian influence in this region and had an impact on the preservation of the Sephardic traditions and language in their purest form.[6] The early immigrants of the 1820s were individual young men who were attracted to the countries of Latin America soon after their independence in search of better economic opportunities. They landed in Belém, which was the closest port across the Atlantic, being unaware of the difference between Brazil and Hispanic America (S. Katz 1992).

---

6. The Haketia language (a mixture of Spanish, Hebrew, and Arabic) of the Jews of Tetuan and Tangier was influenced by modern Spanish, especially since the war between Spain and Morocco in 1859–60.

The study of Samy Katz (1992) shows that the average age of the immigrants from Morocco was twenty-five years, and that 75 percent of them came from Tangier and Tetuan. Immigration was enhanced by the economic opportunities in Brazil as well as by the deteriorating conditions of the Jewish population, especially during the Spanish-Moroccan war (1859–60) and following the return of the Muslim rule after two years of relative prosperity, under the auspices of the Spanish occupation of Tetuan.

Belém was situated at the outfall of the Amazon River, on the Atlantic coast. With the discovery of the elastic qualities of the rubber trees that grew only along the Amazon River, the two states of Pará and Amazonas were transformed from peripheral regions to centers of rapid development. The growth of the rubber industry started in the 1840s and reached its peak during the rubber boom of the 1870s. Jewish peddlers penetrated into the jungles selling goods to the laborers and gradually established business firms and communal organizations in Manáus and other cities, reaching as far as Iquitos in Peru.

According to Victor Mirelman, "Many of these merchants succeeded economically. Some went back to their home cities in Morocco to marry and then returned to Brazil, but others intermarried and slowly lost their Jewish identity" (1992, 242). In his study on Iquitos—the most distant location reached by the Moroccan Jews along the Amazon River—Ariel Segal shows that Jewish identity did not disappear after marriage with Indian Catholics but, similar to that of the descendants of *conversos*, was transformed to a new identity that absorbed local cultural traits (1999).

With the crisis of the rubber industry, the Moroccan Jews turned to the large cities—Rio de Janeiro and São Paulo. In the 1880s Brazil consolidated its immigration policy, which aimed to populate its vast area and to supply laborers to the coffee industry because of the shortage of labor that followed the abolition of slavery.[7] The constitution of the Brazilian Republic (1891) granted religious freedom and civil equality to all inhabitants, and a large number of Moroccan Jews obtained Brazilian citizenship (Avni 1992, 105–6).

Several Moroccan Jews reemigrated from Brazil to Argentina, settling in Buenos Aires or in the different provincial towns. Their socioeconomic adjustment was similar to that of the larger groups of immigrants from the Middle

---

7. The slave trade was abolished in 1817 and ceased in the 1850s. Slavery was abolished in 1888.

East and the Balkan countries that started to arrive to Latin America at the turn of the twentieth century. They came to be recognized by the host societies as *turcos* (Turks), although they did not carry Ottoman passports. Emigration from Morocco was generally a Jewish phenomenon and differed from the mass migration from the Middle East, particularly from Syria and Lebanon, that represented all the religious denominations.

Immigrants from the Ottoman Empire

The dominant Sephardic communities in the contemporary Latin American Jewish society arrived in Latin America from countries that had been part of the Ottoman Empire. They belonged to two language groups: Ladino-speaking Jews from Turkey, Greece, Rhodes, Macedonia, and Bulgaria, and Arabic-speaking Jews from Syria and Lebanon. Immigrants from Palestine were part of either groups and in addition spoke Hebrew.

The migratory movement was distinctly divided into two waves: the first took place prior to World War I, when the Ottoman Empire was still considered a unified political entity. The second started immediately after the war, when political and economic distinctions between the new national entities became more apparent.

The first wave began in the 1890s and reached its peak between 1908 and 1914. It was caused by the deterioration of socioeconomic conditions, fear of the compulsory conscription to the army and the Balkan Wars, as well as by the economic opportunities offered by the receptive countries (Kerpat 1985). The first to arrive were young single men who followed their non-Jewish countrymen in search of better living conditions. Guided by adventure or chance, they arrived at the remotest corners of Latin America. Their economic success promoted immigration of relatives and friends and created the first link in the future chains of migration. A typical story is that of Alberto Levy of Monastir, Macedonia, who left his home town in 1900, and after wandering in different countries arrived in Santiago, Chile, where he was offered a job as a tailor in the frontier town of Temuco. His letters home attracted other Jews and eventually led to the establishment of the first Sephardic community in Chile (Nes El 1984, 48–49).

The small nuclei of Sephardim, established prior to World War I, became the spearheads of the migratory movement, paving the road for those who followed in the second wave (1919–1930). The Sephardic communities in Latin America became havens for Turkish Jews who had lost Ottoman protection and previous autonomy, or for Syrian and Lebanese Jews, caught between the French mandatory powers and the emerging Pan-Islamic nationalism that identified them with the Zionist movement.[8]

Immigrants from Izmir to Argentina and from European Turkey to Cuba illustrate the second migratory flow that followed World War I. Many of them were victims of massacre and plunder during the Greek occupation of Thrace, Macedonia, and Anatolia (1919–1922). Fleeing from their hometowns, they traced the paths of relatives and neighbors who had emigrated before the war. The communal organizations that were founded by early immigrants in Buenos Aires and Havana became responsible for the newcomers, as stated in the annual report of Chevet Ahim (the Sephardic community of Havana): "The year 1924 was the year of the Jewish Sephardic immigrants . . . who knocked at the door of our society. These immigrants were no longer young adventurers in search of riches. They were families with small children fleeing the misery that was caused by the change of regime in the Balkan states, who sought refuge in the free American countries."[9]

The collapse of the Ottoman Empire and the difficulties that ensued were the "push" factors that convinced Sephardic Jews to seek a new home in foreign lands. The success of former emigrants and economic opportunities across the Atlantic were the "pull" factors that marked the routes and destinations of the migratory movement. A third factor, however, played a central role in the history of Jewish migration to Latin America: the proximity of the United States—and the transformation of its immigration policy.

Immigration in the 1920s

The early immigrants from the Middle East and the Balkan countries arrived in Latin America while the gates of the "promised land" were still open to them,

---

8. On the situation in Syria and Lebanon as a background for emigration, see Stillman (1991, 47–63) and H. Cohen (1972, 48–50).

9. Asociación Unión Chevet Ahim, Memoria Annual 1924, Havana, YIVO Archives, New York, Leizer Ran Collection.

provided that they were found healthy and were not liable to become a public burden. According to Liz Hamui de Halabe, "the first to arrive and settle in Mexico did so from a lack of knowledge of the geography of the American continent or because they were refused entrance into the United States" (1997b, 129). A common cause for refusal was trachoma; immigrants denied entry by the US health inspectors turned to other destinations where control was more lax (Teubal 1953).[10]

The Quota Acts of 1921 and 1924 limited considerably the number of immigrants admitted to the United States and became a major factor in the growth of the Jewish communities in Latin America. It is estimated that, between 1920 and 1930, 75,505 Jews immigrated to Argentina, 30,000 to Brazil, 6,000 to Uruguay, and 3,700 to Chile (Avni 1992, 179–80). The majority of these immigrants came from Eastern Europe, particularly from Poland.

Mexico and Cuba were portrayed by travel agencies in Europe as stepping-stones to the United States and were used as ports of illegal entry to the "promised land." Since US authorities severely enforced the restrictions on immigrant smuggling, Jews were compelled to transform the way stations into permanent homes. It is estimated that the Jewish population of Mexico grew from 2,000 in 1921 to 9,500 in 1930 (DellaPergola and Lerner 1995, 28). In Cuba approximately 17,700 Jews from Eastern Europe entered the country, but only 8,000 remained after 1930—the rest continued their journey (legally or illegally) to the United States. According to official statistics, 5,640 immigrants from Syria and 3,112 from Turkey were registered in the 1920s. Jewish sources prove that Sephardic Jews constituted the large majority among the immigrants from Turkey but were hardly represented among those from Syria and Lebanon. The number of Sephardim registered by Cuban Jewish sources around 1930 was 4,000 (Bejarano 1992, 44–58; República de Cuba, Secretaría de Hacienda, Sección de Estadisticas 1903–30).

Emigration from Eastern Europe depended on the assistance of Jewish welfare agencies, such as JCA (Jewish Colonization Association), HIAS (Hebrew Immigration Aid Society), and Joint (American Jewish Joint Distribution Committee).

---

10. Interview with Jack Barrocas, Karmiel 1983, Institute of Contemporary Jewry [ICJ], Hebrew University, Jerusalem.

These agencies responded to the US Quota Acts by relocating Jewish emigrants to Latin America. Ashkenazi immigration was thus connected with official networks with links in Europe, the United States, and the receptive countries.

The Sephardic migratory movement did not rest on official organizations but functioned on the basis of informal networks of relatives and *paisanos* (compatriots) that directed immigrants from the same hometown to specific towns in the interior regions or to specific neighborhoods in the large cities (see, for example, Bejarano 1978, Akmir 1997, 67–77, and Klich 2006). The map of the Sephardic settlements in Latin America, like that of other immigrants from Muslim countries, was gradually constructed by several individual chains of migration, in which kinship fulfilled a central role (see appendix to this chapter).

The Late Migratory Waves

The migratory movement of the 1920s came to a halt because of the restrictive policies imposed by the governments of the receptive countries, as a consequence of the world depression and the ensuing unemployment and xenophobia. The closing of the gates of the Latin American countries was a crucial problem with respect to refugees from Germany (Avni 1987a), but it had an impact also on the prospects of Jewish emigration from other countries.

During the Holocaust period Latin America played an important role in the rescue of Jewish refugees. Officially, most countries maintained their restrictive policies, but individual refugees were able to obtain entry permits by using loopholes in the immigration laws, personal contacts with local politicians, or purchase of illegal documents.[11]

Jeffrey Lesser presents the paradox of Jewish immigration to Brazil under the government of Getulio Vargas, which was explicitly hostile to the Jews. On the one hand the government issued a secret instruction to consular officials in 1937 to deny visas to persons of Semitic origin, but on the other it facilitated the entry of significant numbers of Jewish refugees (1995). During the same period, Sephardic Jews from Rhodes who owned fashionable garment stores in Rio de Janeiro developed good relations with their clients in the upper class. They were

---

11. On the different approaches of the Latin American countries see Milgram (2003).

able to use their contacts with wives of high government officials—including the First Lady—to rescue their relatives by bringing them to Brazil (Flanzer 1997, 86).

The Sephardic refugees and survivors who found shelter in Latin America came from Axis–controlled countries such as Greece, Rhodes, Italy, Bulgaria, and Yugoslavia. The result was a certain increase in the number of Sephardim of European origin, most of whom joined the Ladino-speaking communities.

Immigration from the Middle East, particularly from Syria, started as a consequence of the pogrom in Aleppo (after the vote on the Partition of Palestine in November 29, 1947) and the establishment of the State of Israel. Finding a temporary refuge in Beirut, many joined their relatives in the well-established communities of Aleppans and Damascenes in Buenos Aires and Mexico. Others joined "mixed" Sephardic communities, becoming more influential than the veteran Ladino speakers.

In Panama the Jews from Aleppo became the largest Jewish group, dominating Shevet Ahim—the Sephardic community that was established by immigrants from the Middle East in 1933. Emigration from Syria converted Panama into the only community in Latin America where the Ashkenazim form a small minority. In 1986 it was reported that out of 1,000 Jewish families, 700 were members of Shevet Ahim, 152 of the Spanish Portuguese community Kol Searith Israel, and only 80 families belonged to the Ashkenazi community Beth El (Dayán de Mizrachi and Arjona 1986, 23–34).

The final wave of Sephardic immigration was motivated by two events that occurred in 1956: the independence of Morocco and the Sinai campaign. Unsheltered by the French or Spanish colonial authorities, the Jews of Morocco faced a period of uncertainty, and many opted for emigration. Jews from Spanish Morocco turned to Spanish-speaking countries, and many relocated to the Spanish enclaves in Ceuta and Melilla—two Moroccan towns that remained under the sovereignty of Spain. Others emigrated to Latin America, reinforcing the old Moroccan settlements in Brazil and Argentina. The major destination, however, was Venezuela, converting the community of Caracas into the most active concentration of Moroccans in Latin America (Vilar 1972, 21).

In Egypt, immediately after the occupation of Sinai by Israel (in November 1956), the government imprisoned hundreds of Jews, and thousands (especially stateless and aliens) were deported and their properties confiscated. Others started a voluntary exodus that continued until after the Six-Day War (1967).

Brazil was the second destination of Egyptian Jews (after Israel) with 10,000 immigrants in 1957 (Leftel 1990).

Ruth Leftel, who studied the history of the Egyptian Sephardim in Brazil, revealed the diplomatic negotiations of HIAS with the government of Jucelino Kubitschek and the personal intervention of the president in authorizing a special immigration quota to the Jewish refugees from Egypt (1993).

The late migration was basically a process of family reunion, or—in the case of the Egyptian Jews—a family transplantation. It completed the cycle of emigration of Sephardic families from the Middle East, the Balkan countries, and North Africa to Latin America and thus strengthened the clannish character of their communities.

Economic and Social Patterns

The arrival of the early Sephardic immigrants from the Ottoman Empire, especially to Argentina, Brazil, Uruguay, Cuba, and Chile, was preceded by a period of mass European migration that resulted in agricultural expansion and a considerable growth of the rural and urban populations. The expansion of agriculture was oriented toward the cultivation of staples (such as cereals, coffee, and sugar) for export, but at the same time it increased the internal market that catered to mass consumption. Immigrants from the Ottoman Empire—Catholic, Greek Orthodox, Muslims, and Jews—were integrated into the local economies primarily as distributors or producers of consumer goods for the lower socioeconomic classes.

During the first migratory wave (until 1914), immigrants were more adventurous and less burdened with family obligations. They penetrated into distant areas, accompanying the process of agricultural expansion as itinerant vendors, and eventually moved into their own businesses. Moroccan Jews in Argentina used to train their newly arrived relatives and send them to the provincial towns to open new branches of the family firm. Victor Mirelman observed that while Jewish groups in Argentina tended to concentrate in the capital, there were more Moroccan Jews in the interior cities (1988, 33–35). Another unique feature of this community was that a few graduates of the Alliance Israélite Universelle in Tetuan were hired as school teachers for the agricultural colonies of the Jewish Colonization Association in Argentina.

The patterns of economic integration of the Sephardic Jews from the Middle East and North Africa were similar to those of the Lebanese, Syrian, and Palestinian immigrants. The majority started as itinerant peddlers, in the rural areas as well as among urban dwellers, supplying a variety of household goods but specializing in textiles and clothing. Selling on credit by installments, they acquired a permanent clientele among the lower-income population that could not afford the expensive merchandise in the stores. The comparative studies compiled by Ignacio Klich and Jeffrey Lesser in their pioneer work *Arab and Jewish Immigrants in Latin America* demonstrate that in spite of the different circumstances in the receptive countries, the non-Latin minorities encountered similar economic opportunities and their social adjustment was accompanied by similar images and stereotypes (1998; see also Klich 2006).

In the eyes of the host societies, all the immigrants from the Middle East and North Africa were classified as *turcos,* regardless of their faith or nationality. The immigrants themselves had no sense of Ottoman unity, as they came from countries in which ethnic and religious minorities were segregated from each other under the *millet* system. Klich and Lesser point out the rejection of the label *turco* by Armenians and Arabs as well as by Maghribi Jews, arguing that *turco* is an imposed rather than self-constructed label (1996).[12]

Walter Zenner observed that the concentration of Aleppan Jews in a small number of commercial occupations was linked to the transmission of ethnic identity: "The maintenance of Syrian Jewish identity is related to participation in transnational family, kin, and commercial networks" (2000, 106). The process of adjustment was thus influenced not only by economic opportunities and other circumstantial factors in the receptive countries, but by factors defined by Simon Kuznets as "the heritage of the immigrating minority": the desire of a small cohesive minority to survive as a distinct group, to avoid unity with the majority society or with other religious or ethnic minorities (1960, 1600–1; 1972, 16–17).

The preservation of the minority's distinctness as an economic factor was manifested in the unofficial networks created by the immigrants to facilitate their economic and social integration while preserving their cohesiveness. Information

12. On the Jews under the *millet* system, see for example Shaw (1991, 43–44); A. Levy (1992, 42–44); Stillman (1991, 4).

was transmitted to the new immigrants upon their arrival: "whoever descended from the boat had a relative or friend who prepared him for peddling."[13] An interview with Cali Maya reveals the mechanisms of internal links between the immigrants from the same hometown:

> I was a little girl and we did not work outside the house. Among the Sephardim . . . women stayed at home. The friends were Jewish families that arrived in Camagüey and we already knew each other from the town in which we had been born. . . . The majority of the Sephardim in Camagüey were peddlers. They sold their products in Camagüey, in the neighboring towns, and beyond those as well. I remember that all these peddlers came to my father's store where he sold clothes for men and women, and he would sell them merchandise on credit. In those days there was much humanity, not only credit. When some single boys arrived they were kept at home, were offered food, a place to sleep, until they could compose themselves a bit. (Bejarano 1996a, 16)

A similar pattern is reflected in the memoirs of Isaac Dabbah Askenazi, one of the early immigrants from Aleppo to Mexico:

> These Jewish-*Halebis* [from Aleppo] who were first to settle, have an immediate clientele: that of their coreligionists whose economic possibilities are still limited to the activity of selling on credit. . . .
> The physical proximity, with all being concentrated in the same neighborhood, the similarity of activities, the commercial relations established between peddlers and merchants, in addition to the circumstances of being all from the same country of origin, influenced the life of all the members of the community, who preserved tight relations with each other. (1982, 125)

A study of the Sephardim in Buenos Aires shows that during the 1930s the population was polarized between a few successful merchants and industrialists and the poor classes that needed social assistance. The pace of upper mobility was not equal among the different groups. Among the Syrian Jews, the Aleppans

---

13. Interview with Isidoro Behar, Richter Library Special Collection, University of Miami. Courtesy Robert M. Levine and Mark D. Szchuman. See also Hamui de Halabe (1997b, 131).

were more prosperous than the Damascene. They benefited from commercial contacts with relatives in Manchester and New York that facilitated the development of wool and textile industry and provided jobs to members of their group. The Ladino-speaking community was divided between the more successful Sephardim from Rhodes and the poorer Jews from Turkey (Bejarano 1982; Brauner Rodgers 1999; see also Teubal 1953).

After World War II, however, the socioeconomic differences diminished considerably, and the community tended to concentrate in the middle classes. Among the older generation, the majority remained occupied in commerce and trade, while the second generation started to move to the professions (Sidicaro 1970). A similar trend was observed among Sephardim from Turkey in Cuba: the majority was concentrated in commerce, with a large percentage remaining peddlers until the Castro revolution in 1959. At the same time, however, their children used academic education as a means of achieving greater social mobility, with sons of peddlers or petty merchants becoming accountants, doctors, and engineers (Bejarano 2002, 108).

When the government of Fidel Castro started to nationalize private business, the majority of Cuban Jews preferred to emigrate, leaving all their material properties behind. The rapid adjustment of the Sephardic Cubans in the United States, and especially in Miami, was facilitated by the advantages of having acquired good education and commercial ties prior to their exodus. Raquel Egozi Behar explained in her interview that the only baggage they could take with them when they left Cuba was what they carried inside their minds: "I used to say to my children: 'You have to study, because what you know is the only heritage you are going to possess in your life.'"[14]

A similar feature characterizes the groups of late arrivals, whose emigration was motivated by the Holocaust or by the political transformations in the Middle East and North Africa. The level of their secular education, as well as their socioeconomic position, had been much higher than that of the immigrants of the 1920s. Having lost their properties, they were able to use their skills to adjust to the new circumstances, and their mobility was relatively rapid. According to Rachel Mizrahi, "A large number of the Jewish refugees of Arab countries

14. Interview with Raquel Egozi Behar, Miami 1984, ICJ.

established themselves in São Paulo, a city with ample possibilities for absorbing immigrants of other origins. Their experience in business, academic education and command of foreign languages enabled the Jews from Egypt, Syria and Lebanon to establish themselves in their own firms or in multi-national concerns open to professionals who are experts and bilingual" (2003, 189–91). Economic success, especially when accompanied by strong ethnic identity, was reflected in the impact of the late immigrants on the Sephardic organization.

Communal Organization

The Sephardim from Muslim countries came from societies in which their belonging to a Jewish community was recognized by law and rabbinical authority was rooted in tradition. In Latin America they had to re-create their Jewish world on a voluntary basis and to adapt themselves to the model of other minority groups as well as to legal requirements. In most countries immigrants were expected to supply their own social needs, and to protect their coreligionists from becoming indigent (Bejarano 1996b).

Latin America was also an encounter with Jews from a different background and other patterns of organization. Although in several countries the Sephardim were the pioneers of Jewish education, the Ashkenazim from Eastern Europe became the dominant Jewish groups. The latter established a large variety of organizations that included also *landsmanschaften* (organizations based on a common hometown) and religious institutions, but the patterns of their organization were basically secular with a social or political orientation.

The Sephardic organization was ethnic and religious. Each group identified with its community of origin and tended to preserve separate institutional organizations. This tendency, however, was conditioned by size: large groups, coming from Aleppo, Damascus, Spanish Morocco, or Turkey were able to establish their own communal frameworks. Others had to unite or to join dominant groups, gradually losing their original identity. In a recent study, Rachel Mizrahi describes two synagogues established in the 1920s in the same street in São Paulo by Jews from the Middle East. One was dominated by Arabic speakers from Sidon and the other by Hebrew speakers from Safed. The latter was associated with the rite and tradition of the Sephardic communities in Jerusalem and Safed; gradually, however, they absorbed members from the Balkan countries, from Morocco, Egypt, and Beirut that diminished the influence of the founders (2003, 132, 210–11).

Several Sephardic organizations started as *minyans* in private homes, but as they were not officially constituted, they did not keep records of their early activities. The history of the Sephardim in Buenos Aires and Mexico followed different patterns but ultimately resulted in similar institutional frameworks, which were typical also of communities in other countries. They formed centralized communal organizations that provided all the religious, social, and cultural needs of Sephardim from the same origin, based on the traditional model of the *kehila* (Jewish community) in their old home.

The first communal organization for Jews was officially created in Mexico City in 1912, as a united entity for all the Jewish residents in the country in view of the insecurity and economic difficulties created by the Mexican revolution. The founders of Alianza Monte Sinai came from different countries and cultural backgrounds, but gradually the Jews from Damascus took the leadership (Alianza Monte Sinai 2001, 43–59). The conflicts between the members of the community on the form of religious observance were aggravated by the arrival of Jews from Eastern Europe. In 1922, following a dispute on the reading of the book of Esther, the Ashkenazim decided to separate themselves "from their Arab brethren" and to establish their own community (Gojman de Backal 1993). Two other groups followed, creating the Comunidad Sefaradí for the Ladino speakers and Sedaka Umrape (today Magen David) of Aleppans.

Sephardic organization in Buenos Aires started with small nuclear institutions, designated to fulfill specific functions and serving persons of the same origin and living in the same neighborhood. Among these institutions were synagogues, Talmud Torah, social clubs, and a variety of welfare institutions that assisted widows and orphans, visited the sick, and provided medical assistance. Each ethnic group, however, was united around the cemetery, with a mutual understanding (also with the Ashkenazim) that it was not allowed to bury Jews from other communities of origin. The immigrants from Morocco were the first to organize (in 1891), and their cemetery was acquired in 1900; the Damascene inaugurated their cemetery in 1913 and the Aleppans in 1923. The Ladino speakers started to consolidate their identity as a unified group in 1929, when ACIS (Asociación Comunidad Israelita Sefaradí de Buenos Aires), which had been found in 1914 by Jews from Izmir as a neighborhood synagogue, purchased a cemetery for all the Sephardim from Turkey and the Balkan countries.

The rise of a new communal leadership under the impact of the Holocaust motivated a process of reorganization of the Ladino-speaking population residing in Buenos Aires. An agreement between the Jews from Izmir and Rhodes (1942) converted ACIS into a centralized communal organization that catered to all the religious, social, and cultural needs of the Ladino speakers. Each of the four communal groups was gradually consolidated around the organization that owned the cemetery, preserving four distinct communal frameworks with a parallel structure and functions (Bejarano 1978).

Although all the Sephardic communal organizations were based on religion, they differed from each other in the level of religiosity. The Jews of Syria, especially the Aleppans, were always considered the most strict in religious observance and succeeded in transmitting to the future generations their conservative way of life. Among the Ladino speakers, the first generation was traditional, but it was much more tolerant toward the laxity of the younger generation.

The religious patterns of the different ethnic groups derived from the heritage that they carried from their communities of origin, as well as from their exposure to modernization and secularization on the eve of emigration from their communities of origin. Modernization in the Ottoman Empire was introduced with the reforms of the nineteenth century that granted equality to all the citizens within the limits of their respective ethno-religious communities. The process was shaped by European influence and was oriented toward Western civilization. It did not lead to assimilation but developed within the boundaries of the Jewish community. In Turkey, the center of Ottoman rule, the *Haham Bashi* (chief rabbi) maintained his political authority, but the spiritual influence of the rabbis declined. Secularization, however, was not a rebellion against rabbinical authority, but a gradual transgression of religious observance.

The Ottoman reforms had little impact on the distant province of Syria, where modernity penetrated at a slow pace and Jews were hardly exposed to secular influences. The rabbis of Aleppo continued to be venerated by their community, and their authority did not diminish. As late as 1906 they were able to excommunicate violators of Sabbath (Stillman 1991, 223; Zenner 2000, 45–46).

The Aleppan rabbis in Latin America were able to re-create their past authority, struggling against the influences of secularism and assimilation. Rabbi Shaul

Setton arrived in Buenos Aires in 1912 and discovered that "life in this city is exceedingly wanton, and everybody does as he pleases." Under the influence of Rabbi Aharon Goldman, the spiritual leader of Moisesville (the first Jewish colony in Argentina) Setton promulgated a ban against conversions in Argentina (Zemer 1994). The ban, which is still valid among Orthodox Jews in Argentina, was the first step toward a systematic rejection of mixed marriages from the Syrian communities. Rabbi Setton was also the first *Haham* who imposed a strict control on kashruth. He established a Talmud Torah that imparted religious education as a complement to that of the public schools. He used his religious authority in the two Syrian communities to pressure parents not to send their children to school on the Sabbath ([1928] 1981, 135).

Rabbinical authority in the Aleppan community declined after the death of Rabbi Setton in 1930, with the nomination of rabbis of a different ethnic origin and the rise of a modern communal leadership that aspired to bridge the gap between tradition and modernity. In her study on Aleppan leadership in Buenos Aires, Susana Brauner Rodgers points out the identification of orthodox tendencies with ethnic heritage. The conservative leaders, who struggled against the innovators, looked for a rabbi who would recognize "the spiritual and religious requirements, in order not to abandon the Aleppan patterns of life that are the heritage of our forefathers" (Brauner Rodgers 1999, 139). The arrival of new immigrants from Aleppo in the early 1950s, and the nomination of Rabbi Itzhak Chehebar as the spiritual leader, marked the return of the Aleppan community to its strict religiosity.

The combination of an Aleppan revival, prompted by the new encounter with immigrants of the old home and the personal skills of a rabbi who was capable of establishing a strong rabbinical authority, occurred also in Panama. Rabbi Sión Levy, who arrived from Jerusalem in 1951 when he was only twenty-four years old, was, until his death in 2008, the influential spiritual leader of the whole community: "The primary good that for him represents the preservation of our customs and the observance of Judaism, is that this is what permits us to continue to be Jews" (Dayán de Mizrachi and Arjona 1986, 105).

Among the Ladino-speaking communities and the Moroccans, the rabbis were much more open to the influences of modernization and more tolerant in their attitude toward religious transgressors. The problem was that only a few communities, such as Uruguay, Mexico, and Cuba, enjoyed the presence of a spiritual leader who shared with the members of the community the same rite and customs. In most countries, the lack of a *Haham* from Tetuan or from Turkey debilitated religious life. The study of the community of Buenos Aires concluded that the lack of spiritual leadership and religious education left the Moroccan and Ladino-speaking communities without instruments to transmit their heritage to the next generation. The situation changed in the early 1950s, but the results of the early years are still evident (Bejarano 1978, 128–32).

The loss of religiosity, however, does not mean the loss of Sephardic identity. As in the Ottoman Empire, Jews remained in the boundaries of their community, even if these boundaries are invisible, as in the case of the Jews from Rhodes in Brazil, who were apparently assimilated into the Brazilian society but continued to share a way of life, to preserve their cultural heritage, and to maintain their social and family life inside their "invisible group" (Flanzer 1997).

Zionist Organization and Relationship with Ashkenazi Communities

The Zionist movement presented a common ideal for all the Jewish people, with no ethnic divisions. It functioned outside the communal frameworks and was a meeting point between Ashkenazim and Sephardim as well as among the different Sephardic groups. Attitudes toward Zionism, however, were rooted in the cultural and political heritage of each community.

The Zionist movement in Latin America was dominated by the Ashkenazi sector, which generally controlled communication with the main offices of the movement in Europe and Eretz Israel. The Sephardim were less involved in political Zionism and were far from the conflicts between parties that divided the Ashkenazi activists. Unlike the Eastern European secular orientation, the Sephardim perceived the Zionist idea as an integral part of their religious belief: "What is our religion, if not a beautiful hymn of fervent Zionism? What is all the Bible, if not an effort of our great pastor Moses to organize and lead Israel from the Galut to the Holy Land? Is this not a Zionist labor? Can one believe in the Torah without venerating Zionism . . . and our prayers are simply implorations to the Divine Lord to guide and facilitate our return to Zion" (Bensignor 1929, 15–16).[15]

---

15. The author emigrated from Havana to Buenos Aires, where he became president of ACIS.

Attitudes toward Zionism were not equal among the different Sephardic sectors and were influenced by their contacts with the movement in the countries of origin. They tended to organize cultural activities more than to collect funds for the building of Eretz Israel. The first recorded activity of Sephardic Zionism was the participation of the Moroccans in Argentina in the first local Zionist Congress in 1904 (Mirelman 1982, 192; *El Sionista*, January 1, 1904). In 1917 a Moroccan Jew started the periodical *Israel*, which had a Zionist orientation.

The early enthusiasm of the Moroccans, however, had little continuity in later years. The leadership of the movement, in Argentina as in other countries, was generally in the hands of the Ladino-speaking group—from Bulgaria, Rhodes, and Turkey. Among the Syrian Jews, Zionism was more popular among the Damascene than among the Aleppans. Another group that played a central role in the organization of Zionist activities among the Sephardim was that of the immigrants from Eretz Israel. Although small in number, they became a central link with the centers of the Zionist movement in Jerusalem.

Sephardic activists who participated in the Ashkenazi-controlled Zionist organizations tended to withdraw and organize separately. A typical case is that of Chile, where Ladino-speaking Sephardim took an active part in the local Zionist congresses and were elected to the board of the Zionist Federation. In 1933, however, they created a separate "Sephardi bloc" (Nes El 1984, 143–59). The main barrier between the two sectors was linguistic: the Ashkenazim used Yiddish in all their activities, in the Jewish press, and in the correspondence with the central offices in Jerusalem. Sephardic sources are full of protests against the use of Yiddish, and that seems to be the main reason for the separate organization.

In 1925 Sephardic activists founded the World Union of Sephardic Jews, with the objective of creating a Sephardic framework inside the World Zionist Organization. In response, the WZO sent, for the first time, a Sephardic emissary to Latin America. Dr. Ariel Bensión traveled throughout the continent in 1926 and established branches of the organization Bené Kedem (Sons of Orient) in different countries. His aim was "To group together the Sephardim under the flag of Zionism. To lead them as one element, with only one soul, only one language and only one idea to the Zionist Congress" (1926, 7–14).

Bensión's mission did not succeed. Shortly after his visit the organization he created disintegrated, and unity with the Ashkenazim was not achieved. Rabbi

Shabtay Djaen, from Yugoslavia, was sent to Latin America in 1927 as an emissary of the World Union of Sephardic Jews. He remained in Argentina for a few years as the spiritual leader of the Ladino speakers and the Moroccans (Bejarano 1998, 41–42). Rabbi Djaen was a modern rabbi and a fervent Zionist, and he was critical of the backwardness of the local Sephardim. At the same time, however, he accused the Ashkenazim of neglect of the Sephardi sector: "This part of the Jewish people in this country was almost forgotten. . . . The Ashkenazim and Sephardim assemble only in the cemetery, being divided as two worlds: not like Jews but like Russians and Turks."[16]

During the 1930s and 1940s, under the impact of the Holocaust, the Sephardim intensified their Zionist activities and participated in the umbrella organizations that were created at that time to protect the Jewish community against anti-Semitic attacks and represent it vis-à-vis the authorities. The umbrella organizations were generally led by Ashkenazi activists, but common interests brought the two sectors together. The World Zionist Organization had discovered the financial potential of the Latin American communities and intensified its activities around the national campaigns. Its work among the Sephardim, however, was quite limited.

The Zionist revival of the Sephardim came with the establishment of the State of Israel, which was a turning point in the history of the Sephardic Jews in Latin America. For those coming from Muslim countries, the establishment of a Jewish state was the destruction of the bridges with communities of origin. Israel became a source of spiritual inspiration, but also a society with a large Sephardic population with which they could identify.

Conclusion

The patterns of adjustment of the Sephardim from the Ottoman Empire in Latin America were shaped by cultural and social traditions and identities brought over from their communities of origin. These, in their turn, were a product of global and local factors that consolidated the identities of the Sephardic Jews according

---

16. Memorandum to the 12th Zionist Congress in Argentina, May 15, 1930, Archives of Vaad Haeda Hasfradit, Jerusalem, Rabbi Djaen file.

to the country or town in which they lived. Throughout the twentieth century the Sephardic Jews in Latin America absorbed the influences of the majority societies in their respective countries, and the identity of each group cannot be disconnected from the social and political milieu in which it lives. The immigrants of the first generation brought with them the elements of continuity with the communities of origin. Their children had to defend their heritage against the currents of assimilation.

The capability of each Sephardic group to perpetuate its ethnicity depended on external and internal factors. The former are related to the influences of the majority societies and to the impact of other Jewish groups, the latter to the unique features of each individual community with respect to other co-ethnics.

The impact of the majority societies on the ethnicity of the Sephardim is influenced by their own ethnic composition. In the countries that received mass migration, like the "European" Argentina, Uruguay, and Chile, as well as the multiethnic Brazil, the immigrants and their descendants became a dominant element in the population, counterbalancing the influences of the conservative oligarchies. Although mostly Latin and Catholic, the immigrants and their descendants created large middle sectors that absorbed the Jews and had a strong impact on the tendencies of assimilation within the majority society. Ladino speakers, similarly to the Ashkenazim, are much more influenced by these tendencies, with a growing rate of intermarriage that is similar to that in other Western countries. The Arabic speakers, and especially the Aleppans, defend themselves against the currents of assimilation by social seclusion.

In countries with a large Indian or Mestizo population, such as Mexico, Peru, or the Circum-Caribbean Venezuela and Panama, Jews form part of a small, white, upper middle class that is not accepted by the Creole oligarchies but distinguishes itself from the poor masses, which are largely of mixed race. In these countries, all the Jewish groups tend to be secluded, with Ladino speakers being much more conservative than in the "European" lands.

The internal factors demonstrate that each group resembles its co-ethnics in other countries more than other Jewish groups in its own country. Religiosity is related to ethnicity, with the most observant being more attached to their ethnic tradition. A crucial factor in the preservation of religiosity is the presence of capable rabbis. The Syrian communities were able to re-create rabbinical authority because of the post-1947 migration and by the establishment of local *yeshivot* and the studies of young members of their communities in Sephardic rabbinical schools in Israel or other countries. The Ladino speakers are faced with the choice between Sephardic rabbis of a different ethnic group, generally from Morocco, that are too orthodox for their liking, or congregations of Conservative Judaism that bridge the gap between their Jewish and local identities but result in the loss of their Sephardic identity. The case of Buenos Aires shows that many Sephardim are religiously "assimilated" into the Ashkenazi sector, but their Sephardi identity is preserved as a cultural residue.

APPENDIX

Table 1.1.
Distribution of Sephardic population, by communities of origin

COUNTRY	MAJOR COMMUNITIES	COUNTRIES OF ORIGIN
Argentina	Buenos Aires Rosario Cordoba	Morocco Syria (Aleppo and Damascus) Turkey (Izmir, Aydin and Istanbul) Rhodes and Italy Greece, Bulgaria, Yugoslavia Palestine (Jerusalem)
Brazil	São Paulo Rio de Janeiro Porto Alegre	Morocco Syria (Aleppo and Damascus) Lebanon (Beirut, Sidon) Turkey Rhodes and Italy Palestine (Jerusalem, Safed) Balkan Countries Egypt
Uruguay	Montevideo	Turkey Syria Italy Palestine Yugoslavia, Bulgaria
Mexico	Mexico City	Syria (Aleppo and Damascus) Turkey (Istanbul, Silivri) Balkan countries

Continued on following page

Table 1.1. (Continued)
Distribution of Sephardic population, by communities of origin

COUNTRY	MAJOR COMMUNITIES	COUNTRIES OF ORIGIN
Venezuela	Caracas	Morocco Israel Egypt
Cuba	Havana Camagüey Santiago de Cuba	Turkey (Silivri, Istanbul) Turkey (Kirklareli, Edirne)
Panama	Panama City	Curaçao Istanbul Syria (Aleppo) Israel
Chile	Santiago	Turkey (Izmir, Istanbul) Macedonia (Monastir) Greece (Saloniki)
Peru	Lima	Syria Turkey
Colombia	Bogota	Turkey Greece Syria
Paraguay	Asunción	Turkey Palestine
Bolivia		Turkey
Guatemala		Turkey Syria

Note: This table was prepared in the framework of a research project on Sephardic communities in Latin America, Division of Latin America, Spain and Portugal, Avraham Harman Institute of Contemporary Jewry, Hebrew University of Jerusalem. It is an elaboration of a table in M. Cohen (1980, 89).

2

Nuevos mundos halló Colón, or What's Different about Sephardic Literature in the Americas?

EDNA AIZENBERG

Was Columbus Jewish? The question debated ad nauseam over the years, reaching fever pitch around the time of the 1992 fifth centennial, surfaced again some time ago on the website of LAJSA, the Latin American Jewish Studies Association. Yes, he was, claimed one adamant message; that's why the Church doesn't want to canonize him even if he "found" new worlds. No, he wasn't, retorted another, and anyway, it doesn't matter whether he was Jewish or not, what matters is that Hispano-Catholic society still has trouble accepting the Jewish, *lo judío*, Columbus's or otherwise.

I am not going to enter the fray and debate Columbus's supposed ancestry, but the heated yes-and-no exchange does serve me as a way of entering the topic of this volume, "Sephardim in the Americas." Or as I would like to rephrase it slightly, "What's *different* about Sephardim in the Americas?" (I will be using the term "Sephardim" in its broadest sense.) Since the journeys of Columbus's caravels, Latin American Sephardic identity has been marked by a *fruitful difference*, fruitful for artistic creation, fruitful for the insertion of Jews in societal imaginaries.

Why this difference? I would like to propose a couple of reasons. From the beginning, unlike Sephardim in other places of their dispersion, Sephardim in Luso–Latin America were embedded in an Iberian matrix; they entered, or reentered, much of what many of them had left. They may have even discovered it for the rest of the world; they were certainly there right from the start.

31

Think if not of Columbus, then of his Hebrew-speaking translator, Luis de Torres, baptized right before the journey, or a century later, of New Spain's Judaizing poet Luis de Carvajal, who left us testimonies of faith in his passionately beautiful Castilian tongue. This Iberianness and presence *ab initio*, allowed for a possibility of belonging—as fraught as it was with danger in inquisitorial times. More important for literary purposes, it allowed for a myth of belonging not available elsewhere. Sephardim, but also Ashkenazim and even non-Jews, made use of this myth—some would claim that non-Sephardim ahistorically appropriated it—but my interest is in the myth's productivity, whatever its twists and turns.[1]

The Iberian link gave Sephardim the right to be part of Latin America, of its Luso-Hispanic cultures and languages. Here are their voices: Jews discovered Brazil, says Márcio Souza (Scliar and Souza 2000), the Hispanic-Portuguese Moroccan Amazonian Sephardi, a sort of latter-day *converso* writer about whom I will say more. "I'm a Sephardic Jew," says Isaac Chocrón's novelistic alter ego Daniel Benabel, "so African, so Spanish, and so Venezuelan, that the Yiddish Jews from Brooklyn would consider me a heretic. . . . We inherited our superstitions and our sense of pride from the Spanish; and in Venezuela we continued to transform what we inherited from the Moors and the Spanish" (1975, 230). His fellow Venezuelan author, Sonia Chocrón, also follows the Iberian thread, digging deep into the language and legends of Castile in her verse collection *Toledana* (1990), connecting to her Sephardicness, and through it renewing her country's linguistic and poetic modes.

And in Mexico, writer Rosa Nissán, whose quasi-autobiographical novels are shot through with the sounds of her family's *djudeo-español* language, proverbs, and songs poignantly asserts: "'Even in exile, the Sephardim wanted to continue to belong to their adoptive mother. The umbilical cord that connects them to Spain has not been severed.' *Sefarad!* Which in Hebrew means Spain" (2002, 554–55). Vicki Nizri, another Mexican, likewise talks through her Ladino-speaking novelistic characters, *que guardaron a España en el corazón y en la memoria* (who kept Spain in their heart and memory). "*Por tu madre, Moshón,*" murmurs one of them when she gets off the immigrant boat, "*¿estamos*

---

1. See Alcalay (1999) on the appropriation of Sephardic pasts.

entre djidiós? Todos ablan muestra lingua?" (2000, 30, 38; On your mother, Moshón, are we among Jews? Everyone speaks our language?). Of course, the Spanish-Portuguese heritage did not always mean instant belonging even in post-inquisitorial days—Sephardim were still a minority within a Jewish minority in a vast Catholic sea. Ladino, which not all Sephardim spoke, as there were Arabic, and Turkish, French, Italian, and mixes of them, could be a distancing mechanism—oh, that funny and quaint archaic Spanish. But the weight of Iberia was so great that Ashkenazic intellectuals repeatedly re-created themselves as *neo-Sephardim*, a term not everyone likes.

Like it or not, this re-creation was their way of becoming integrated or reconnected with their Luso-Hispanic milieu. I have in mind in Argentina immigrant-generation authors such as Alberto Gerchunoff with *Los gauchos judíos* (1910) and Carlos M. Grünberg with *Mester de judería* (1940). And closer to us is Juan Gelman, whose linguistic experimentation with Ladino in his book *Dibaxu* (1994) brought him back to the roots of the Spanish language at the moment of his own separation and exile. In Brazil there is Moacyr Scliar with his novel *The Strange Nation of Rafael Mendes* (1987), and in Venezuela, Alicia Freilich, author of *Colombina descubierta* (1991). Even the non-Jewish Borges got into the act, styling himself a Portuguese Sephardic Acevedo—his mother's surname—as a means of imagining a cosmopolitan multicultural Latin America to which he could belong, not a narrow authoritarian one.[2]

If the Iberian connection nurtured an intellectually invigorating Latin American Sephardic difference, so did a related idea: the idea of utopia. *Nuevos mundos halló Colón*, Columbus found new worlds: from the perspective of the Native Americans we know he did not, but unlike fellow Sephardim in their various dispersions, Sephardim in Luso–Latin America were coming to the continent of promise. *A la Amérika* (con "k" en Ladino). *Fazer a América em português*.

At the start there was Aaron Levi, alias Antonio de Montezinos, whose electrifying account of meeting up with the Ten Lost Tribes in an El Dorado beyond the Colombian *cordillera*, electrified Europe through the 1650 Spanish language bestseller *Miquweh Israel: Esto es la Esperança de Israel* (The hope of Israel). Its author was the distinguished Sephardic intellectual Manoel Dias Soeiro,

---

2. On neo-Sephardim in literature and on Borges, see Aizenberg (2002, 2005).

better known as Menasseh ben Israel. Let Jew and Indian make common cause to defeat the accursed Spanish, the Judeo-Indian brethren had suggested, and found a realm of peace for the persecuted stock of Abraham (1987).

Or perhaps El Dorado was in the Amazon, where *látex, caucho,* rubber was king. La *fiebre del caucho,* rubber fever, together with political changes in North Africa, brought Sephardic Moroccan Jews to the Brazilian and Peruvian Amazon at the end of the nineteenth century. Márcio Souza, born there, has written about these Jews of Bélem, Manaus, Pará, and Iquitos, situating them at the intersection of reality and fiction, like the locale itself. This was *Eretz Amazonia,* as Samuel Benchimol (1998) has marvelously dubbed it, a magical kingdom that nurtured memoirs, books, and oral testimonies by settlers and their descendents, among them Benchimol and Abraham Ramiro Bentes in *Das ruínas de Jerusalém à verdejante Amazônia* (1987). "Havía um movimento, uma propaganda," Cléa P. Pilnik, another Amazonian Sephardi recalls, "que lá era uma terra prometida" (There was a commotion, and the word spread that it was a promised land over there) (Freindenson and Becker 2003, 26). Combining reality and unreality, novels like Scliar's *Strange Nation of Rafael Mendes* (1987) and Antonio Elio Brailovsky's *Identidad* (1980), about a Judeo-Hispanic Mexican El Dorado, fed on the idea of Latin America as a Sephardic Shangri-la, proving how powerful and malleable the idea is (see also Segal 1999).

La tierra prometida could also be urban: on the avenues of Montevideo, where, Teresa Porzecanski writes in her *Perfumes de Cartago* (1994), her Syrian Sephardic ancestors hoped to find respite from ancient sorrows; or in the streets of Guatemala, where Victor Perera's Spanish-Jerusalemite-Damascene father came to pick gold from the paving stones, a tale retold in Perera's *The Cross and the Pear Tree: A Sephardic Journey* (1995); or on the *ruas* of Sao Paulo, a haven for Alberto Moghrabi's expelled Egyptian family in *Pequenos contos de enredo indeterminado* (2001) (see also Rubel 1992).

Unfortunately, utopia had its counter side, its darker side. The Promised Land was not always flowing with gold and rubber. Columbus left the New World in chains, his first settlement in the Americas destroyed. But aside from individual failures, which could happen anywhere—Perera, for instance, portrays his aging uncle mournfully surrounded by stacks of yard goods in a forlorn Guatemalan town—the Latin America El Dorado sometimes fell particularly hard because of the ongoing inquisitorial impulse, most horribly displayed in the brutal twentieth-century dictatorships and the mutilated disappeared in the republics of the South. Humberto Costantini, Ricardo Halac, Teresa Porzecanski, José Isaacson, and Reina Roffé all reacted to the terror unleashed during the 1970s and 1980s in Argentina and Uruguay through the prism of their Sephardic legacy, sometimes finding comfort, sometimes not. "Eli, eli, lamma sabactani," Humberto Costantini, who suffered exile during the dictatorship, cries out in a poem to the "benevolente, itálico Adonái" of his Turin ancestors, nostalgic for warm family celebrations, but bitter at the well-mannered bourgeois assimilation that sapped revolutionary fervor (1989, 160–62).

Porzecanski in *Perfumes de Cartago* and Roffé in *La rompiente* (1987) also fondly reconstruct moments of bygone Sephardic life, their way of expressing, and resisting, fragmentation and decline. José Isaacson's poems to his rationalist forebear in *Cuaderno Spinoza* (1977) and Ricardo Halac's play, *Mil años, un día* (1993), set in the age of Isabel la Católica, similarly use the metaphor of Sepharad to call for intellectual dignity at a new inquisitorial time. As in the case of the myth of belonging and the idea of utopia, the use of the antidictatorial Sephardic prism went beyond Sephardic authors. Witness Marcos Aguinis's *La gesta del marrano* (1991) about Francisco Maldonado da Silva, the real-life martyr to the Spanish Inquisition in Peru.

This then, belonging and utopia dreamed and undone, is the legacy we have, on which we can build. So where do we go from here? One of Columbus's late writings was given the name *El libro de las profecías* (1991). It is an apocalyptic compendium of biblical and patristic verses predicting the conquest of Mt. Zion and Jerusalem by—surprise of surprises—Fernando and Isabel, and the ensuing end of days. Although we may live in another apocalyptic age, when many again believe Armageddon is upon us, I will not engage in eschatological ruminations about Sephardic literature in the Americas. I will limit myself more modestly to a few future-oriented comments to end my essay, not our days.

To begin with: I think we need more studies, comprehensive ones. Ricardo Feierstein and Jacobo Sefamí have moved in that direction, Feierstein on *Literatura sefardí en Argentina* (2003), and Sefamí on *Memoria e identidad en la literatura sefardí y mizrahi en Latinoamérica* (2002). What strikes me about their articles, beyond their significant classificatory impulse—who are Latin American Sephardic writers and what do they write—is their gesturing toward a new form of looking at *all* of Latin American Jewish literature *from the perspective of the*

Sephardic, moving away from the more common Ashkenazi-centered other way around (see also Feierstein 1988).

I'm not setting up any kind of antagonism here, not at all. But can looking at Latin American literature in general, through a Sephardic perspective, lead to novel insights at a moment of special vigor in Sephardic studies? I think it can.[3]

Sephardim set the foundations and imaginative tropes for Latin American Jewish—and non-Jewish—literature. Geographical and linguistic-cultural belonging, utopian hopefulness, and inquisitorial undoing have a distinct Sephardic color in Luso–Latin America, and we need to read the literature from this viewpoint, even as we continue to savor the Slavic-inflected flavors of Yiddish. Then again, as if proving my point, Yiddish in Latin America is filtered through old, Jewish-tinged Spanish, as when Gerchunoff translates the Yiddish *reb,* mister, into *rabí.* Also, through modern Spanish, creating what I once dared to call "Spanyish," perhaps a neo-Judezmo? I am thinking of works like Feierstein's *Mestizo,* where Yiddish and Spanish mix, *se mestizan,* to form a contemporary, Judeo-shaded Spanish. "Neo-Sephardism" might be an operating term here—a Hispanic Jewish writing being created in Luso–Latin America, on a strong historical Sephardic base. How exciting to think about and study such a literature!

Reading Latin American Jewish literature through Sepharad achieves other wonders as well. It brings in Southern European, Middle Eastern, and African elements, challenging Central and Eastern European exclusions and hegemonies (see Alcalay 1999 and Sefamí 2002). "Soy un judío sefardita," Isaac Chocrón has said, "tan africano, tan español y tan venezolano, que los yiddish de Brooklyn me considerarían hereje" (1975, 230). What about that African heritage, what about *los perfumes de Cartago* that Prozecanski lets us whiff, *o los perfumes de Tánger, o Salónica o Damasco?* How does studying them change our understanding of what it is to be and write Jewish in Luso–Latin America, to be and write Latin American? For one thing, the "Afro" in Latin America might well mean more than its usual connotations.

And finally, although I've alluded to this throughout, I'd like to close with the matter of language. In Luso–Latin America the inventive potentialities of an

---

3. I have in mind in the US books by Ammiel Alcalay (1999), for instance, or anthologies by Stavans (2005), Matza (1997), and I. Lévy (1989).

Iberian Jewish language, bred on the Peninsula, have taken hold as nowhere else: poetry in Ladino (Gelman), *djudeo-español*-tinted novels (Nissán, Nizri), archaic Castilian-tinted stories and verses (Gerchunoff, Grünberg, Sonia Chocrón), perhaps even the "Spanyish" I mentioned. Most recently there is Hebrew-saturated, Arabic-flavored, Mexican-Spanish prose, as in Jacobo Sefamí's novel of mourning, *Los dolientes* (The suffering) (2004). And, to stretch it further, the Spanish-hued Hebrew of Latin American *olim*, immigrants to Israel, were given literary expression some years ago in Gabriela Avigur-Rotem's *Motzart lo haya Yehudi* (Mozart was not a Jew) (1992). The promise may not be infinite, but it is very, very wide. Oh, what Columbus let loose when he boarded those little caravels!

3

Sephardic and Syrian Immigration to America

Acculturation and Communal Preservation

JANE GERBER

A rousing exhortation to the Sephardic immigrant community appeared in a letter in the Ladino newspaper *La America* in the early twentieth century:

> We are now in America, let us become Americans! Let us study the language and history of our Country! Let us direct our activities toward business and the manual trades. Let us plan courageously for a permanent future in this country. Let us bestir ourselves, thus showing our co-religionists the Ashkenazim and the non-Jewish community, who look upon us as strange beings of little worth, . . . that with the blood of Maimonides, Judah Halevi and the Abravanels still coursing through our veins, we shall refuse to remain outcasts. Let us unite our forces and form societies, unions and social clubs! Let us plan a brave future for ourselves in this country! (Papo 1987, 36)

It suggests some of the complexity of the Sephardic immigrant experience in North America. Part of a wave of almost two million Jews reaching North American shores between 1890 and 1924, Sephardic Jews were scarcely noticeable to contemporaries and chroniclers. Totaling approximately 45,000 souls by 1924, the Sephardim formed a tiny minority within the Jewish wave of immigration that was itself a minority among the millions of other groups reaching the shores of North America. Their Old World experiences and varying communal pasts colored their immigrant story, providing a prism through which one can derive novel perspectives on the history of American Jewry in general and Sephardic

Jewry in particular. The Sephardic American story is essentially several stories that are intertwined, with the adjustment of the Balkan and Turkish Jews following a different trajectory from that of the Arabic-speaking Syrian migration.[1]

The Sephardic and Syrian Jews arrived in North America at approximately the same time—the first quarter of the twentieth century. Both continued to immigrate to America throughout the century. While the two groups were each internally diverse—Syrians hailed from Damascus and Aleppo and held strong loyalties to their respective cities of origin—the Sephardim were more numerous and more linguistically and geographically heterogeneous. Despite their inner and mutual differences, they were generally regarded as a single immigrant group by outsiders and indiscriminately designated Orientals, Turks, or Arabs. In their area of first settlement, the Lower East Side of New York, Sephardim and Syrians lived side by side with Ashkenazim, sometimes even as one of many boarders in the apartments of East European Jewish families. Sephardic and Syrian Jews also shared a similar background of originating in close-knit, patriarchal families, although Syrians were more traditional and religiously observant and endogamy was especially important to them. Both streams of immigrants diverged from the American Jewish immigration mold of the time: Ashkenazim tended to arrive in family units, sometimes groups that had constituted an entire Jewish small town in Eastern Europe. In contrast, Sephardic and Syrian males outnumbered females in their immigration stream by as much as ten to one. Despite their many similarities and the common association of the two groups as one part of the Jewish family, the paths of Sephardim and Syrians did not converge in America. Three generations after their initial entry, most Sephardim have been largely absorbed into the broader American Ashkenazi Jewish community. They

1. The Ladino-speaking Jews from the Balkans and Turkey, comprising the majority of the Sephardic immigration, will be referred to as the Sephardim in this study, while the Syrian immigrants, hailing primarily from the city of Aleppo, will be referred to simply as Syrians. Technically, the former are descendants of Spanish émigrés of 1492, while the latter (the Syrians) are composed of indigenous Jews who have resided in Syria since antiquity, Sephardic immigrants who reached Syria after the Spanish expulsion in 1492 and continued to come from Iberia the sixteenth century, and the European Jews, primarily from Italy, known as the *Francos* who settled in Syria in the eighteenth and nineteenth century. The three groups of Syrians all spoke Arabic and shared many customs that bound them as one community, despite their internal differences.

have long since forgotten their ancestral language of Judeo-Spanish or Ladino. Their extended family organizations have withered and their separate fraternal organizations are virtually extinct.[2] In contrast, the contemporary Syrian descendants of the same early-twentieth-century migration possess the strongest, best organized, and most cohesive community among American Jews today. Their third and fourth generations thrive as Americans *and* as Syrian Jews nurturing a strong sense of Syrian Jewish identity, while becoming fully American. Most live together in a cohesive community in Brooklyn and have preserved many of their unique social, religious, and musical customs. How each confronted and adapted to America to follow such divergent paths will be part of our inquiry.

Sephardic Jews hold a special place in American Jewish history as the "founding fathers" of the American Jewish community. Fleeing the Iberian Peninsula and the long arm of the Inquisition, Spanish and especially Portuguese Jews appeared as Crypto-Jews among the earliest Hispanic explorers and settlers in North and South America. By the seventeenth century, enterprising and intrepid Sephardic Jewish merchants and artisans, many of whom were either formerly *conversos* or descendants of *conversos*, joined their Crypto-Jewish brethren in the Caribbean colonies established by the French, the British, and, especially, the Dutch. They were active in the triangular trade that linked Brazil or other South American points, the Caribbean islands, and the newly settled ports of North America with the ports of London, Amsterdam, and Lisbon in far-flung commercial, human, and cultural networks. These Sephardic Jews of the colonial period were part of the worldwide maritime commercial circuits of their day that cut across imperial lines. As is well known, a group of Sephardic merchants fleeing Brazil upon its conquest by the Portuguese in 1653 became the first group of Jews to settle in the Dutch outpost of New Amsterdam/New York. Although Sephardim were outnumbered by Ashkenazim as early as 1740 and never exceeded

---

2. The case of Seattle is the exception that proves the rule. Until recently, several generations of Sephardim remained together and continued to worship in their two Sephardic synagogues, younger generations choosing to settle down near their parents and grandparents and retaining some familiarity with some words of Ladino. Their experience was exceptional in the immigrant story of Sephardim from the Balkans.

a total of twenty-five hundred souls at any one time, they nonetheless set the institutional patterns that characterized American Jewry for the first century and a half of its existence. Sephardic congregations provided the sole form of worship for Jews (Israel 2002; Bernardini and Fiering 2001);[3] Sephardic social and economic integration offered a model adjustment in American society without the necessity of protracted emancipation debates so characteristic of developments on the European continent. Portuguese was the language in which the minutes of the synagogue were kept in New York. Their economic success and social mobility in the colonial period, together with the occasional dramatic arrival of a Crypto-Jewish immigrant such as the colorful Aarón López of Newport following a narrow escape from the clutches of the Portuguese Inquisition, have endowed the Sephardic Jews of colonial America with an aura of affluence, aristocracy, and drama that have continued to color the American Jewish collective memory. Predominantly merchants, the Sephardim of colonial America maintained intricate trade links with their global diaspora. Alternately depicted as martyrs, pioneers, and Iberian aristocrats, the descendants of the Sephardic founders of American Jewry and their flagship congregation, Shearith Israel, the Spanish and Portuguese Congregation in New York, would remain the leading voice of the Sephardic community and the most obvious natural patron of the Sephardic newcomers of the twentieth century. In assuming the lion's share of responsibility for the assistance and acculturation of the newcomers from the Ottoman Empire, they were assuming a burden that they perceived as one of Sephardic solidarity and communal responsibility or charity.

The so-called Sephardic first chapter in American immigration was followed by the "German chapter" as the sources of Jewish immigration shifted decisively to Germany and Central Europe in the early nineteenth century.

Just as the first period of American Jewish immigration was more German than Sephardic in origin, despite the nomenclature that later historians attached to it, so, too, the so-called German immigration was more Central and East

---

3. The recent emergence of Atlantic Studies has provided new impetus to the scrutiny of the flow of peoples, products, and ideas from Europe to North and South America and the Caribbean, bringing Sephardic Jewry into somewhat sharper focus. On the crystallization of the concept of "Port Jews" see Cesarani and Romain (2006) and Cesarani (2006).

European than German in origin by the 1870s. By the early 1880s, a tidal wave of the Jewish poor and oppressed was pouring out of Eastern Europe, bringing close to two million East European Jews to American shores by 1924. The Sephardic and Syrian Jews who arrived at the same time were virtually invisible among these Ashkenazic multitudes. Their numbers were miniscule: an estimated ten thousand Sephardim (of whom approximately one thousand were Syrian) reached America by 1913. Estimates of the American Sephardic population ranged between thirty-five and forty-five thousand in 1924. By 1934, those estimates rose to seventy-five thousand. The Sephardi-designated population included Arabic-speaking Jews from Syria and Yemen, Ladino-speaking Jews from Greece, the Balkans, and Turkey, and Greek-speaking Jews from Janina (de Sola Pool 1913, 209).[4] They differed from the large Ashkenazic immigrant group not only in volume but also in language, physiognomy, and family status.

After World War I, growing restrictionist sentiments, becoming ever more vocal since the 1890s in America, gained political power in Congress. Calls for a limitation on the absolute numbers of newcomers permitted to enter the United States mixed with more racist proposals to control the sources of immigration in order to maintain set proportions among the American population groups on the basis of national origin. The restrictionists hoped to limit severely or to cut off immigration from Italy, the Balkans, Russia, and other parts of eastern and southeastern Europe in favor of immigration from western and northern Europe. This could be done through basing the country quota allotment on the percentage of the number of immigrants already in the United States from that particular country at a given date, that is, 1890, 1900, 1910. Arguments about what cut-off date to employ were critical in determining these quotas. Thus, for instance, a cut-off date that would set the distribution of immigrant slots based on a percentage of the American population in 1890 would produce a markedly different quota from an assessment based on population breakdowns from 1900 or 1920. Nativists and restrictionists finally succeeded in 1924 in winning their congressional battle: the 1924 National Origins Immigration Act established a

---

4. The official estimates on Jewish immigration compiled by Jewish officials did not consider Sephardim who arrived before 1900 nor the identity or numbers of those who arrived at ports other than New York (Angel 1973).

system of immigration quotas based on the 1890 population figures, thus giving preferential immigrant status to Western European immigrants (the so-called "good immigration" from Germany, England, Ireland) while severely limiting or practically barring people who were perceived to be "inferior" immigrants. At the same time, a ceiling was set on the absolute number of visas that would be allocated for entry to America. This legislation virtually closed the doors of America to all applicants from eastern and southeastern Europe just as the clouds of fascism and Nazism were gathering. The 1924 immigration quotas were disastrous for the Sephardim as well as the Ashkenazim. Whereas England (Ireland had its own large quota) was allotted over 62,000 immigrant slots per annum, and Germany was granted 45,229, countries where most Sephardim resided were extremely restricted in numbers. The needy masses of Turkey were granted only 123 allotted places per annum, Syria received a quota of 100 places, Greece was allocated 135 spots, and Bulgaria was apportioned 200 places, Russia was granted only 1,892 and Poland, 8,972. Both Ashkenazim and the Sephardim of Europe were thus left to confront the Holocaust with no hope of asylum in America. Most other countries, following the American precedent, tightened their own immigration laws in the 1930s. With American doors shut tight, Sephardic migration assumed different directions—to Mexico, Cuba, France, Spain, Argentina, or wherever there might be some possibility of gaining entry. The most logical and nearest refuge for the Jews of the Eastern Mediterranean was obviously Palestine, but it too was virtually closed by the British mandatory policy culminating in the White Paper of 1939.

Sephardic and Syrian immigration to America from the Balkans and Greece continued in diminished form after the 1924 quotas were enacted, not to resume until after World War II. In the interim, both groups underwent a period of Americanization as contacts with the old world declined and economic and social integration accelerated, particularly as a result of their active participation in the American war effort during World War II.[5] Thus the first quarter of

---

5. As in the case of other Americans, the war proved to be a formative experience for Sephardim in molding an American Jewish identity. In its aftermath, the move to the suburbs resulted in the greater dispersal of the Sephardim of Balkan origin. In contrast, the postwar Syrian Jews experienced expanded institutional development in Brooklyn as a new influx of Syrians, Egyptians,

the twentieth century forms a distinctive chapter in American Sephardic history requiring special attention. Decisions and actions taken and attitudes adopted in those formative years were to shape the future of the two groups in America.

After World War II, immigration of Sephardim resumed. Few European Sephardic Jews survived World War II in the Balkans, with the notable exception of the Jews of "old" Bulgaria who emigrated en masse to Israel. A tiny remnant of Greek survivors gained entry to America as a result of family reunion initiatives in the immediate postwar period. With the disappearance of the Sephardim of Europe, the main reservoir of Sephardim now resided solely in the world of Islam. The creation of the State of Israel in 1948 was accompanied by a mounting tide of violent Arab nationalism, forcing almost one million Jews to flee their ancestral homes. As the European colonial presence in the Muslim world unraveled, most Jews from Muslim lands fled to Israel or, in the Algerian case, to France. Smaller groups of Middle Eastern Jews from Lebanon and Egypt settled down among the Syrians in Brooklyn, retaining their separate identities. They turned to the Syrians for community services and tended to be absorbed into the Syrian community.

During the 1960s American immigration policy began to liberalize, and a new wave of Sephardic immigration, Israelis from Middle Eastern countries, began. No precise figures exist on the internal composition of this immigrant group (Shokeid 1988). The last large influx of non-Ashkenazic Jews to America began in the late 1970s with the flight of two separate and distinct communities—Iranian Jews, in the wake of the Islamic Revolution of 1979, and Bukharan Jews from Uzbekistan who emigrated with the fall of the Soviet Union in 1989. The approximately seventy-five thousand Iranians settled primarily in Los Angeles and New York. An estimated fifty thousand Jews from Uzbekistan settled principally in New York. During the 1990s the remnant of the Jewish community of Syria were released from their forced confinement in Damascus and joined their relatives in the Syrian Jewish community of Brooklyn.

This brief enumeration suggests several important characteristics of Sephardic migration to America: the influx of Sephardim was concentrated at the

---

and Lebanese bolstered their numbers at the same time that postwar economic expansion brought new affluence to the community.

beginning and the very end of the twentieth century. A long period intervened during the twentieth century during which the Sephardim and the Syrians were exposed to the full force of American culture. The two groups responded differently to the century of acculturation, based on the historic and cultural baggage that they brought with them. Sephardim were heterogeneous and less observant than the Syrians. The Syrians hailed overwhelmingly from the city of Aleppo. In contrast to the Syrians, the Sephardim possessed no important traditional leadership at their helm. Although both groups prized their distinctive cultures and spoke their own language, which set them apart from the Ashkenazic majority, only the Syrians were able to maintain their differences beyond the immigrant generation.

All estimates of the current size and internal breakdown of the contemporary American Sephardic population are extremely unreliable. American law prohibits any inquiries about religion on its census questionnaires, and the internal Jewish censuses do not break down Jewish populations on the basis of national origin. Questions of mother tongue on the US census questionnaires, while helpful, are not definitive indicators of religious and cultural identity. Identifying someone as Jewish based upon his stated mother tongue of Arabic, Spanish, or Greek (or more recently as Russian, Farsi or Uzbek) is highly unreliable. Middle Eastern and Balkan Christians arrived in larger numbers than Jews in the early twentieth century. Similarly, Muslims from Central Asia and Iran have been a dominant group in those waves of immigration in recent years. Only immigrants born in the Ottoman Empire who designated Spanish as their mother tongue on the census questionnaires can automatically be assumed to have been Jewish. Further complicating any attempts to identify the internal breakdown of Jewish immigration is the fact that the Hebrew Sheltering and Immigrant Aid Society (known as HIAS), the Jewish welfare agency responsible for assisting the new Americans, did not maintain separate records on Sephardic Jews. The HIAS identifying rubric "other countries" as place of origin is too vague to help us determine the provenance of a particular Jewish immigrant subgroup. In the parlance of HIAS, Jews from the Middle East and the Balkans were all "Orientals," a designation that Sephardim were to find disconcerting, if not racist. Finally, with the widespread intramarriage between Ashkenazim and Sephardim (which many regarded as equivalent to an intermarriage), particularly among the Balkan Sephardim arriving in the early twentieth century and later Israeli immigrants, it is impossible to define who is Sephardic. It is generally assumed that Sephardim (the broad designation that includes all the above separate groups) number approximately 350,000 souls in the contemporary American community. Some of them are affiliated with Sephardic institutions, but most have entered the American Ashkenazic mainstream. Only the Iranians, Bukharans, and Syrians consistently maintain strong separate identities and have an *approximate* idea of their numbers. In the final analysis, what unites the many disparate groups and waves of immigrants who are loosely designated today as Sephardic is that they are *not* Ashkenazic. Either they or their parents originated in lands that were under Muslim rule for many centuries and consequently share many liturgical and some cultural characteristics. Their many historic and internal differences belie the notion of a single Sephardic community in the United States, a reality that was also the case one century ago when the modern Sephardic immigration to America began. As a result of the huge disparity in numbers between Ashkenazic and Sephardic immigrants to North America, coupled with the general ignorance on the part of otherwise excellent historians of all matters pertaining to Sephardim, the Ashkenazic experience has dominated the American Jewish immigration narrative until today.[6]

Like most non-Jews, Sephardic (as well as Ashkenazic) Jews were motivated to immigrate to America by economic factors. Like their fellow countrymen, they were galvanized to leave their ancient communities because of poverty. The opportunities America offered had become legendary in Europe and the Ottoman Empire, some no doubt embellished by reports of early visitors to the New Orleans Centennial Exposition in 1885 and the Louisiana Purchase Centennial Exposition in St. Louis in 1904. In addition, the impact of the Balkan Wars on the Jews was devastating. During these bitter conflicts, the Jews were caught between the warring peoples of the dying Ottoman Empire and frequently were accused by the emerging successor nations of being pro-Turkish. Specific catastrophes such as earthquakes or the fire in Istanbul in 1910 and the

6. Recent overviews by Diner (2003) and Sarna (2004) continue to place Sephardim solely within the colonial American context. The historiographic lacuna should be remedied in some measure by Aviva Ben-Ur's book, *Where Diasporas Met: A History of Sephardi Jews in the United States, 1654–2000* (2009).

conflagration that destroyed the entire Jewish business and residential section of Salonica in 1917 finally convinced many tightly knit Sephardic families to loosen their hold on their sons to send them to America to seek a better life. Jews also suffered from the World War I campaigns in the Middle East as well as from a series of natural disasters and plagues that swept through the Ottoman Arab provinces. Nationalism was inflamed in the aftermath as the Treaty of Lausanne and the emergence of the Turkish Republic in 1923 brought massive population dislocations. Jews were displaced in Salonica, for example, to make way for the influx of approximately one hundred thousand Greeks who were thrown out of Turkey in a vast population transfer of Greeks and Turks. The resulting atmosphere in Greek Salonica was virulently xenophobic, leading to further deterioration in the position of the formerly Jewish majority in that great port city. Thwarted by the territorial adjustments of the postwar settlement, Bulgarians also turned upon their Jewish neighbors in Thrace and Macedonia. The redrawing of national boundaries in the Balkans and the creation of the new state of Yugoslavia further aroused nationalist movements as Jewish security became ever more tenuous.

With future prospects dim and few economic opportunities available, single Jewish men throughout the Eastern Mediterranean were encouraged to leave their homes to smooth the way for the eventual migration of their families to America. In addition, many young Jewish graduates who had enjoyed the educational benefits of the newly established schools of the Alliance Israélite Universelle in the Middle East and the Balkans found few economic opportunities to meet their rising expectations and fresh skills. The Alliance graduate also frequently experienced a new sense of freedom from the traditional family or restlessness to stake his or her future elsewhere. In the case of the Syrians, immigration to North America formed one link in a transnational communal chain stretching from the Middle East, through Manchester in England, to New York, Mexico City, Panama, or Brazil and Argentina (Zenner 2000, chap. 7; Mirelman 1987, 24–25; Lesser 1992; Hamui de Halabe 1989). The number of Jewish émigrés from the "old world" grew exponentially as nephews followed uncles, younger brothers followed older brothers, with single Syrian men outnumbering women. Brides were frequently selected in the old country from among related families and dispatched to America to buttress the ties binding business and family, the old world and the new (Sutton 1988).

While all subject peoples were smarting under the yoke of a corrupt and decaying Ottoman regime, the Jews faced new problems as the empire teetered on the verge of collapse. For centuries, Jews and Christians had enjoyed cultural and religious autonomy in the Ottoman Empire, enjoying a low level of toleration under Islamic laws of discriminatory majority-minority relations. In the nineteenth century, the future of the Ottoman minorities appeared brighter as a result of the enactment of a series of legislative reforms that promised them greater personal security and more equitable treatment before the law. These reforms, known collectively as the Tanzimat, introduced Western legislative traditions that, in many cases, superseded the sharia and overthrew the old relations between the minorities and the majority Muslims. Trends toward greater equality for minorities also upset the fragile historic balance among the minorities; greater freedom for Jews was greeted with consternation and even hostility on the part of the Ottoman Christians, while greater freedoms for Christians was regarded with suspicion on the part of Muslims. Indeed, as the Jewish status improved in the nineteenth and early twentieth centuries, new economic rivalry between Christian and Jew emerged. Blood libels against the Jews appeared with increasing frequency in the Greek Orthodox, Armenian, and Coptic communities of Arab lands, probably as a result of the growing influence of the Western powers in the area, with their European anti-Semitic baggage. The Ottoman Christians repeatedly attacked the Jews in the Balkans as blood libels were fabricated in the Arab provinces. Indeed, so alarming was the anti-Jewish violence and so numerous the signs of impending ethnic explosion in the Eastern Mediterranean that American Jewish philanthropic groups assumed in 1914 that fully one quarter million Jews from the Balkans, Turkey, and the Near East could be expected to flee to America within the foreseeable future.[7]

The coup de grâce that set off Sephardic (as well as Christian) immigration was not the increasing poverty and instability in the area, however, but a new and unanticipated perceived threat to the Ottoman minorities. Prior to the mid-nineteenth century, it was customary for Ottoman Jews and Christians to

---

7. The influx of Jews to America from Ottoman lands became particularly noticeable during the Italo-Turkish war of 1911 and the Balkan Wars of 1913–14. Only the outbreak of World War I stemmed the tide of emigration.

be exempted from military service. While the Tanzimat era introduced many improvements in the Jews' political status, the reforming legislation also entailed new obligations. In 1855 the traditional discriminatory poll tax levied on non-Muslims, the *jizya*, was abolished and replaced by a military substitution tax known as the *bedel askariye*. For a payment, Jews and Christians (as well as Muslims) could buy their way out of military service. But the constitutional revolution of the Young Turks in 1908 raised, for the first time, the specter of conscription of all males, regardless of religion. This special payment in lieu of military service imposed a special burden on the masses of Jewish poor, unable to pay the annual exemption tax as wars and conscription increased. In 1910 the *bedel askariye* was abolished and Muslims and non-Muslims alike were drafted. The threat of conscription and the religious problems raised by service in the Ottoman army provided the final push to emigrate. The fear of imminent army service, alongside the widespread destruction in the area as a result of the Turco-Italian War of 1911 and the Balkan Wars that raged in 1912–14, convinced the Jewish youth from the villages of Anatolia, the Jewish quarters of Aleppo and Istanbul, and the ancient Greek-speaking Romaniotes of Macedonia and Thrace to join the larger wave of Christian émigrés to America.

From the outset, the Sephardic immigration differed from that of the Ashkenazim. Whereas Ashkenazic immigration tended to be in family groups, Sephardic immigration was usually of single males. Thus the plight of the Sephardic immigrant in a strange land was much more acute, his adjustment more painful. At the same time, Syrian migration was much smaller than the stream from the Balkans, and Syrians found themselves isolated among the immigrant Jewish masses. While Syrians and Sephardim shared many customs and rituals, they were internally divided by language and could scarcely communicate with one another, let alone with the Ashkenazic Yiddish-speaking immigrant majority among whom they settled. Their mutual incomprehension has been compared to the tower of Babel. Most of the Sephardic immigrants spoke Judeo-Spanish (Ladino), but they were not Hispanic, and while the Syrian Jews were Arabic-speaking, they shared no ties with the Arabic-speaking Syrian Christians simultaneously settling in New York (but on the Lower West Side) in larger numbers. Divided by language and customs from their co-religionists and by religion from their fellow countrymen, they formed separate worlds unto themselves despite being concentrated in one of the most densely populated districts in the world. Minor differences from the old country were accentuated in their new setting, making it virtually impossible for the different Sephardic groups to reach agreement on community-wide issues. The 1926 Jewish community report on Sephardim in New York reflects uncomprehendingly on some of these layers of misunderstanding: "The men of Kastoria in their synagogues employed a slightly different cantillation that was unpleasing to the men of the island of Chios. Incidentally, it is in the Oriental temperament to be suspicious even of the slightly unfamiliar, with the result that because of a localism that was the development of centuries, men from towns only thirty miles apart were prone to regard one another with distrust."[8]

k

Unlike the Judeo-Spanish Jews of Ottoman lands, the Syrians were quite homogeneous. Most of the Syrians arriving in New York hailed from one town, Aleppo. They proudly shared the same legacy, one that went back hundreds, if not thousands, of years. Their familial ties were also particularly intense. While both the Sephardim and the Syrian Jews began as peddlers, moving upward to ownership in one branch of the textile industry, linens and infant wear, Syrian Jews tended to remain in the same trade as their parents and grandparents. Commerce was not an avenue to professionalization nor was eventual prosperity seen as an instrument aiding them in attaining higher education. Family remained the focus of their culture. The first American challenge that both groups confronted was their estrangement from the American Jewish majority; they wondered who would assist them in the predominantly Yiddish culture of the neighboring Jewish immigrant community. Moreover, being so few in numbers, how would they manage to preserve their distinctive subcultures forged over almost two thousand years of diasporic existence in Syria, Yemen, or Greece, and one half a millennium in Turkey? Their dilemma was very specific: if they joined together simply as Sephardim, their unique defining traits would be lost. But if they did not federate and unite, their broader Sephardic identity would be lost as well, as they

---

8. A summary of Louis Hacker's 1926 report, "The Communal Life of the Sephardic Jews of New York City," can be found in *The Jewish Social Service Quarterly* 3, no. 2:32–40. In 1926, Hacker counted thirty-six separate Sephardi fraternal societies, primarily concerned with sickness and death benefits.

melded with American Jewry. More immediate questions of survival and liveli-
hood took precedence.

It was customary for HIAS, the Jewish welfare agency entrusted with immigrant resettlement, to send its social workers to the piers in New York or Philadelphia to examine the ship manifests to help the incoming Jews overcome the
first hurdles in their initial entry to America and to prevent their falling victim
to charlatans or promoters. But the roster of Sephardic names, such as Russo,
Alhadeff, Matarasso, Matalon, or Hasson, bore no resemblance to the Ashkenazic names with which the social workers were familiar. Frequently of different
physiognomy from Ashkenazim, with no understanding of Yiddish, Sephardic
Jews fell below the radar screen. An article in the *New York Tribune* of September 22, 1912, "New York City Is a City Apart Where Live Jews Who Know No
Yiddish," reflects this quandary of the established Jewish community and their
doubts that these "Turks, Greeks and Arabs" were really Jewish.

The differences between the old-timers and the Sephardic newcomers went
further. The newcomers pronounced Hebrew differently, tended to be suspicious
of outsiders, and loved different foods. For the Judeo-Spanish Jews, spicy foods
such as *pescado con tomate*—fish in a sweet-and-sour tomato sauce—or *pescado
con huevos y limon*—fish in egg-lemon sauce—were the Sabbath meal staple rather
than the Friday evening East European favorite gefilte fish. The Syrians, in particular, stressed family unity and religious orthodoxy. The problem of cultural
estrangement among different Jews was not limited to New York City. Rabbi Marc
D. Angel recalls his mother's accounts of how the Ashkenazim in Seattle taunted
their Sephardic neighbors by calling them *Mazola*, since the latter used vegetable
oil instead of chicken fat in their cooking. The Sephardim responded by calling the
Ashkenazim *schmaltz* (chicken fat) (1982, 45). Even when the prayers of the various
groups were the same, they were accompanied by different gestures (Sutton 1979,
23). These differences also raised questions about the Jewishness of the worshipers.
Thus Joseph Sutton recalls of his Syrian immigrant experience: "During a mid-
week prayer service in an East European synagogue, my father, ritually clothed in
taleet, a prayer shawl, the *tefileen*, phylacteries, was approached by an Ashkenazic
congregant. Since he didn't understand what was being said to him in 'plain Yiddish' the man who had spoken to him asked in evident amazement, 'Bist du a Yid?'
(Are you a Jew?). Similar stories fill the memoirs of Sephardim in other United
States cities." Memoirs and oral interviews as well as the Ladino press repeatedly

dealt with the hurt of these slights, citing both its humorous and its painful aspects. Decades later, Sephardim and Syrians still recalled the sense of hurt the newcomers felt (Sutton 1988). One of the reasons editor Moise Gadol proffered for supporting the Ladino press was that Ladino in Hebrew script would prove the Jewishness of subscribers and readers to the Ashkenazim. The failure of Ashkenazim to recognize the Sephardic newcomers as fellow Jews is echoed in the following 1916 description of a Lower East Side street scene by social worker Samuel Auerbach, a description especially noteworthy, as the reporter was Istanbul-born:[9]

> See the signs on these institutions. They read "Café Constantinople," "Café Oriental," "Café Smyrna," and there are other signs in Hebrew characters that you perhaps cannot read. Are they Jews? No, it cannot be; they do not look like Jews; they do not speak Yiddish. Listen: what is that strange tongue they are using? It sounds like Spanish or Mexican. Are they Spaniards or Mexicans? If so, where did they get the coffeehouses, an importation from Greece and Turkey? . . . On your way home you think and wonder who these alien people can be who speak Spanish yet are not Spaniards; speak Greek, yet are not Greeks; have Turkish as their mother tongue and wear turbans, yet are not Muslims.

Divisions and misunderstandings abounded. These differences were still pronounced in 1926 when acculturation had been proceeding for more than one decade. As a 1926 social work report noted: "Although the Sephardic Jews have in the main settled in those parts of the city inhabited by their Ashkenazic coreligionists, the former find themselves as alien and apart as if they had settled somewhere in China or Sweden. It is quite difficult for the Yiddish- and German-speaking Jews, who surpass all others in number, to reconcile themselves to the belief that there can be other Jews who do not employ the same means of linguistic utterance" (Ben-Ur 2009, 10). For Syrian Jews, the slights from the Ashkenazic community were similarly acute as Arabic-speaking Jews were fewer in numbers and even more unfamiliar.[10]

9. For a nuanced discussion of the issue of co-ethnic nonrecognition, see Ben-Ur (2009). Ben Ur notes the verbatim resemblances between the Auerbach article and a June 1914 report by David de Sola Pool.

10. On the Syrian situation, see Zenner (2000).

It was commonplace in the history of immigration for all immigrant groups to seek out the part of the host population that shared common ethnic or religious bonds with them. This host often became the most important reference group in their Americanization process, even when the shared ethnicity represented quite different things to the two groups.

Like all immigrants, the Sephardim turned to their fellow townsmen and kin for assistance. Poor, young, and predominantly single, the Sephardic newcomers sought solace among their own people but it was not quite clear who were "their kinsmen" beyond those from the same village or town. The newcomers established their own groceries to supply the olives, cheeses, and sweets familiar to the Turkish or Syrian palate. Record stores imported favorite records of popular Turkish singers, advertising the arrival of new records in the Ladino press. Before long, Sephardic restaurants and cafés, even separate ones such as Rosie Mizrahi's restaurant for the Syrians, appeared on the Lower East Side, providing a cheap meal in a welcoming atmosphere with fixed menus reminiscent of home cooking in Aleppo or Turkey. The Sephardic cafés and restaurants provided a refuge where lonely Sephardic males, many of whom lived as boarders in apartments of Ashkenazim, could meet fellow Sephardim. The unemployed among them could be found at all hours of the day and night smoking, drinking Turkish coffee, and playing backgammon (*sheshbesh*) or gambling. The spectacle of such idleness did not escape the scrutiny and dismay of the established Sephardic and Ashkenazic communities, prompting the leaders of HIAS to establish a special agency to deal with the needs of the Sephardim. To this end, an Oriental Bureau began to function in 1911. Understaffed and underfunded, the bureau closed in 1915. Disturbed by the breakdown of religious and family life among the Sephardic immigrants, and especially concerned about the welfare of the women among them, the Sisterhood of the Spanish and Portuguese Synagogue, Shearith Israel, sprang into action, assuming the responsibility of providing for the spiritual and social needs of the newcomers. In establishing a neighborhood house, first on Orchard Street on the Lower East Side of New York some time prior to 1910, then, as its activities expanded, in enlarged quarters on Eldridge Street in 1918, the Sisterhood became deeply involved in the immigrant community. As the Sisterhood of the synagogue acknowledged in its 1912–13 report, "While we maintain that the problem (i.e., the Oriental Jews) is one for the general community to solve through existent institutions, we will undertake to conduct at 86 Orchard Street . . . a neighborhood

House, which, in connection with our work for the betterment of Jews from all countries, shall also be a center for the Oriental colony downtown."

Sentiments of solidarity with the newcomers on the part of the Shearith Israel Sisterhood could not hide the fact that their charitable activities on behalf of the new Sephardim were intermixed with a sense of noblesse oblige. The affinity between the "old" and "new" Sephardim—the old-line New York members of Shearith Israel and the Ladino-speaking Jews of the Balkans—was only skin deep. For one thing, the descendants of the first colonial American immigration had virtually disappeared by the twentieth century. The Shearith Israel crowd was thoroughly Americanized, a majority of its membership was Ashkenazic, and the veteran Sephardim among them retained few vestiges of distinctive Sephardic culture beyond a sprinkling of Judeo-Spanish prayers in their ritual and a great deal of pride in their ancestors. Few in numbers, they appreciated the fact that the newcomers could add fresh blood, vitality, and authenticity to their diminishing Sephardic ranks. The Shearith Israel bulletin of February 1912 welcomed the new immigrants from the Balkans and the Middle East, commenting: "The great increase in the number of Sephardic Jews in America is a happy guarantee of the survival and spread in the United States of the ancient *minhag* of our congregation" (Angel 1982, 89). There was more than a touch of irony in the fact that these "helpers" regarded the Balkan Sephardic immigrants, the direct descendants of the exiles of Spain of 1492, as "Orientals" or "Levantines," hoping to reserve the appellation "Sephardi" for themselves. The immigrants, in turn, found being labeled Orientals or Levantines denigrating. Although the term "Levantine" was soon discarded, "Oriental" continued to be used to designate the newcomers, much to their chagrin, for many years. As Dr. Marc Angel, a grandson of Sephardi immigrants explained of the immigrant sensitivity:

> Some of the old line Sephardim felt uneasy because the new immigrants called themselves Sephardim. They were afraid the term would fall into disrepute and urged the newcomers to be called "Oriental." The immigrants, at first, accepted the new designation, but later came to resent it deeply as a slur against them. The impression had been created that the Sephardim were noble and rich while the Orientals were poor and ignorant . . . The irony of it was that many of the immigrants were pure-blooded Spanish-speaking Sephardim who were called "Orientals," while Shearith Israel members who were Ashkenazim and of mixed blood, were considered as the true Sephardim. (Angel 1973, 101)

In addition to socioeconomic differences, the newcomers exhibited many of the cultural and linguistic traits of their non-Jewish Middle Eastern neighbors that were at variance with the American ethos. The newcomers, especially the men among them, were concerned that the greater freedom and multiple roles played by Jewish women in America would undermine their traditional family hierarchies. At the same time, the women among the immigrants admired the greater freedom of American Jewish women in the economic as well as the personal sphere and envied their higher rates of political involvement and Hebrew literacy. Tensions existed among the Sephardic newcomers themselves over the degree of Americanization that was desirable. These mutual suspicions and apprehensions were expressed in the letters to the editor in the Ladino press. Differences of class between Sephardim and new Sephardim were also pronounced. The ignorance and poverty of the newcomers, coupled with their lack of polish and many superstitious folkways, posed a challenge to the "uptown" Jews, not dissimilar to the challenge that the East European Jewish newcomers posed to the established German Jews.

While the Jews of Turkey and the Balkans reluctantly accepted assistance from the old Sephardim in New York, Syrian Jews from the outset rejected such aid and set up their own networks to help each other, using their family diaspora of relatives as their primary reference group and support system. They also established a short-lived Arabic press for themselves. Their mutual assistance was buttressed by their mode of combining business and family. When they traveled on business Syrian merchants would spend extended stays in the many far-flung Syrian outposts, frequently setting sons or nephews up to serve as agents in such outposts to facilitate the success of the family business. Partnerships with suppliers in the various Syrian diasporas were especially strong, with family members serving as both the suppliers and the wholesalers. Leaving the family business was tantamount to leaving the community. To rebel against the family took the form of moving away from the neighborhood and the community. Matchmaking and business went hand in hand, further cementing the already strong Syrian Jewish bonds.[11]

11. Typescript of an article entitled, "Reinterpretation of a Tradition by a Transnational Elite," delivered at the American Anthropological Association, 2000, Walter P. Zenner Archives, American Sephardi Federation, Center for Jewish History, New York. The importance of matchmaking in business relations figures prominently in Sutton's oral interviews (1988).

Pride and hypersensitivity to putative insults from the Ashkenazim as well as from the Old Sephardim characterized both groups of Sephardic newcomers. Louis Hacker, the social worker whose 1926 report has shed so much light on the immigrant generation observed that, "The Oriental Jews, unless they be decrepit, blind or maimed ask and take no charity, and to maintain themselves—no work is too hard . . . they consider themselves a people apart; they are 'Spanish Jews' with a distinct historical consciousness and, often, an inordinate pride." The immigrants were particularly sensitive about accepting charity, even if it originated with Sephardic brethren. They spoke proudly of their illustrious ancestry of courtiers and poets; they glorified their medieval past, painfully contrasting it with their contemporary downtrodden state.[12] Moise Gadol, who was originally an immigrant from Bulgaria and was the editor of *La America*, urged the Sephardic newcomers to hire their own rabbis and teachers directly from Turkey in order to preserve and to nurture their distinctive culture and to reestablish their former glory. He exhorted them to assist one another to show both the "Portuguese Jews and the Ashkenazim that we Sephardim of the Orient are the descendants of the Spanish Jewish greats and we are capable of united action."[13] Although Syrians proceeded to hire their own religious leaders, Sephardim lagged behind in this respect.

From the outset, the Sephardic Jews built parallel institutions to the Ashkenazim, ones that were not just American but were built on Jewish models. Thus, for instance, they not only formed fraternal organizations like all immigrant groups, but Sephardic branches of general Jewish organizations such as Bnai Brith, Sephardic Zionist organizations, the Oriental Jewish Maccabee

---

12. See Ben-Ur (2009), in which the divide between "Old Sephardim" and "New Sephardim" is sensitively and extensively discussed. Joseph Papo explores the relations of the immigrants with the established Sephardi community, citing the difficulty that the established community experienced in accepting the newcomers as members of their extended family. Papo argues for the essentially patronizing attitude of the old Sephardim in "Sephardim in North America in the Twentieth Century" (1993).

13. The abortive attempts of the Sephardic Jews to form some sort of union in America is the leitmotif of Papo's 1993 study. For typical arguments of Gadol in this vein see *La America*, November 11–15, December 9, 1910; April 11, May 12, June 20, July 7, 1911; January 12, March 8, May 12, 1912; February 21, 1913; October 10, 1919.

Association, and the Young Men's Sephardic Community Centers. These institutions illustrate the importance of the Ashkenazim as both reference group and model. It is, however, in the immigrant fraternal organizations or *landsmannshaften* that the fragmented or very local identity of the Sephardim was most clearly expressed. The Ladino speakers had scarcely settled down when they set up relief committees and self-help societies to offer loans, free medical services, burial plots, and some rudimentary Jewish education for the young. These societies were organized on the basis of city of origin—Monastir, Kastoria, Salonica, Janina, Dardanelles, Ankara, and elsewhere. The societies provided a link to the old country, a means of extending one's social ties beyond family connections as well as a warm, comfortable, and familiar social setting. The societies served as an ideal place where a new immigrant could vent his or her nostalgia while offering a continuation of some of the social services that existed in the communities of origin. Most important, the societies offered an arena in which the immigrants could adapt to America without being exposed to possible embarrassment or ridicule. Society minutes were initially kept in Greek, Judeo-Spanish, or Arabic depending on the native language of the newcomers. Originally most of the societies bore Hebrew names: the Greek-speaking Jews of Janina formed Hebra Ahava ve-Ahva Janina (Love and Brotherhood Society of Janina) in 1907, which, by 1910, boasted two hundred members, its own cemetery plot, and religious services for the High Holidays and the Festivals (Dalven 1990).[14] At the same time, the Ladino-speaking Jews from Greece formed the Kastoria Society.

After 1910, the number of societies proliferated. The Jews of Rhodes possessed the Yeshuah ve-Rahamim Society while Syrian Jews congregated in Rodfei Zedek. Salonica Jews formed Etz ha-Hayyim; the Turkish Jews separated into multiple organizations—the Dardenelles Society Mekor Hayyim, the Dardanelles Social Club, the Haskala Club of Gallipoli, the Ankara Union Club, and the Oriental Hebrew Association. The last-mentioned organization organized a

---

14. The original synagogue of the Greek Jews, Kehillah Kedosha Janina, still functions on Broome Street in New York's Lower East Side, offering the only surviving Romaniote services in America and currently undergoing a renewal of activities with the establishment of a small museum and website. It organizes public programs on its unique heritage for a wider public. Yanioti Jews or their descendants, however, are widely dispersed, decreasing in number and most no longer know the ancient Romaniote Jewish liturgical tradition.

Purim Ball in 1914 that boasted five-hundred attendees, including several Turkish officials! By 1926, more than thirty Sephardic societies existed. Sephardim even formed their own socialist party in 1914—the Oriental Federation and Socialist Educational Society. In addition, Sephardim launched a Sephardic Democratic Club as well as the Independent Voters' Political. A separate social club composed of Sephardim living in New York's 26th election district was also active.

The tendency to fragment into subgroups and fraternal societies, so common to Jewish immigrants in general, was lauded by the Sephardic press as a means of gaining recognition from the New York organized Jewish community (the Kehillah). Separate congregations, a natural phenomenon in light of the many differences in ritual and religious practice, also dotted the Lower East Side. Although the societies bickered among themselves, they nevertheless offered solace and a sense of familiarity to their members. One major drawback of this extreme particularism was that it tended to accentuate the minor differences among the Sephardim, keeping them in small clusters and tightly knit social groups. They possessed neither the leadership nor the means and critical mass in each subgroup to provide adequate educational settings to assure that their separate traditions would be perpetuated outside the home or social group beyond the first generation of immigrants. Reluctant to relinquish their local societies and their local identity for a broader organizing unit in the formative years, when such an organization might indeed have been a preservative of the traditions of the old world, the attempts at Sephardi community federation foundered repeatedly and failed to achieve communal effectiveness and a semblance of unity over the long run.[15] As long as the Judeo-Spanish press persisted, its pages were

15. The saga of the attempts to achieve a federated community have been chronicled by Papo (1987) in his study of the Sephardic Jews in America. Most of his material derives from the Ladino press and from his long career in Jewish communal work. His analysis describes the frequent indifference of the Sephardim to forming a united community that could offer community-wide services that transcended the small societies. To some degree, similar issues of divisiveness and apathy plague the American Sephardi Federation until today. Its aim of fostering a Sephardic cultural identity and presence in American Jewish life has continued to meet with resistance from individual groups that cherish their autonomy, on the one hand, and the growing indifference to distinctiveness beyond a generalized Jewish identity, on the other. Sephardism is more a sentiment of general pride of roots than one of practicing and preserving a distinctive language and customs at this juncture.

primarily a vehicle for Americanization, not a means for perpetuating the old-world culture. Only the Jews of Syria seemed intent upon maintaining their Syrian ritual and culture, perceiving that such a retention required living together, building their own separate educational and social institutions, importing their own teachers, if necessary, and moving en masse as one group from their area of first settlement on the Lower East Side to Brooklyn.

The Judeo-Spanish social and political clubs established by the Sephardic immigrants present a clear contrast to the institutions built by the Syrians as they began to get on their feet economically. The fact that the Syrians in America originated primarily in one town was an important unifying factor from the initial stages of their immigration and adjustment. There was probably no family of Syrians in New York that was not related to the other Syrian families, just as there was no Jewish family in Aleppo that was not related to the others by marriage. But the roots of the unique Syrian evolution ran deeper than blood ties. Aleppan Jews took pride in a long tradition of strong rabbinic leadership. The community not only respected their dynasties of rabbinical luminaries but also venerated them. It was a leadership of a particular sort. For generations, Aleppan rabbis blended religious and political roles, such as the Laniados of Spanish-Italian origin or the Ha-Dayyans who trace their lineage all the way back to the house of the seventh century *Rosh ha-Golah* (exilarch) Bustanai and through Bustanai to King David. Syrian scholars in the old country were learned in Talmud and Kabbalah. The lay leadership was especially supportive of their religious leadership, turning to it for *segulot* (talismans and amulets), enjoying the richness of its tales of miracles and trusting in those miracles. The Syrian chief rabbi, a position introduced in the nineteenth century, was a figure who wielded political power before the Muslim authorities while working in tandem with the Jewish lay leadership. This Syrian combination of close rabbinic/lay relationships persisted in New York, providing for continuity and ongoing guidance in the critical formative decades of Americanization.

Unlike what has been described by Zvi Zohar as the accommodative stance of the Sephardic leadership in general to modernity (1996), Syrian orthodoxy has exhibited what Zenner has characterized as "militant conservatism" (2000). As modern currents began to enter the Middle East, the Syrian rabbis retained their conservatism. Several rabbinical families migrated to Jerusalem from Aleppo in the 1880s, moving on after receiving rabbinical training to satellite Syrian communities in Anatolia and the Syrian diasporas in North and South America.

They thereby formed a rabbinic international axis over one century ago, deeply influenced by Ashkenazic right-wing orthodox currents acquired in Jerusalem, especially at Porat Yosef Yeshiva. Interestingly, this same conservative leadership, many of whose rabbis had some worldly business background, retained an influential position among Syrian immigrants and was attuned to changing currents within the community, such as Zionism and the thorny question of intermarriage. They were not always flexible, but they never rendered themselves irrelevant. This partnership of conservative religious leaders and savvy lay businessmen willing to follow their leaders provided a bulwark against the most corrosive effects of Americanization. With the arrival in New York in 1932 of Rabbi Jacob Kassin (1900–1994), already a recognized scholar and kabbalist despite his youth, the Syrian community gained a towering leader who served the New York Syrians for the next sixty-two years.

The Sephardim were not as fortunate. The monthly meetings of the myriad Sephardic societies could not substitute for the absence of the kind of daily services so necessary to all age groups in an immigrant community. Sephardim may have accepted the help of the old Sephardim with some ambivalence, but they did so because it was necessary and they were too divided to provide substantial community services for themselves. By 1915, more than 350,000 immigrant Jews lived on the Lower East Side, constituting one of the most densely populated area in the world. The Ashkenazim were providing immigrant services in places such as the Educational Alliance that were eagerly consumed by the vast majority of the Ashkenazim. The Sephardic Neighborhood House on Orchard Street established by the Shearith Israel Sisterhood, affectionately known as Turkey House, offered another venue for similar activities for the use of the Sephardim. Professional social workers and volunteers provided a host of religious and educational activities, including a Talmud Torah, religious services (because the Spanish and Portuguese Congregation Shearith Israel was uptown and therefore inaccessible), a roof playground and gymnasium, and classes in the English language. Significantly, the Syrian Jews do not appear in the records to have availed themselves of these services. They seem to have provided for themselves, establishing instead very strong economic networks that bolstered their families. Americanization was a key goal of the settlement house phenomenon.

One important mandate of the Shearith Israel Sisterhood was to help the newcomers attain employable skills. In this regard, they organized mock job interviews and offered instruction in dressmaking, millinery, and handicrafts. For Sephardic women, employment outside the home had been unthinkable in the old country. In New York, out of necessity, some Sephardic women began to join the labor force, while many did piecework within the house. Old country networks played a less important role in the Sephardic immigrant economy than in the Syrian. The most important commercial enterprise to employ Sephardic immigrants was the cigar factory of the Shinasi brothers, located on Hudson Street in Lower Manhattan's West Side. The Shinasi brothers provided the outstanding Sephardic example of the rags-to-riches American story. Arriving penniless from Manissa in 1892, by 1911 they owned two cigar factories in New York and were doing business that netted millions of dollars, selling one of their factories in 1916 for 3.5 million dollars. More than two hundred Turkish Jewish men and women were employed there. At the time of his death in 1919, Shelomo Shinasi bequeathed a fortune for the establishment of a hospital in his name in his native city. Similarly, four hundred of the seven hundred workers in the Sephardic-owned Interstate Electrical Battery Company in New York were Turkish Sephardim. Another noteworthy economic venture by a group of Turkish Jews, reported in *La America* in 1913, was the establishment of a company to set up a chain of stores that would sell clothing and groceries. This cooperative mercantile association promised to hire Turkish Jews. As they began to pull themselves out of their initial poverty by the mid 1920s they also started to move out of the Lower East Side of New York in several independent directions—to Harlem, the Bronx, and New Lots in Brooklyn. Family businesses in retail trade eventually gave way to professionalization as Sephardim adopted the general American Jewish route to higher education.

⚜

Syrian economic behavior followed a different trajectory. By and large, Syrian Jews rejected the American melting pot model. Until recently, they eschewed higher education and professionalization, preferring to maintain their family businesses that linked them globally in a few lines of commerce. They specialized and succeeded in branches of the economy that required no higher education, moving from the roles of peddlers to shopkeepers and dry goods manufacturers and traders to international traders in electronics, linens, lingerie, and infant wear—always within the family context. They migrated between centers of Syrian domicile, using sons, nephews, and brothers as agents, with the family always at the heart of their commerce. The connections between marriage and business were clearly articulated with economic success and the emphasis on kinship strongly emphasized and valorized.

The residential patterns of the two groups soon began to diverge as well with Sephardic Jews following those of other Americans. Their move out of the immigrant neighborhoods occurred on an individual or family basis as their economic situation improved. They tended to disperse along the lines of the Ashkenazic American Jewish migration patterns. In dispersing, their former ties, such as the fraternal organizations, weakened accordingly. In contrast, as the Syrian economic situation improved, Syrians moved en masse to Williamsburg in Brooklyn in the 1920s, again en masse in the 1930s and 1940s to Bensonhurst in Brooklyn, and finally, to the neighboring Flatbush section of Brooklyn. All the while, they remained together as a community, investing in local institutions, expanding existing housing stock, building an ever more elaborate nexus of schools, and introducing an increasingly diverse number of services for themselves. Their two synagogues and one yeshiva multiplied rapidly. Today the Syrian neighborhood includes more than a dozen synagogues—all Orthodox and following Syrian liturgy and Syrian pronunciation of Hebrew—at least ten Orthodox Day schools, several publications, study groups, restaurants, bakeries, caterers, a formidable Bikur Cholim society, a summer community at the ocean on the New Jersey shore, and a dynamic and expanding Community Center. One never has to leave the community to obtain almost all one needs. All of these keep the Syrians united—and apart from other Jews.

One other area of Americanization provides a suggestive subject for further study. Parenting and "culture" were two issues that the Sisterhood of the Spanish and Portuguese Synagogue took especially seriously in its programs of assistance to the newcomers, offering the immigrants kindergarten classes, a parents' group, an orchestra, and music lessons. In keeping with the social mores of the leisured classes in the early twentieth century, it was considered a sign of breeding for a young woman to play the piano. Thus piano lessons were introduced in the settlement house that the Sisterhood established for the Sephardim on the Lower East Side. Uncomfortable with the Ladino language of the newcomers, considering it a jargon much in the same manner as the German Jews regarded the use of Yiddish, the uptown Sephardim offered the immigrants lessons in

Castilian Spanish in order to introduce what they called "proper" Spanish to the Jews of Turkey. The perception of necessary survival skills that were offered to the Sephardim in the early part of the twentieth century as the immigrants were introduced to America were thus undifferentiated, in many vital respects, from American Jewish values of that time, with a strong emphasis on assimilation to the broader American way.

In providing for themselves with little American Jewish mediation, the Syrians accomplished a remarkable feat. They provided cultural services for themselves, insisting, for example, on the transmission to their youth of their unique musical tradition of *pizmonim*, which has played a defining role in the preservation of the traditions of Aleppo. The Syrian traditions were, at an early period, given pride of place in their own network of Jewish day schools. This network has expanded during the past generation to include most male and female children in the community.

Sephardic immigrants, unlike the Ashkenazim, bore no animosity toward their former homeland. Indeed, donations sent back to the old country included contributions to build and support local institutions, such as hospitals, in Greece and Turkey. Positive feelings toward Turkey persisted on the Lower East Side: Sephardic organizations even petitioned the American government to exempt them from conscription during World War I lest they be forced to fight against the Turks. Turkish officials were invited to Sephardic assemblies and celebrations, and the Ladino press repeatedly invoked the Ottoman Empire with gratitude for the haven that had been granted the exiles from Spain in 1492. Like other immigrant groups, Sephardim had left their families behind in the Balkans and Greece and continued to send remittances home until the destruction of the European communities in the Holocaust. Their pride in a distant past and gratitude for events long removed from their everyday needs might have provided emotional ballast as they struggled to get a toehold in America, but it scarcely afforded effective tools to withstand America's enticements and assimilatory pressures.

The organization of the Sephardic masses in America was chaotic at best. While individual leaders would exhort the immigrants to learn English and attend meetings, repeatedly urging people to pay membership dues to a fraternal society and to join forces to form one community, the Federation of Sephardi Jews established in 1912 soon foundered. It lacked leaders, money, and most of all, the will of its few members to unite their separate societies founded on old world affiliations into one Sephardic community. The Ladino press repeatedly deplored the fact that most meetings were woefully under-attended. Several attempts were made to unite the Sephardic community in the 1920s, 1930s, and 1940s. Each attempt was unsuccessful. Suggestions to drop the names of individual societies, joining them into a merged unit under one umbrella organization, also met with little success. In 1972, an American Sephardi Federation was established. By that point, Sephardic Jews were basically indistinguishable from the majority of the (Ashkenazic) American Jewish community. Ladino, like Yiddish, was generally incomprehensible to the native, American-born generation. Salonica was a distant memory, recalled more as a result of its tragic destruction by the Nazis than as the cradle of a unique cultural experience. The name of Kastoria is preserved in the continuation of joint burial plots from an earlier era. Up to today, efforts at Sephardi unity in America are elusive. The parts are, however, greater than the whole. True, the Bukharan and Persian Jewish communities are visible and distinctive, but only time will tell whether this vitality is more than a first-generation immigrant phenomenon.

The immigrant experience of the Judeo-Spanish Sephardic Jews has been submerged within the success story of the greater American Jewish community. Having successfully Americanized, they filled the expectations of their "old" Sephardic uptown patrons and hosts. One sign of their successful Americanization is that so little attention has been paid to them and so few remnants of their rich folk culture have survived. In contrast, the 2009 Syrian Jewish community constitutes a unique ethnic group among the Jews of America. Syrian Jews are integrated Americans, already three and four generations in the United States; they dress like and live like their Ashkenazic brethren. Yet their intermarriage rates are much lower than other American Jews, their religious affiliation tends to be Syrian/Orthodox, and their economic profile is still enmeshed in a pattern of interfamilial ties. The community has been willing to heed the calls of their rabbis to build a fence around themselves through a formidable institutional network and an unwillingness to countenance intermarriage or even conversion within their community. They continue to live together, pray together, and support the transmission of their distinctive culture through a set of strong educational and social institutions. The Syrian success at maintaining their identity, so fundamentally different from both the Ashkenazim and the other Sephardim, continues to confound the sociologists. Arriving at the same time, in more or less the same numbers, starting out with the same basic skills and demographic profile, the Syrians and the Judeo-Spanish Sephardic paths have diverged in most essential ways. One century after their arrival, the Sephardic community is preserved mostly in the memory and a sprinkling of Ladino vocabulary among a disappearing generation. As one Sephardi observer has poignantly exclaimed: "I am a third-generation Sephardic Jew, Monastirli on my mother's side and Yanioti on my father's. I speak no Judeo-Spanish and no Greek. I can faithfully duplicate only a few traditions of the Yanioti Passover, such as the style of the *Dayenu* chant; others are but shadowy memories. Like many third-generation ethnics, food provides my closest attachment to my heritage. . . . Between me and authentic cultural practice, then, lies an unbridgeable gulf" (Matza 1992, 11).

Part 2   **Ideological Divergence**

Zionism, Religion,
and Transnationalism

4

Cultural Zionism as a Contact Zone

Sephardic and Ashkenazi Jews Bridge the Gap on the Pages of the Argentine Newspaper Israel

RAANAN REIN *and* MOLLIE LEWIS NOUWEN

"For practical reasons," Argentine Jews should not immigrate to Palestine, declared a contributor to the Sephardi Zionist newspaper *Israel,* because the arrival of too many people could cause both a moral and economic catastrophe in that Middle Eastern territory (Jan. 12, 1920). Like other articles in *Israel,* a newspaper founded by Moroccan Sephardim in Buenos Aires, not only did this one explicitly call for readers not to emigrate, but it even went so far as to suggest that Argentina was preferable to Palestine.[1] Jews had made Argentina their home and wanted other Argentines to recognize them as members of the nation. Sometimes Zionism was not about Palestine—it was about creating identities in the Diaspora.

The authors are grateful to the Elías Sourasky Chair of Iberian and Latin American Studies and the S. Daniel Abraham Center of International and Regional Studies, both at Tel Aviv University, for their support. We would also like to thank Margalit Bejarano for her useful comments on an earlier version of this text. In this chapter, the word Sephardim is used for those Jews who descended from those expelled from Spain and those who immigrated to Argentina from Arab countries. All translations are by the authors.

1. One of the cases in which the newspaper showed its support for migration to Palestine was the publication of a manifesto, signed with the pseudonym Rubeni, where the author asked for the migration of one hundred Jewish-Argentine families and included a detailed plan to carry it out. In this case, the editor added words of support (see *Israel,* April 1, 1921).

For the editors and contributors to *Israel*, Zionism was about their lives in Argentina. Even though it was a global movement, Sephardim and Ashkenazim in *Israel* united around an apolitical strain of Zionism that emphasized their place in Argentina. Between 1917 and the late 1930s, these Jews of diverse backgrounds used Zionism to create a new Jewish identity, based as much on a common mythic past as on the hope of a shared future in Argentina. Hence, the Zionism of those surrounding *Israel* did not suggest that Argentine Jews should return to Palestine, the historic home of the Jews, but rather that Argentina could become the homeland of both Sephardim and Ashkenazim, just as Zionism could unite the Jews of the Diaspora. On one hand, then, the new Zionism expressed in *Israel* reflected the desire of the contributors to be recognized as part of the Argentine nation and not as radical or militant, nationalist Jews; on the other, it presented a usable past for the Jews as well as a pattern for future unification of Sephardim and Ashkenazim in that country.

Through Zionism, the Sephardim and Ashkenazim grouped around *Israel* created a common Jewish past as the basis for an imagined community. They created a nation of origin, allowing them to fit in with other immigrant groups. In this sense, Palestine fulfilled the same role for the Jews that Italy did for the Italian immigrants (the largest immigrant group in Argentina). The idea of a place of origin was clearly more important than its actual existence.

The Jews at *Israel* affirmed their own national past through Zionism, yet the desire for a future Jewish state was less clear before the outbreak of World War II. The newspaper did include photographs of Palestine and requests for donations to the Zionist cause, yet despite the difficulties that many immigrants faced in Argentina, few showed any sign of leaving it.[2] Both Palestine and the impetus to move there seemed remote. As Argentines, they were linked to the daily life of their own country, not to a vague idea of a possible future Jewish state in the Middle East.

2. See, for example, in *Israel* (August 13 and December 3, 1920), information about the campaign to collect funds for the Zionist Federation of Argentina and the visit of Max Nordau, who came to Argentina to raise money for the construction of a Jewish home in Palestine (June 9, 1920).

Studying Latin American Jews

Many themes relating to Latin American Jews have yet to be studied in depth, particularly the history of those unaffiliated with communal organizations, and the roles of class and gender.[3] Most studies of Latin American Jews to date have focused on Jewish communal institutions. Because at least 50 percent of the Jews currently living in Latin America are unaffiliated, the scholarship centered exclusively on those belonging to communal organizations effectively leaves out the story of at least half of the people it attempts to study.[4] At the same time, a large part of the specialized literature creates the false impression that Jews in Latin America were homogeneous and free from social stratification. In these texts, Latin American Jews are usually presented as if they had moved quickly and easily into the middle and upper classes. This incorrect premise has led numerous scholars to disdain any work that concerns itself with poor or working-class Jews.[5] Another area often neglected in the study of ethnicity in Latin America, and Jews in particular, is that of gender. Research on Jewish women has tended to concentrate on their roles as either prostitutes or intellectuals, even though Jewish women played many different roles.[6] As Sandra McGee Deutsch pointed out for the Argentine case, "Jewish women are virtually absent from the secondary historical sources. Studying them is vital for its own sake, to recover the voices and tell the untold stories of the unheard half of the Jewish population" (2004). The same argument is valid for children and sexual minorities.

In the studies of Jews in Latin America, most scholars focus on the Ashkenazim. Those who do research on Sephardim have emphasized their differences

3. This contention is discussed at length in Lesser and Rein (2006, 2008).

4. Among the few works that deal with unaffiliated Jews are Rattner (1977); Sofer (1982); Lewis (2008).

5. Rafael Kogan, Angel Perlman, and David Diskin, for example, were both important followers of Juan Perón in the 1940s and key figures in the organized labor movement in Argentina, yet they have received little attention from scholars (see Rein 2009). For a bibliography on Jews and the labor movement, see Bilsky, Trajtenberg, and Weinstein (1987).

6. For works dealing, in one way or another, with Jewish prostitution, see Avni (2009); Bra (1982); Mirelman (1988, chap. 9); Guy (1991); Glickman (2000); Vincent (2005); Trochon (2006).

from Ashkenazim, ranging from social contact zones to culture to ideology. Margalit Bejarano, an expert on Sephardim in Latin America, wrote that unlike the Ashkenazim, "Sephardi Judaism existed inside social circles and closed cultures, whose points of contact with the 'other' Jewish world would have been scarce" (1978, 124). Bejarano later qualified her opinion and affirmed that relations between Ashkenazim and Sephardim were more fluid in the early years of immigration to Argentina, before the establishment of the Sephardic organizational infrastructure, and in various cities of the interior. A recent study of the Tucumán Jewish community confirms this argument (Cohen de Chervonagura 2010).

Likewise, Silvia Schenkolewski-Kroll, a scholar of Argentine Zionist history, stated that "the Sephardi public lived racked by internal divisions, and apart from the Ashkenazi public, because of differences in origin, mentality, and above all, language. The two groups only cooperated in moments of crisis or great achievement, such as fund-raising for those affected by the disturbances [in Palestine] in 1929" (1996a, 33; see also Bejarano 1978).[7]

Most research about ethnicity in Latin America tends to present ethnic groups as homogenous and asserts that ethnic group members attach special importance to the imagined country of their ancestors. Yet the reality has often been quite different. The "Jewish" community included Sephardim and Ashkenazim, who in turn were divided by country and city of origin.[8] The "Arab" community included Christians and Muslims from Syria, Lebanon, and Palestine, and Japanese, Chinese, and Indian immigrants all somehow fit into the "Asian" category. Upon reading much of the historiography, one might get the impression that these ethnic groups, with their ties to the "old countries," did not contribute

---

7. Contemporary works also complained about the lack of cooperation between Sephardim and Ashkenazim; see for example, León Schussheim's article in *La Luz* (June 19, 1931). The Ashkenazi weekly *Mundo Israelita* often referred to the relations between the groups (see, for example: February 7, 1931; June 20, 1931; February 16, 1935; November 31, 1935; March 22, 1941).

8. Two of the experts on Sephardim in Argentina rightly complain about the simplistic generalizations that place the Jews of Aleppo, Damascus, and North Africa and the speakers of Judeo-Spanish (Ladino) in the same category. See Rubén E. Beraja and Ernesto Slelatt's article entitled "Panorama Sefaradí en la Argentina" (*La Luz*, September 26, 1980). Margalit Bejarano examines the limited Sephardi historiography in Latin America in her 2005 article. See also Hamui de Halabe (1997a); Brodsky (2003).

to the creation of national identity in their own countries. Thus, studies of Latin American Jews, for example, have tended to assume that support of the Zionist organizations has always been about the State of Israel and not an expression of hyphenated identities in their countries of residence (Schenkolewski-Kroll 1996a; Avni 2005; Liwerant 1991; Friesel 1956).

The Sephardi newspaper *Israel*, founded in 1917 and published irregularly (though uninterruptedly) until the 1970s, painted a more complete picture of the variety of Zionist identities in Argentina. Our analysis of the content of the periodical questions whether participation in Zionist activities was necessarily linked to the imagined motherland of Jewish Palestine. Many scholars have asserted that Zionism was a central component of Jewish-Argentine identity; few have questioned this assumption. We need to reexamine Zionism and the varying attitudes toward it in Argentina. We suggest that "Zionist activity" in Argentina, particularly in the early twentieth century, was a strategy that gave Jewish Argentines a mother country in the same way Italian Argentines were from Italy, or Spanish Argentines were from Spain. Through their support for Zionism, Jews could become like other Argentines in the heterogeneous immigrant society.

By studying *Israel*, a newspaper founded by Spanish-speaking Jews from Morocco, we explore the creation of an alternative collective Jewish identity in Argentina in the 1920s and 1930s. During this period, Jewish Argentines created both a historical narrative and a complementary or hyphenated identity within a continuum, with one ideal type of Jewish identity at one extreme and one ideal type of Argentine identity at the other.[9] Although such a contention may be new to Latin American Jewish historiography, it has recently been raised in debates on Jews in Arab countries, to judge from the works of Yaron Tsur and Hagar Hillel, who examined the Zionist publications *Israel* in Egypt and *L'Avenir Illustré* in Morocco. The authors described these newspapers as expressions of a Zionist identity that did not necessarily require immigration to the Holy Land. These Zionist identities admitted that the readers and contributors would continue their lives in the places where they lived, integrating into the societies around

---

9. For an exhaustive debate on the theories and research about group identity and collective memory, see Gershoni (2006).

them even as they supported the national project developing in Palestine (see H. Hillel 1995, 2004; Tsur 2001).

For the contributors to *Israel*, being Zionist was more important than origin, native language, or even whether one was Sephardi or Ashkenazi. Although *Israel* was founded by Jews from Morocco, its contributors were not clearly divided between Sephardim and Ashkenazim. For those surrounding the newspaper, Zionism and being a good Argentine were central to their individual and collective identities. They identified primarily as Zionists, and only after that as Sephardim or Ashkenazim.

Israel demonstrated that the division between Sephardim and Ashkenazim in Argentina was not as deep as many researchers have claimed.[10] Traditionally, the Sephardim from the Middle East and North Africa and the Ashkenazim from Central and Eastern Europe were described as groups with few points of contact and little interest in each other. Scholars explained the lack of interaction as being caused by the differences in origin, language, and ways of practicing Judaism. Although these arguments were valid in a variety of contexts, *Israel* revealed another side of the story. As many Sephardim as Ashkenazim appeared in the newspaper as contributors as well as in the social pages, photographs, and advertisements. Therefore there was contact between the two groups—they read and wrote within the same newspaper, creating a social network of people that interacted with each other and attended the same social events and meetings of their common organization. Through *Israel* and their Zionist identities, Sephardim and Ashkenazim could unite around a common objective.

Few scholars have attempted to study the heterogeneous groups together, partly because they expressed their Judaism in different ways. One of the main problems is the institutional documentation that historians have traditionally used to tell the story of Argentine Jews. The communal organizations where historians find their sources—mutual aid societies, hospitals, synagogues—were often formed by people who shared an origin or language, making links between groups difficult. For example, a synagogue created by natives of Damascus or a

---

10. For a historiography of the Jews in Argentina that emphasizes the division between Sephardim and Ashkenazim (with little space dedicated to the former), see Avni (1991); Mirelman (1990); Lewin (1983); Weisbrot (1979).

political group whose meetings were held in Yiddish used different languages and, being based on region of origin, necessarily attracted different groups. Consequently, the use of documents generated by each group led to the conclusion that Sephardim and Ashkenazim lived almost separately, with hardly any daily contact between members of the two groups. Scholars need to start looking at different sources—and at traditional sources in different ways—in order to begin to understand how Sephardim and Ashkenazim interacted on a daily basis. Historians have studied the organizations created by one group or the other, but they have paid little attention to the frameworks that could contain both groups. Perhaps if we begin to analyze frameworks of this kind, we will be able to locate new paths and documentation that will allow us to establish the extent of the interaction between the two groups.

Moreover, the historiography mentions few links between Sephardim and Zionism, casting Zionism as an almost exclusively Ashkenazi project.[11] Scholars have contrasted the politically active Ashkenazim with the supposedly more conservative and religious Sephardim. *Israel* forces us to rethink these hypotheses and the place of Sephardim and Zionism in the Latin American context.

Between 1890 and 1930, tens of thousands of Jews arrived in Argentina, the vast majority in the city of Buenos Aires and its surrounding areas. In the 1936 census, 120,195 Jews lived in the capital, of which 86.9 percent were Ashkenazim, primarily from the "Pale of Settlement," an area now part of Poland and the Russian Federation. The remaining 13.1 percent were Sephardim, who came from the Middle East and North Africa and spoke Arabic, Spanish, or Judeo-Spanish (a Spanish-based language with Hebrew letters), sometimes called Ladino (Mirelman 1990, 26, 179; Epstein 2008; Brauner 2009; Brodsky 2003). The 5.4 percent who were Arabic speakers came from Syria, Lebanon, Palestine, or Egypt, while the Ladino speakers from Turkey, Greece, and Bulgaria made up 4.5 percent of the population. The Spanish speakers from Morocco, Spain, Tangiers, Algeria, Gibraltar, Portugal, and Tunisia were a tiny minority of 420 people, that is, 0.6 percent of the Jewish population of Buenos Aires.

11. For discussion of Zionism in Latin America (with little mention of Sephardim), see Avni (1987b, 1985); Schenkolewski-Kroll (1991, 1993, 1996b). On Zionism among the Sephardim, see Bejarano (1984); Mirelman (1987).

Israel, then, was a publication started by a minority (Moroccans) within a minority (Sephardim) within another minority (Jews). Moroccan Sephardim were uniquely suited to building a bridge between the Sephardim and Ashkenazim because they spoke Spanish and had begun arriving in Argentina in the 1860s, far earlier than most other Jewish groups. Some even taught in the colony schools set up by the Jewish Colonization Association (JCA) in Argentina's rural interior. It was also Jews from Morocco who led the creation of the Congregación Israelita Latina in 1891, the first effort to organize the Sephardim. Evidently, because of their education and wealth, the situation of Jews that came from Morocco was better than that of other Sephardim.

Israel: More than Moroccan Sephardim

From the first issue, in which one article expressed the desire to unify and reflect the aspirations of the entire Jewish community, *Israel* was clearly not directed just at Moroccan Sephardim (April 1917). One of the oldest Jewish publications in Spanish, and the first Sephardi periodical in Argentina, *Israel* was founded by Samuel A. Levy and Jacobo Levy, two Jews of Moroccan origin who lived in Buenos Aires. The newspaper began as a monthly in 1917, became bimonthly, and by 1918 was published weekly from the Once neighborhood (Schallman 1971).[12] Samuel Levy, a prosperous accountant and the son of immigrants from Morocco, became the sole owner soon after the founding of the newspaper after Jacobo Levy's death.[13] By the second half of the 1920s, Levy was joined by Zebulon Levy and José Libermann on the editorial staff. Zebulon Levy, the administrative manager between 1926 and 1935, often appeared in the social column, usually because of his many trips through the interior of Argentina and other South American countries to visit Jews in diverse towns and cities. In a way, Levy was a "pilgrim of the collective identity" offered by the newspaper, connecting the dispersed Jewish settlements and transforming them into what is known as

---

12. In 1917, A. Sethon began publishing *Al Gala*, a short-lived Zionist newspaper in Arabic (see Sieskel 1991).

13. Samuel Levy was born in Argentina in 1886 (see Mirelman 1987, 18).

the Argentine Jewish community. At the same time, he was also a businessman in search of subscribers and advertisements for *Israel*.

José Libermann, author of the book *The Jews of Argentina*, was editor-in-chief in 1927 (1966, 117). Like Zebulon Levy, he was a constant contributor to the newspaper. Libermann often translated works from Yiddish into Spanish for *Israel*, including novels and even a fragment of a play by Sholem Asch. During the 1920s and 1930s, the two Levys and Libermann ran the newspaper, yet in his book Libermann makes no mention of his work there. Did he argue with the Levy family? Was he unwilling by the 1960s (when the book was published) to acknowledge his role in a newspaper created and run by Sephardim? Perhaps the Zionist identity offered by *Israel* in the 1920s and 1930s was considered less legitimate in the world that had seen the Holocaust and the establishment of the State of Israel—reason enough for Libermann to want to forget his work in *Israel*. Whatever the reason, it seems that both Sephardim and Ashkenazim were interested in keeping silent about the existence of the publication and its significance. There was no place in their collective memories for a Sephardic periodical with a distinct Zionist message.

Israel was part of a rich print culture in early-twentieth-century Buenos Aires that taught recently arrived immigrants about their new social context and served as a point of contact for those who had already integrated into the immigrant society (Baily and Miguez 2003, xix). Immigrants from a variety of backgrounds used periodicals to create their imagined communities, to communicate with each other, and to attempt to forge common interests between diverse subgroups within their communities. Usually, periodicals tried to appeal to groups with shared ethnic backgrounds or a similar political orientation. The Jews were no exception.[14] *Israel* did not fit easily into the world of the Jewish press, which was dominated by political newspapers and bourgeois magazines; it fell somewhere in between. With its articles about Zionism, Zionist congresses, and famous Zionists, *Israel* mirrored other political publications, mostly in Yiddish, that combined in various measures Zionism, socialism, communism, and the workers' movement (Fainstein 1990). Yet like the bourgeois newspapers, it also included social

---

14. On the press as an instrument for the creation of communities, see Anderson (1991).

pages and photographs of community members, often at weddings or celebrations. *Israel*'s inclusion of elements of both political newspapers and bourgeois magazines made it unique in its period.

It was unique also as far as gender issues were concerned. *Israel* seemed to take a relatively modern and progressive attitude. As Sandra McGee Deutsch has shown in her recent book on Jewish Argentine women, in the early 1920s, *Israel* published a column signed by "Ruth" and dealing with women's issues. On the one hand the column was very much pro-marriage and upheld the traditional family model. Thus, it expressed the commonly held view that "there was nothing sadder than an old maid, who lived a 'dry and solitary life'" (Deutsch 2010, 134; quoting from *Israel*, August 13, 1920). On the other hand, it kept calling for more respect for women, both married and unmarried. One of the columns quoted a woman who nostalgically told of the attention she received as a *novia* from her future husband. She referred to this period of courtship as the best time of her life (September 24, 1920). The same column also included a letter from a female reader who complained about wealthy men for looking for "a beautiful 'social doll'" to marry. The letter compared this attitude to prostitution, which was still legal in Argentina. Several months later, "Ruth" claimed that Argentine girls "will never permit their parents to select their *novio*. Even further: they don't even want to ask for advice" (Deutsch 2010, 149; quoting from *Israel*, March 4, 1921).

Jews of different backgrounds often lived in the same neighborhoods and shared the same workplaces and cultural spaces. *Israel* was notable among the Ashkenazi and Sephardic voices because it encouraged Jewish intermarriage in order to overcome barriers between Yiddish, Judeo-Spanish, and Arabic speakers.

Israel directed itself toward a much larger readership than the Moroccan Jews in Buenos Aires, a group that was not large enough to maintain the ten thousand subscribers that the newspaper claimed it had (Mirelman 1990, 26). In 1925, two different announcements appeared in the paper asserting that it was read by sixty thousand people, because each of the ten thousand copies was read by six other people (July 3; October 2 and 9). Although it is impossible to check those figures, which were surely exaggerated, neither can one assume the opposite, that there were only a few hundred subscribers. In addition to the Sephardim who came from Spanish Morocco, Algeria, and Turkey, the newspaper would also have attracted Jewish immigrants who were learning Spanish, those who had immigrated to Argentina as children and were by now fluent in Spanish, as well as second-generation Ashkenazim who knew the language already, even though their parents primarily spoke Yiddish (April 2, 1920).[15]

In January 1920, *Israel* became a daily newspaper, presenting itself as the first and only Jewish daily in the world, alluding to this step as an expression of progress and modernity.[16] *Israel* must have had some success (and money) to attempt expanding, yet the experiment failed after seven months, citing problems with the printing presses and the impossibility of replacing them, and the newspaper reverted to being a weekly (July 13, 1920). As the only newspaper created by Sephardim until the appearance of *La Luz* in the 1930s, *Israel* exemplified the strategy of a political minority—Sephardi Zionists—within the Jewish minority in the larger immigrant society of Argentina.[17]

In the second issue of *Israel* as a daily, the editors published a sort of mission statement: "We consider it necessary to create a manifestation of the Jewish spirit in the Spanish language. We consider it necessary to make ourselves understood in the national language [Spanish] of this great people who have taken us in" (January 2, 1920). Already, three years earlier, the editors had described their enterprise as a defense of ideals—Jewish, Argentine, and universal—and ended with the following phrase: "And, without tempering our assertion with any vanity, we would say that with our newspaper we have contributed to [fomenting] love of the Argentine nation" (April 1917). Upon referring to themselves as "Jewish-Argentines," the directors of *Israel* had begun to use the hyphen, creating a hyphenated identity decades before the invention of this identity concept.

It was impossible to discover how many subscribers and readers *Israel* had. Yet an analysis of the columnists, advertisers, social pages, and photographs

15. Other Zionist publications in Spanish include *El Sionista*, published bimonthly from June of 1904 and lasting 47 editions. *El Macabeo* appeared for a short while in 1920, and *El Semanario Hebreo* from 1923–1933, though irregularly.

16. During this period, a four-page version of *Israel* appeared only on the weekdays, except for the Passover edition, which was entirely filled with advertisements.

17. La Luz was founded in March 1931 by David Elnecavé, who had previously edited a Zionist newspaper in Istanbul, to help bring more Sephardim into the Zionist movement. It is interesting to note that the Jewish Egyptian *Israel* was published in three languages: Arabic, French, and during a brief period, also Hebrew (see H. Hillel 2004, 9–14).

indicates that *Israel* attracted Sephardim and Ashkenazim as readers, both in Buenos Aires and in the interior (the newspaper had correspondents in all of the provinces), as well as in other Latin American capitals. In each anniversary issue, Sephardi Jews not involved in the writing or administration of the newspaper sent letters and notes with kind words about the good work carried out by *Israel* and its support of Sephardi Jews in Latin America in general, and in Argentina in particular. Thus, *Israel* went beyond the borders of its country of origin. In addition, subscription lists for the newspaper always noted the prices for subscriptions outside Argentina, indicating that *Israel* had a public larger than just Moroccan Jews in Buenos Aires.

Sephardim and Ashkenazim: Could Zionism Unite Them?

Even though researchers have paid little attention to relations between Sephardim and Ashkenazim in Latin America, it was the preferred theme of the contributors to *Israel*. Numerous articles about Ashkenazim lamented the lack of interaction between the two Jewish groups and the impossibility of acting together. One article asked: "Isn't it truly painful to see the divide that exists between the two groups?" (February 13, 1926). Another declared that "The little interest [the Ashkenazim] show for certain co-religionists is lamentable" (March 30, 1928; April 6, 1928). Because the complaints appeared in *Israel*, they seem exaggerated, given the strong ties the newspaper had with Ashkenazim. The Sephardi contributors to *Israel* hoped to accumulate power and influence by uniting with the Ashkenazi majority, for whom Zionism was important.

When the Sephardi contributors identified themselves with the Ashkenazim, they sometimes found themselves in a situation of inferiority. In an article dedicated to the lecture tour of a Sephardi Zionist speaker, contributors alluded to a condescending observation about the essence of the Sephardim that had appeared in the Yiddish press. An Ashkenazi journalist, supposedly very knowledgeable about Sephardi culture, had written, "No one can ignore that, culturally, South American Sephardim are not in a good state, particularly in terms of national organization. Apart from its religion, Ashkenazi Judaism has a culture that elevates it: theater, press, literature. . . . Sephardi Judaism, by contrast, has neither its own culture nor language, which fact facilitates assimilation. In

Sephardim, national sentiment persists longer. Therefore it is vital to assimilate them into the cultural movement of Palestine, the spiritual center of nationalist Judaism." In response, the contributor from *Israel* replied: "very true" (January 22, 1926). From his or her anonymity, the writer at *Israel* agreed with the argument wielded by the journalist in Yiddish that the Sephardim in Latin America lacked something, both as Jews and as Zionists, and thus were in need of culture on a level with the Ashkenazim.

There were political reasons for including this quote in an article in *Israel*. The key to the consensus was in the last phrase, where Sephardim were urged to join the spiritual and cultural Zionist movement. Through Zionism, they could redeem themselves and transform themselves into "Jews" on the same level as the Ashkenazim. By putting them on the defensive, the Yiddish writer demanded that the Sephardim demonstrate the force of their commitment. These debates raged among Sephardim in the mid-1920s, during the creation of the World Union of Sephardi Communities and the visit of Sephardi Zionist envoy Ariel Bensión to Buenos Aires (Bensión 1926).

Israel proposed a variety of models for the relations between Sephardim and Ashkenazim. In 1931, one contributor related the story of the two groups in Rosario del Tala, who had come to ask themselves if there was an essential difference that was responsible for the divide between the two groups (October 16). According to the writer, there was no essential difference, judging by the rise in marriages between Sephardim and Ashkenazim, something that would have been unheard of earlier. Yet the contributor still saw a difference between the two groups and wondered whether the separation was based on concrete reasons, or if it continued because of tradition. In the pages of *Israel*, Sephardim fought for a union with Ashkenazim through Zionism.

Writing and Connecting: Sephardim and Ashkenazim in the Pages of *Israel*

As many Ashkenazim as Sephardim appeared in the newspaper, according to the four databases we compiled on contributors, advertisers, and people who appeared in the social pages and accompanying photographs. All told, the databases include about fifty-five hundred names, and clearly demonstrated that

Ashkenazim and women both played a vital role in *Israel,* together with the Sephardi men who made up the core group of contributors.[18] In addition, many Jews from outside Buenos Aires seem to have played a significant part in the life of the newspaper, particularly from Rosario (Province of Santa Fe), Córdoba (Province of Córdoba), and Asunción and Montevideo, the capital cities of Paraguay and Uruguay.

We paid particular attention to four important dates in the lives of Jews in Argentina—the two national holidays (May 25 and July 9), Rosh Hashanah (usually September–October), and the anniversary of the Balfour Declaration of November 2, 1917 (which pledged British support for a Jewish home in Palestine). We selected these dates because of their importance in the expression of collective national and ethnic identities. Through them, we observed the ways in which people remembered and fostered these identities and memories.[19]

In the social pages, the lists of attendees at various events reveal that most were confined to either Sephardim or Ashkenazim, although some did combine members of the two groups. When the Gluksman family's son was circumcised in Buenos Aires, for example, or at the Serfati wedding in Reconquista (Province of Santa Fe), members of both groups attended (November 12, 1920). In Entre Ríos, many of the members of the Sephardi Cultural and Recreational Center were Ashkenazim. At the wedding of Rosa Nahon and Isaac Chocron, which the announcement noted was an event "in which the most select families of our community gathered," most of the attendees were Ashkenazim, even though

18. It was difficult to determine the exact number of Ashkenazim and Sephardim associated with the newspaper because of names like Cohen or Levy, for example, which could be from either group. Sometimes almost half of the names for a given year were difficult to categorize, distorting any attempt at exact numbers or percentages. In addition, the databases are incomplete because we were unable to locate all issues.

19. For fascinating examples of the ways Jews emphasized their patriotism for Argentina through eulogies of national heroes and enthusiasm for Independence, see these articles: "La Colectividad está pronta a celebrar entusiastamente y con fervor patriótico con el pueblo de la R. Argentina la gloriosa fiesta de Mayo" (May 25, 1920); "Desde ayer la bandera israelita flamea junto a la argentina en todo el país, asociándose a la gran fecha patria" (July 9, 1920); and "Las próximas Fiestas Mayas" (May 21, 1921). Of particular interest is the number dedicated to May 25, 1926. The editors placed a photograph of the president of Argentina on the cover, who had autographed it specifically for *Israel.*

the bride and groom were Sephardim (October 2 and 9, 1925).[20] Sometimes, as the Nahon-Chocron wedding illustrated, social status was more important than whether one was Sephardi or Ashkenazi (October 30, 1925; September 23 and 30, 1927; May 20, 1932). At most of the weddings noted in *Israel*, however, attendance was limited to one group or the other. In the social pages, unlike the other databases (contributors, advertisers, photographs), the lists of attendees revealed the extent of interaction between the two groups. Yet even if there was no physical contact for many Sephardim and Ashkenazim, each group read and learned about the other through the pages of *Israel*.

Jewish identity, and Zionist identity in particular, was a force that united (not divided) in *Israel*, suggesting that the relations between Sephardim and Ashkenazim were not as strained as other scholars have hypothesized. While they might have had different ideas about what it meant to be Jewish and how to express it, in *Israel* they could adopt a common Jewish identity, and even though they came from different regions and traditions, through the newspaper they created a new group that sought to move away from divisive Sephardi or Ashkenazi identities.

Argentina as a "Zionist Homeland"

Israel was different from the other Jewish and Zionist publications in Argentina because of its particular Zionist orientation and because Zionism was not as firmly rooted among the Sephardim as it was among the Ashkenazim. Unlike other Zionist newspapers, neither Palestine nor political Zionism was the focus. *Israel* first appeared on March 24, 1917, seven months before the Balfour Declaration (which reignited worldwide interest in Zionism), providing clear proof of the strong Zionist convictions of its founders, the Levys. Even though the First Zionist Congress in 1897 had generated interest in the Diaspora, and Jews had formed two Zionist groups in Argentina—the Tiferet Tzión (1905) and the Poalei Tzión (1906)—dedication to the Zionist cause had been limited to very narrow circles (Mirelman 1976).[21]

20. Also see the announcement on the Liberman-Segal wedding, where the rabbi and many guests were Sephardim (June 4, 1926).

21. For information on the early activities of the Poalei Tzion, see Schers (1992).

Many scholars have interpreted the Zionist activities in Argentina in a one-dimensional manner, despite the fact that *Israel* demonstrates that it was much more complicated. At the First Argentine Jewish Congress in 1916, for example, Nachman Gesang suggested that one of their aims should be to bring up the term "Jewish" in Gentile circles, so that Jews could be identified as such and not as Germans, Russians, or members of any other nation; he did not exactly preach the need to populate Palestine (Schenkolewski-Kroll 1996a, 13). For both Sephardim and Ashkenazim, International Zionist Congresses were an arena for meeting other Zionists, not necessarily a place for planning future emigration to Palestine.[22] And while *Israel* reproduced speeches from the congresses that proposed emigration, the idea did not appear in the articles written by permanent contributors. Through the Zionist Congresses, Argentine Jews came into contact with Jews from other countries, particularly the United States and Europe. Thus, when the Argentine delegates to the International Congresses were mentioned in the articles in *Israel*, it was in the context of national pride, in order to emphasize their status as Argentines, and not because they had delivered a speech or proposed an initiative. Even though Zionism was a world movement, for the editors at *Israel* it was their local context that mattered—they used Zionism and the Zionist Congresses to bring the Jews of Argentina closer to other Jews in the Diaspora.

Choosing the name *Israel*, and not a title that included "Zionism" or "Zionist," demonstrated that the idea of a homeland for the Jews was more important than its location or how it would be established. Palestine was the ancient home of both Sephardim and Ashkenazim, and with the title *Israel*, the founders expressed their hopes for a united Jewish future. However, there was no indication that the future necessarily had to be in Palestine. Jews could make their homes in the countries of the Diaspora, like Argentina, and Israel could be any country that welcomed and united the Jews. Zionism was a way to make a new country a Jewish homeland; the physical location was less important. The editors added the phrase "Argentine Jewish World" under the masthead; in this way, the name and motto of the newspaper pointed to the complementary identities of the directors—Jews, Zionists, Argentines. Argentina had taken them in, and it

---

22. See the report on the Sixth Zionist Congress (*Israel*, November 12 and 19, 1920).

was their home, so whenever they referred to "our country" in *Israel*, they meant Argentina. Thus, in the fourth anniversary issue, the newspaper emphasized that the founders of *Israel* had been inspired by the "democratic ideals of our country, the Argentine Republic," which took in the people of Israel with good faith. On the same page, they explained the need for publishing a Jewish daily in Spanish, "the national language" (April 2, 1920).

The Zionists surrounding *Israel* were interested in the creation of Argentine Jewish identities, not in a separate Jewish state. Sephardim and Ashkenazim could remember a mythic past and look to a common future that could occur anywhere. Just because Argentina was part of the Diaspora, it did not mean that it could not be a home for Jews, and they wanted others to recognize them as members of that nation. Even though Zionism was a political movement for other Argentine Jews, *Israel* revealed a group that chose Zionism as an identity, not a political manifesto.

Obviously, not all Argentine Jews shared this conception. The editors of the newspaper often questioned political Zionism and its meanings, while asserting their own right to be Zionists. In an article reprinting quotes and comments about the Jewish National Fund Meeting (Keren Kayemeth) in Argentina, the unidentified writer defended the right of Sephardim to be Zionists. "Many say that we Sephardim are not Zionists and are uninterested in the ideals of State, Nation, Culture, Language, and any number of other elements that ennoble a people." The writer then proceeded to describe the differences between the Zionism of Sephardim and that of the main Ashkenazi current. "I can say, without fearing that I am wrong, that we are not militant Zionists" (January 22, 1926). He or she attributed this phenomenon to the much smaller number of Sephardim, in actual fact, compared with the Ashkenazim, and to the lack of pogroms or expulsions in the recent history of the Sephardim. To identify themselves as Zionists meant that Sephardim had to define themselves in comparison to the Ashkenazi majority, and many Ashkenazim did not consider them sufficiently Zionist.

The author of the article suggested a more comprehensive definition of a Zionist, one that took into account both Sephardim and Ashkenazim. Like other articles that addressed Ashkenazi complaints, this particular one rejected the arguments about the lack of Sephardi vision in the creation of a Jewish homeland. According to the contributor, some Ashkenazim wanted to impose their own organization and ways of thinking on the Sephardim. Yet, for the author,

Sephardim had different and no less valid ways of expressing their Zionism. The problem in communication stemmed partly from the differences the two groups showed when implementing their policies. The contributor analyzed the differences with concrete examples, but at the same time rejected those who labeled Sephardim as less Zionist.

In May 1927, the Sephardi Zionist group Bené Kedem instructed the readers of *Israel* to buy *schekalim* (symbolic membership tokens in the World Zionist Organization) to show their support for Zionism and the Jewish settlement in Palestine. Those who bought the *schekalim* could then vote for the representatives to the Zionist Congress. The full-page announcement told Sephardi readers that they should buy the *schekalim* because "around the world, particularly among the Ashkenazim, we have already sold and continue to sell millions of *schekalim*." In this case, when Zionist sentiment was measured in *schekalim*, the Ashkenazim had the advantage. The directors of the donation campaign attributed the smaller number of Sephardim-bought *schekalim* to their lack of organization but also warned that if they waited, they might find all of them sold. In order to sell more, the members of Bené Kedem wrote that they intended to visit the homes and stores of all Sephardim in order to be competitive and show their Zionist spirit (May 27, 1927). Here, the division between Sephardim and Ashkenazim seems clear: the Sephardim had to demonstrate their support to the Zionist cause to the Ashkenazim, who had already shown themselves to be good Zionists.

Conclusions

Through *Israel*, Sephardim expressed their Jewish and Argentine identities and demonstrated that some Sephardim did have social contact with Ashkenazim. In their new country, some adopted a hyphenated identity through Zionism, as Argentine-Jews or Jewish-Argentines. Between 1917 and the mid-1930s, the editors at *Israel* situated themselves within the Argentine nation while expressing multiple identities simultaneously—Sephardi or Ashkenazi, Zionist, and Argentine. *Israel* illuminated one piece of the mosaic of Jewish Argentine identity and its processes of gestation and change. In this context, the newspaper should be seen as both an agent of change and an articulation of collective identity, or at least as a tool in the struggle of a group of Jews, headed by Moroccans, to integrate their own identity proposal within the larger Argentine-Jewish discourse. Because it was dealing with a young Jewish community in Argentina, *Israel* constituted a fascinating attempt at forging a new collective identity, with mythic roots in the common, yet remote, past of all of the Jews of Argentina, and trying to connect it to the Argentine immigrant society.

Throughout its existence, *Israel* negotiated with the collective memories and identities offered by different groups of Argentine Jews. Like other ethnic groups in the nation, Jews had to juggle competing and coexisting identities and narratives. The Jews of Aleppo and Damascus, for example, the majority among Sephardim, were for the most part conservative and, for many, religion was a central component in their lives. They showed suspicion toward Zionism at the beginning. However, Susana Brauner (2009) found that the 1930s marked a change in attitudes among Sephardim about Zionism, particularly after the creation of the State of Israel. The growing support for Zionism among the Jews of Syrian origin did not question or go against their identities as Argentines. The multiple identities complemented each other—they did not collide.

Israel leads us to rethink the essence of Zionism as well as the relations between Sephardim and Ashkenazim in Argentina and in Latin America in general. How did different groups of Jews interpret or define Zionism and Zionist identity? Zionism was a political movement, yet *Israel* shows us that many Jews adopted it as an apolitical Jewish identity. This interaction between politics and identity demands more study, as do the zones of contact between Sephardim and Ashkenazim. The two groups related to each other in a variety of ways, sometimes even competing with each other. It remains to be seen whether the interactions occurred between small groups of people or if the contact was widespread in both official and unofficial frameworks. *Israel* therefore forces us to reexamine the supposedly unbridgeable gap between the groups and demonstrates how Zionism could also serve as an apolitical strategy for both Sephardim and Ashkenazim to make Argentina a Jewish homeland.

5

Syrian Jews in Buenos Aires

Between Religious Revival and Return
to Biblical Sources, 1953–90

SUSANA BRAUNER

> The future has become the present. Sick and tired of the bread of tediousness,
> intoxicated with the waters of the nontranscendental, we find ourselves, at the
> end of the twentieth century, hungry and thirsty for God.
>
> Among our chastised people, the Baalé Teshuvá [returned to biblical
> sources], on their return to our cultural heritage, have ceased to be a rarity
> and have become a daily reality. It is mandatory to satiate that thirst.
>
> —DINES, "Prólogo"[1]

A distinct religious revival process was undergone by the Syrian Jews
who came from the cities of Aleppo and Damascus to Buenos Aires from the
mid-1950s to the beginning of the 1990s. The secular leadership, open to modern world values, was weakening, while new religious leaders and sectors that
promoted strict compliance with biblical precepts was gaining strength. Such
leaders and sectors claimed that only their beliefs and practices could ensure
Jewish intergenerational continuity.

A combination of variables made certain developments possible. First, a
strengthening influence was exerted by some rabbis, who were acknowledged
as holding the interpretative monopoly on the ideal standards needed to comply with biblical precepts, as well as on the criteria for admission and exclusion

---

1. Author's translation.

applied to those wanting to stay or to join the community. Second, there arose a new generation of native-born religious leaders who became the dynamic factors in the "return to the biblical sources" movements. Most of these leaders were especially ordained abroad, in rabbinical schools that responded to ultra-Orthodox Jewish formulas (See Friedman 1988 and J. Katz 1984).[2] Their movements spread in Buenos Aires from the mid-1970s. They incorporated a large number of young people who had distanced themselves from religious practices and from communal Jewish organizations. Finally, financial institutions, in combination with the religious power, not only promoted the spread of Orthodox Judaism, but also represented this form of Judaism in the broader context of the Jewish community in Argentina.

In other words, different trends arose from the most moderate sectors—aimed basically at reviving religious and ethnic distinctive features within their own communities—to others that then became more radical and intended to expand their influence to the whole Argentine Jewish community.

This work is based on a wide range of sources: the internal documentation of the main community institutions, the private archives and reminiscences of outstanding leaders, and the national and communal press, as well as interviews conducted with representatives of the various sectors involved.

Between Orthodoxy and Openness

The main Sephardic[3] sectors first arrived in Buenos Aires in the late nineteenth and early twentieth centuries. From the outset, a strong regionalism characterized all sectors. In general, they founded their own institutions independently according to their zone of origin and/or mother tongue, but with similar objectives, so as to render religious services and provide a traditional Jewish education.

2. For Aleppan militant conservatism, see Zohar (1993a) and Horowitz (2000).

3. This term generically describes the Jews whose ancestors descend from those who were evicted from the Iberian Peninsula as well as those coming from the Arab World. On the Sephardim in Argentina, see Bejarano (1986, 1978) and Mirelman (1988, 31–41, 126–28, 152–54, 207–8, 254–57). On Sephardim in Latin America, see Bejarano (2005). On Sephardim, see Stillman and Stillman (1999); Goldberg (1996); Elazar (1989).

All in all, four groups may be distinguished, at least according to the forms of organization they adopted in Buenos Aires: the Spanish-speaking Moroccans; the various Ladino-speaking Jews, including the Turks, the Greeks, and people from the Balkan countries; the Syrians of Aleppo, together with others whose mother tongue was Arabic, generally from Egypt and Jerusalem; and the Syrians of Damascus, together with those coming from Lebanon.

Although there is no official data, it was estimated that in the mid-1980s the Syrian Jews constituted around 9 percent (20,000) of the Jewish population in Argentina, 60 percent of the Sephardic population,[4] and nearly 95 percent of the descendants of immigrants from Arab lands.[5] Thus, as in other countries, they were a "minority within a minority," as compared to the majority Ashkenazi[6] Jewish community, and the largest group among the Sephardic communities.

From the beginning of the century until the mid-1920s, the Syrian immigrants[7] focused their efforts on attaining fast economic growth. Each sector established itself in its own neighborhood. It kept close regional ties and established the first institutions that would cover the religious needs of their members: synagogues, religious schools, and a cemetery for each community.

In that context two types of leadership emerged: the religious and the secular. The former was composed of rabbis and teachers, who preserved a significant influence in their respective communities at a time and in a society where religious power seemed to have lost prestige. In these communities, the most outstanding personalities, surrounded by "an aura of holiness," continued to command respect and awe. This was due both to their erudition and to the mystic power attributed to them.

On the other hand, the secular leadership was generally composed of fairly young men, with traditional Jewish upbringing. They belonged to families who were rising on the socioeconomic ladder. We can call them very traditionalist

4. The Moroccans, 4.2 percent; Ladino speakers, 35.5 percent; Aleppan, 28.7 percent; Damascene, 31.6 percent (see Bejarano 1986, 145).

5. On the Moroccan Jews in Argentina, see Epstein (1993).

6. Ashkenazi are Jews from Ashkenaz (Germany) whose leading communities developed in Eastern Europe (see Avni 1992, 148–49).

7. About Syrian communities in Syria, see Harel (2003); Zohar (1993b); Zenner (1987); Stillman (1991).

men, though they were generally more open to changes in the environment and fascinated by the opportunities that the Western world offered them. Eventually, their prestige and reputation increased because of several factors: their initiative and economic support for the development of community institutions, the greater range of relational resources they had with extra-community sectors, and the ties of dependency they started to create through the granting of jobs and loans to the Syrian Jews.

From the 1930s to the 1950s, a large percentage experienced a significant process of upward socioeconomic mobility accompanied by more openness to the broader environment and a larger commitment to international Jewish affairs. Around that time, certain groups in the communities started to abandon traditional religious practices, while the power of the religious leaders was diminishing, at least on the structural level.

With this background in mind, I will analyze the internal processes that both the Aleppo and Damascus communities underwent from the 1950s until the late 1970s, that is, since the arrival in Buenos Aires of the Aleppan Rabbi Itzhak Chehebar, a leader who became one of the pillars of Orthodox Judaism until a stronger influence of the ultra-Orthodox started within the ranks of the organized communities.

The Aleppo Community: From Openness to Religious-Ethnic Revival

Following the appointment of Itzhak Chehebar as chief rabbi in 1953, Aleppan Jews started a revival of religious and ethnic traditions.[8] This movement was aimed at recovering and developing a more segregated community, in which group belonging, as in the ultra-Orthodox sectors, was conditioned by its members' degree of religiousness in all daily affairs. Nevertheless, the movement led by Rabbi Chehebar promoted religious, educational, and economic practices

---

8. For a definition and distinctive features of the "revival movements," see the classic work by Wallace (1956). For an analysis of this process among the Aleppan Jews, see Brauner Rodgers (1999, 2000). For a community interpretation of such phenomenon, see Congregación Sefaradí (1995).

that led to the revival of Aleppan identity and group cohesion.[9] This process differed from that undergone by the ultra-Orthodox groups that thrived during the 1970s and promoted activist politics in order to capture all non-observant Jews, regardless of their ethnic origin.

The first generation leaders, some of whom were men of considerable wealth, had started to be removed from their positions of power and were replaced by the rabbi and lay leaders[10] who supported him. Such leaders of the new generations set themselves the task of adopting the Bible as the guiding framework for all aspects of modern life and increasing strict compliance with the Jewish precepts "according to Aleppan traditions."

Those were controversial years of great internal conflicts between the religious power and the wealthiest sectors. The discussion was based on a common ground of shared beliefs where respect for such beliefs prevailed, but it centered around observance, what was correct or incorrect, what was permitted or prohibited, and, ultimately, on what the limits of transgression were. However, awe and mystic qualities attributed to the charismatic rabbinic personalities succeeded in increasing Rabbi Chehebar's authority even among the most liberal sectors.

The rabbi strengthened his power, making use of incentives and sanctions, with blessings to those who complied "with their religious and traditional duties" (*Mundo Israelita*, August 5, 1967),[11] and with admonitions to those who "transgressed" (*Kesher Kehilati*, August 1991).

Furthermore, contradicting current trends—at a time when religion did not fulfill a primary role among most of the Jews in the country—a long-term strategy was implemented. It aimed at strengthening traditional values as a resource to face modernity.[12] However, modern and updated means were also used in the educational and economic areas (see Rodgers 2005, 173–215).

9. As to the ways of preaching by Orthodox groups, see Kepel (1995, 242–61).

10. In 1960, both sectors competed for control of their central communal organization. The victory of the list of candidates identifying with Rabbi Chehebar's project paved the way for his strengthening as an undisputed authority (AISA 1960, 147–48).

11. There was also a leaflet delivered by hand to the Jewish traders living in Once, amid a campaign launched to honor the Sabbath rest by closing the shops.

12. About secularization theory, see Bell (1977); Berger (1999); Casanova (1996); Martelli (1999).

At the educational level, religious education spread and expanded to all levels, for both genders, in day schools where national and secular education was also offered. It incorporated modern pedagogical methods and the scientific innovations of the era.

At the economic level, the religious power and the new economic elite joined forces. In the 1950s, the boom of the savings and credit cooperatives began.[13] These financial entities had operated as banks with restricted functions, offering credit assistance to the middle-class sectors whose financial needs were not satisfied by the main banks. Some of these cooperatives, whose directors were active members of the leading community associations, also gave their support to different institutional religious, educational, social, and cultural projects. Thus, unlike in past times, both the religious and the new economic elites began to join forces and to legitimize each other mutually.

In brief, the institutional network was expanded through the interdependence of both factors, the economic and religious sectors, which, owing to their permanence throughout time, consolidated very strong leaderships in each field.

In practice, group cohesion intensified; ties to the surrounding society were restricted and the religious uniformity of those who were in contact with the community was strengthened. In other words, the process undergone by the Aleppan community should not be understood merely as the return to a premodern phase. It should rather be regarded as a phenomenon where both resacralizing as well as modernizing features are witnessed—a phenomenon where the Jewish "sacred" texts become the absolute foundation for legitimizing ancient beliefs and standards. These texts should also be seen as the absolute foundation for reformulating the new educational and economic practices. Within this framework of religious and ethnic identity revival, under a charismatic religious leadership, institutional ties with the central organizations of the Jewish-Argentine community and the Zionist Sephardic institutions were preserved only at a formal level. However, ties with other Middle Eastern Jews were strengthened: with the Damascenes in Buenos Aires as well as with other Syrian communities in the

---

13. The cooperative unions provided broader range of loans and services (to their members) that were offered by the main financial institutions (see Brauner, Fraga, and Shuckman 2004; Petriella 1984). About Jewish cooperativism in Argentina, see Zadoff (2005).

Diaspora,[14] with the Sephardic Rabbinic seminaries and religious authorities in Israel and with political representatives of the Israeli right-wing parties.

On the other hand, some people from the Syrian sectors stayed away from the central community institutions. The most religious had joined ultra-Orthodox organizations; the most liberal participated in the founding of Conservative and Reform institutions while others had distanced themselves from all Jewish spaces. It was in that context that in the late 1970s, when a *"teshuvah"* movement (advocating a return to Orthodox Judaism) developed in the Jewish world, new strategies were also implemented to encourage those "who had strayed away" to join in (Kepel 1995, 242–61).

The Damascene Community: Between Orthodoxy and Zionism

Like the Aleppans, the Damascene Jews preserved a strong religious and regional identity. However, their degree of attachment to religious practices was comparatively less strict than the Aleppans and their main institutions or leaders more open and committed to the Zionist cause.[15]

Since the mid-1950s, as in the Aleppan community, the institutional framework was expanded and modernized: starting with improved facilities they moved into the creation of a day-school system at all three educational levels, incorporating updated pedagogical and technological methods.

Nevertheless, the internal dynamics of this sector were quite different (see Brauner Rodgers 2005). On the one hand, the Damascene Jews appointed renowned religious individuals as school directors and as chief rabbi, all of whom remained in office for long terms, but these appointed leaders were not of Syrian origin. In comparison, their power was much more limited than that exerted by Rabbi Chehebar. On the other hand, in the Damascene sector, each synagogue or school or beneficent institution was more independent. The chief rabbi performed, and still performs, a type of external advisory role. In fact, it was the local rabbis who directed religious and educational affairs, even though their

---

14. For an analysis of the Aleppan Diaspora, see Zenner (2000).

15. The Syrian Jews in Damascus were also more open to the Zionist movement (see Zohar 1993b, 57–60; Menachem 1990).

reputation was restricted to their own neighborhood and limited to the synagogue or school where they performed their duties. As a result of this type of weaker leadership, there was not much consensus on the standards required to establish very strict admission or exclusion criteria.

There was more: the Damascene lay leaders who enjoyed high prestige and were prominent beyond the closed boundaries of their neighborhoods were not religiously observant. They were traditionalists though secular leaders, of high repute within their group, who still planned part of the community policies, at least until the 1980s. They had important extra-community relations and were even appointed to high offices in the most representative institutions of Argentine Jewry or in the Zionist movements. As an example, Dr. Sión Cohen Imach, after being appointed as the new president of the principal umbrella Argentine Jewish Association (*DAIA*) in 1970, stated, "Now the Sephardic communities should not attempt to create new regional organizations. They should rather demonstrate they are ready for total integration" (*Israel*, December 1970, author's translation).

Like the Aleppans, the new rising generations of the Damascenes founded financial institutions, credit cooperatives of a regional character, or joined with those of Aleppan origin, fulfilling a significant role in the financing of their own institutional activities (*Israel*, October 1970).[16]

However, in the search for more religious options, some of their members, like some Aleppans, joined ultra-Orthodox entities, directed by Ashkenazi rabbis, who enjoyed special prestige in Jewish-Arabic sectors (see I. Benchimol 1999). The death of the first generation of rabbis also led to a significant spiritual vacuum in Damascene synagogues. Eventually, rabbis from the new generations, educated in the different ultra-Orthodox trends, were appointed.

Syrian Jews in the Ultra-Orthodox Movement

An understanding of the influence the ultra-Orthodox started to exert on both communities requires an awareness of several factors. First, because of the lack of highly religious training, some Israeli rabbis were hired as educational or religious

16. CASA cooperative participated in the opening ceremony of the new building of the community cemetery.

leaders. Second, Argentine students were sent to study in ultra-Orthodox rabbinical schools abroad, and, upon their return, they filled different roles in Buenos Aires. Third, ties with Israel's religious authorities in time became closer. Finally, different ultra-Orthodox organizations composed of Syrian Jews were gradually consolidated as rabbinic training institutions in Buenos Aires, preparing many of the rabbis appointed to conduct the Jewish–Middle Eastern communities.

Among the ultra-Orthodox organizations was Shuba Israel (Israel Return), which was founded in the mid-1940s in a synagogue that belonged to the Aleppan community but was under the leadership of an Ashkenazi rabbi, Zeev Grimberg (I. Benchimol 1999). This organization was much stricter at the religious level, and it succeeded in attracting a large number of Jewish-Syrian youths. It was one of the pioneer organizations that, in Buenos Aires, undertook the task of "making" the Jews "who had distanced themselves return." Directed for many years by different Ashkenazi rabbis, Shuba Israel was one of the sectors more inclined to incorporate some conceptions and rituals of the different variants of Ashkenazi ultra-Orthodox Judaism. It was also more inclined to radicalize the behavior patterns demanded of its members, who reached all the city neighborhoods that had strong Sephardic concentrations.

This group eventually succeeded in incorporating some sectors and in setting up different branches all over Buenos Aires (Flores, Lanús, Barracas, and Once). Its required behavior patterns were in fact stricter than those which the Aleppans had adopted under the direction of Orthodox Rabbi Chehebar, so much so that for the Shuba Israel members, at least until the mid-1970s, such a religious leader "was considered too permissive."

After several internal conflicts, whereby some of its members joined other ultra-Orthodox groups,[17] Shuba Israel, under the leadership of an Iranian rabbi, Eliezer Ben David, had developed educational spaces that trained most of the rabbis who had spread all over the country and who started to adopt new techniques to persuade "assimilated Jews."[18]

17. In 1961, some joined Satmar's Hasidim while others adhered to Jabad Lubavitch (both ultra-Orthodox movements).

18. The same Agudath Israel party describes Shuba's Higher Education Rabbinic School as the space to integrate "sectors of our youth into Jewish life" and to train "new spiritual leaders to

By the mid-1950s, some Syrian youths, under the influence of another Ashkenazi rabbi, Dov Ber Baumgarten, started to join one of the groups that promoted the organization of Chabad Lubavitch in Argentina. Chabad is an ultra-Orthodox Hasidic (pious) movement of European origin headquartered in New York, and at an international level is one of the most influential institutions devoted to "making the Jews who had distanced themselves return." The first to be sent to study in the United States were young men from the Damascene and Aleppan communities. Since the late 1970s, Chabad has become one of the movements attracting Jews of different origins, Ashkenazi or Sephardic, by means of intense mass-media campaigns. They signaled that they were willing to start the *teshuvah* (repentance and return to Judaism) campaign and to live according to standards elaborated by Chabad on the basis of the "sacred texts." Some of those who received training in that movement became rabbis in different synagogues belonging to the Damascene network.

Although each sector of Orthodox Judaism jealously preserved its independence, the inter-institutional ties became closer, like fellow travelers, in order to combat the more liberal religious sectors that had found considerable support in the Ashkenazi environments. They also did so in order to undertake joint measures that would ensure compliance with the biblical precepts in neighborhoods with large Jewish populations and/or in public institutions that would represent Judaism in Argentina.[19]

No less important were the personal, social, and business networks that had originated among individuals belonging to different factions, concentrated in the same neighborhoods in Buenos Aires or connected at family level. They strengthened their mutual influence in daily life. Even in the economic area, central communal associations of both Aleppans and Damascenes, as well as

---

encourage traditional lives in the Latin American communities" (*La Voz Judía*, June–July 1986, author's translation).

19. Joint measures were implemented against conservative rabbi Marshall Meyer, "It is necessary to protect our children from the moral degradation and the bad winds that blow . . ." signed by the Argentine Rabbinic Council (*La Luz*, November 3, 1972), "or campaigns organized by the different organizations" (*Kesher Kehilati*, August 1990, author's translation).

the financial entities tied to them, started to grant subsidies to the benefit of some of the ultra-Orthodox institutions.[20]

The causes for the so-called Sephardic return to the sources in the specific case of Argentina are analyzed in different ways by the protagonists themselves. The main rabbis who led such movements among the Sephardim and, especially those of Syrian origin, related it to a world phenomenon and affirmed that most of the "returning" youths were individuals who enjoyed better economic positions and educational training than their parents had. In other words, they were Jews who were tied to business or financial activity, generally with high school educations and some with university degrees. They also state that they belonged to traditionalist homes, where Judaic continuity was preserved in a "folkloric" way and that they were also searching for "deeper answers to their existence." None of the rabbis associated such movements with the local political state of affairs; that is, with youths who in the 1960s or 1970s had adopted the radical and left ideologies that were popular against the military dictatorships in Argentina. Rabbi Abraham Serruya (1989) wrote, "The great difference that exists between the previous and the current generations is the type of questioning: our parents asked 'How?' and we ask 'Why?'"[21]

In the central Syrian institutional frameworks, such a "return" movement started to be noticed around the late 1970s and was strengthened by the mid-1980s (*La Voz Judía*, December–January 1985–86). On the one hand, it was helped by the opening of day high schools and seminaries in autonomous institutions, where youths could now access a more comprehensive religious education, on the other, by the wide range of activities promoted by a new generation of rabbis, most of whom were born in Argentina. Some of the young rabbis returned to the country, studied at universities, and started to replace those hired in Israel. They also used modern social communication techniques in order to spread the study of the Bible, with interpretations that appealed to reason and had application to the modern world.

---

20. And not only to Syrian institutions. Banco Mayo also granted subsidies to ultra-Orthodox and Ashkenazi organizations (*La Voz Judía*, September–October 1982, author's translation).

21. Author's translation.

Youths and adults who were attracted to these groups expected rational explanations in order to understand how the sacred texts applied to "the current state of affairs." They also sought explanations that might help them to regulate their lives in accordance with a narrow interpretation of the 613 Jewish commandments. Individuals searching for places where they could belong and feel safe were also attracted. It was a time when Argentina was highly political and economically unpredictable. It was, additionally, a setting where "assimilation" was perceived as one of the greatest dangers threatening the continuity of the "chosen people" in the Diaspora.

In this context, Perspectivas (Perspectives), a pluralistic[22] organization, came into existence in 1985. It was promoted by a charismatic rabbi who officiated at one of the Aleppan synagogues, Rabbi Abraham Serruya,[23] who, together with other religious leaders of Damascene and Sephardic institutions who were generally trained as ultra-Orthodox under the Lithuanian Ashkenazi influence, paved the way for a *Baalei Teshuvah* movement. The organization was established as an entity acting as a nexus among the various parts of the Jewish community, open to all Jews. It highlighted the brotherhood of all Jewish people and respected regional differences as merely folkloric or external expressions not essential to religious principles. According to the institutional sources themselves, the idea was to promote an institution similar to those run in Israel.

Perspectivas promoted activities that attracted around 150 to 300 people on Saturdays and at seminars and camping sites. It gave rise to an increase in the number of adhering groups, besides granting more prestige to each rabbi involved in the initiative. Eventually, it spread to other more liberal synagogues of Sephardic origin that had distanced themselves from the Orthodox movement. Furthermore, with the economic support of ethnic financial institutions,[24] rabbis were sent to the

---

22. About the creation of that organization, see *La Voz Judía* (December–January 1985–86).

23. Rabbi Ben David was the spiritual leader of the rabbinic seminary of Shuba Israel, where rabbinic youths were trained (*Kesher Kehilati*, August 1990).

24. One of the principal financial ethnic leaders, Dr. Rubén Beraja, affirmed, "We have to encourage a movement of return to the sources and of reaffirmation of the presence, today as usual, of a traditional Jewish distinctiveness, as a unique and valid basis for Jewish permanence" (*La Voz Judía*, April 1987, author's translation).

Argentine provinces. They succeeded in reviving the community life of Sephardic Jews in some other cities. Also, some of their followers started to serve elsewhere in Latin America—in Brazil, Mexico, and Uruguay. In other words, in Argentina, the Middle East Jews and, from them, large numbers of Aleppans and Damascenes, laid the foundations for the so-called return to biblical sources.

Still, Perspectivas, an organization aimed at reaching the community as a whole, was mostly monopolized by Jews from Arab countries. The attempts to extend its influence to the Ashkenazi synagogues of the capital or the provinces did not yield significant results. Another sector that encouraged the return to sources was the previously mentioned Hasidic movement, led by Chabad Lubavitch, which with more public and mass media exposure succeeded in increasing the number of followers among Jews of East European origin.[25]

In sum, the ultra-Orthodox organizations and the new generations of rabbis who had received training in Israel or in local ultra-Orthodox rabbinical schools appeared among the Jewish community as the legitimate repositories of the Jewish cultural heritage and as the sole entities who could ensure intergenerational continuity and prevent the assimilation that prevailed in many sectors of the Jewish-Argentine population.

The Religious Renaissance in the Syrian Communities

The second-rank Aleppan rabbinic leaders gave place to a religious process that went beyond Rabbi Chehebar's original expectations during the 1950s. While Chehebar's policies were characterized by a strong regional sense, focusing on the need to preserve both Judaism's essential values and Aleppo's traditions, these new leaders were distinguished by the strong universal character of their aims, respecting the customs of origin but preserving ritual by highlighting the brotherhood of the diverse branches of the Jewish people, and by their willingness to incorporate guidelines from the Ashkenazi ultra-Orthodox sectors.

---

25. "Chabad Lubavitch" is the type of pioneer who would use the mass media to spread "the Judaic message." For a communitarian perspective, see *Veinte años: Encendiendo el Corazón Judío* (Jabad Lubavitch 1997). For a critical review, see M. Doño's April 2000 article, "Fe ciega," in *La Voz de Israel*.

Although at first their methods of attracting people were quite open and avoided coercion, they became stricter than the generations that had preceded them and had promoted the religious revival in the 1950s. The path toward a greater degree of self-segregation deepened, and contact with the environment was radically limited. Thus, new frameworks were founded that would give rise to the creation of very closed spaces but that succeeded in attracting a large number of youths willing to change radically their way of living and even to adopt clothing and external symbols that easily distinguished them from the rest of society.

Divergent points of view also started to coexist regarding the State of Israel. The lay leaders and Rabbi Chehebar continued to express their traditional, if ambivalent, support for Israel. Israel was supported in spite of "all imperfections" that the "secular" country might have. However, since the late 1970s the views of the new generations of rabbis prevailed, preventing all kinds of open manifestations in favor of a state that had been founded by secular Jews and Zionists before the "arrival of the Messiah" (*La Luz*, February 12, 1988, author's translation). *La Luz*, a Sephardic journal, affirmed: "The ultra-Orthodox movement presents itself, with less and less shyness, as openly anti-Zionist" (February 12, 1988).

As the "religious awakening" expanded in the Damascene community, it incorporated rabbis trained in several ultra-Orthodox[26] trends, some of whom were appointed in synagogues that had remained leaderless for many years and others who provided religious direction to the main communal institutions. All tended toward invigorating religious life, but not all of them followed the same path. Nevertheless, in preserving the traditional rituals, they came closer to or continued to identify with different versions of Orthodox Judaism.[27] Damascene Judaism became a broad conglomerate with great attachment to religion and a sense of regional belonging but with diverse and even antagonistic currents

---

26. On September 3, 1977, a new synagogue was opened in Barracas, along with the head synagogue already existing in the area, where two other ultra-Orthodox Damascene organizations merged, Asociación Retorna Israel (Israel Return Association) and Iagdil Torá. It was attended by rabbis who represented the diverse sectors in Buenos Aires (*Rumbos*, September 24, 1977).

27. For example, the Or Mizraj Temple appointed a young Aleppan rabbi, though tied to the Chabad ultra-Orthodox movement (*La Luz*, April 1, 1988), and other rabbis of the same sector were appointed in the Puertas de Oración Temple in Once.

coexisting, some with very little contact, and, in practice, responding to several very charismatic local rabbis or lay leaderships.

Some Final Considerations

The Syrian Jewish groups and a new generation of native-born religious leaders became dynamic factors in the "return to biblical sources" movements that spread in Argentina and Latin America. It is worth noting that traditional Jewish distinctiveness, reserved some decades ago to more restricted sectors, started to expand and exert significant influence on the institutional policies of the community as a whole. The economic elites tied to Syrian Judaism, who had joined forces with the rabbinic and lay authorities of their communities, turned themselves into spokespersons for Sephardic Judaism in the larger Jewish-Argentine community, and, using their economic power, they succeeded in imposing religious standards on the institutions to which they granted subsidies. The president of Fundación Banco Mayo, Adolfo Safdíe, affirmed: "I cannot conceive the idea that, in the Jewish institutional sphere, the principles and practices of our people's traditions should not be observed. To cease to respect publicly these basic standards means true self-denial and utter disdain to our own selves" (*La Voz Judía*, July–August 1986, author's translation).

They further succeeded in exerting more influence on the domestic and foreign policies of Argentine Judaism.[28] In this context of religious renaissance, the material and individual successes of Syrian economic elites were also explained in theological terms, as God's blessing to some of the Orthodox leaders, so that, through them, it would benefit those who had taken the right path: "B'H [with G-d's help] blessed many members of our People who are Orthodox with material wealth as has never been witnessed in previous times . . . B'H has delivered it by means of them and, if they do not deliver it, they will be taken as thieves."[29]

Thus leaders who enjoyed great economic power and who became "philanthropic businessmen" received respect similar to that granted to the eminent

28. "The community knows that no Banco Mayo director will attend a meeting which is not 100 percent kosher" (*Kesher Kehilatí*, April 5, 1990; author's translation).

29. Perspectiva paper, unknown date. Author's translation.

religious authorities. These men also underwent a change in their relationship with the domestic and foreign political sphere. From a position that tended to avoid any involvement, they gradually started to incorporate themselves into the political game, accompanying those with an Ashkenazi religious orientation in the internal decisions of the Jewish community.[30] Although they continued to preserve a very low profile on issues related to national politics, they expressed their support to the Argentine government during the Malvinas-Falklands War, and, unlike other Jewish sectors, they avoided speaking out publicly against the violation of Human Rights during the last military dictatorship.[31]

Regarding Israeli politics, Aleppans favored the nationalist right-wing parties[32] or, later, the new Sephardic ultra-Orthodox political party Shas,[33] founded in 1984. In that context it is worth noting that the strengthening of the religious standards demanded by the new rabbinic leaders (who had been trained in ultra-Orthodox seminaries) also aroused very clear intergenerational differences. It led to pressure on the older generations to abandon or redefine religious practices as well as to a number of family and community conflicts.

In other words, although there was a stronger commitment to compliance with biblical precepts, within each community several levels of religiousness have coexisted. This has become one of the sources of latent tension, where not only the older generations regard the new forms as extreme and inappropriate, but also others, who in the name of a more tolerant Eastern Sephardic tradition want greater pragmatism in the guidelines adopted against the challenges posed by modernity and in a Gentile world.

30. In 1987, the first massive Sephardic incorporation to AMIA (Asociación Mutual Israelita Argentina) was announced (*La Voz Judía*, April 1987).

31. Most of the Syrian Jews were not affected by the tragic events that took place in Argentina in the 1970s during the last military dictatorship. Although the community authorities tried not to be involved in politics, and avoided declarations about the dictatorship, some Argentine youths of Syrian origin disappeared, while others had to take refuge abroad (see Rodgers 2005, 176–77).

32. Rabbi Chehebar's support letter addressed to Prime Minister Menachem Begin of Israel says, "that there should be willingness which would also make it possible with God's help to be elected again." (Congregación Sefaradí 1995, 220–21). Author's translation.

33. The Union Party of Sephardic Observant Torá, a movement that proclaimed religious and ethnic revival in the name of Sephardic Jews in Israel.

The processes undergone by such migratory collective groups may be contextualized within the religious awakening of recent decades. In Buenos Aires, as well as in other parts of the world, new religious movements and sects were and still are in full growth.

All in all, it is worth noting that the renaissance of religious practices was not restricted to the communities composed of Arabic-speaking Jews or the Ashkenazi ultra-Orthodox groups (*Mundo Israelita*, October 21, 1978; May 2, 1986). The desecularization process was much broader. Since the 1960s, another Jewish religious trend, the Conservative movement, called "heretical" by the Orthodox groups because of its broad interpretation of Jewish Law, also attracted many nonobservant Ashkenazi Jews. Thus, although the religious monopoly of the traditional views of the Torah was undermined, it was relegitimized from a more liberal religious perspective among those individuals who, while being believers in earlier times, did not follow such traditional practices.

However, it is necessary to highlight that the "returning" Jews also were and are part of a unique and different phenomenon that is not merely a reflection of religious affairs in Israel. In the Aleppan community, the turn to faith emerged much earlier—in the 1950s—when it was still believed that religions were in extinction. In addition, such a revival is part of the development undergone by the second and third generations of two groups of immigrant origin, with a strong sense of regional belonging. It is not a result of the individual search of men and women (regardless of their origin) for new existential answers. In fact, the social paths trodden by both communities are a unique phenomenon in the social history of immigration to a pluralistic, though also homogenizing Argentina, where, in time, the specific attributes of the different migratory groups had started to erode.

In conclusion, in 1990, the Syrian Jewish communities seemed to be at their height. The religiousness of the new generations, the numerical growth of Orthodox and ultra-Orthodox religious manifestations, the popularity of rabbinic leadership, and the material prosperity of some businessmen and institutions that were committed to the renewed zeal, all combined to strengthen the feeling of legitimacy and divine protection in the paths that had been taken.

6

Religious Movements in Mexican Sephardism

LIZ HAMUI HALABE

Throughout the twentieth century, the cultural heritage identified with the Sephardic Jewish experience in Mexico was reflected in the life of three communities that had gone through significant transformations along the four generations: the Mount Sinai Alliance (MSA) composed of *Shamis*, descendants of Damascus Jews; the Maguén David Community (MDC), which groups together the *Halebis*, whose ancestors came from Aleppo, Syria; and the Sephardic Union (SU), which unites the sons and grandsons of the Jews coming from Turkey, Greece, and the Balkan countries. Although the first two groups descended from a *Musarabian* population, considered indigenous to the Middle East region, the influence of Sephardic immigration of the fifteenth and sixteenth centuries left a cultural imprint that allows us to define them by the term *Sephardim*.[1] In Mexico, however, the last of these groups is distinguished by the name "Sephardic" for its Balkan origin and direct descent from Hispanic Jews.

Although each community has its own singularities and has experienced different ethnic-religious movements, we may identify certain common processes

---

1. Margalit Bejarano applies the term, with respect to Latin America, to four groups with different geographic and cultural roots: direct descendants of Jews from the Iberic Peninsula; North African immigrants; Jews from Turkey, Greece, Rhodes, Bulgaria, and former Yugoslavia who spoke Judezmo or Ladino and were identified with Sephardi tradition; and last, Jews from oriental provinces of the Turkish-Ottoman Empire such as Syria, Lebanon, and Palestine, speaking Arabic or Ladino (Bejarano 2005, 12–13).

that the third and fourth Jewish generations in Mexico are going through. The objective of this essay is to carry out a socio-historical reconstruction of religiosity in Sephardic communities before and after 1970, a decade characterized by an onset of ideological particularism—a movement of reevaluation of community space, as well as the reelaboration of axes by which identity is built.

Community Experience Throughout the First Two Generations of Sephardic Jews in Mexico (1900–1970)

The first Sephardic immigrants in modern times arrived in the country during the period known in Mexican history as the *Porfiriato* (1876–1910). Although the colonial period was characterized by a significant presence of Crypto-Jews, the Holy Inquisition Court managed to weaken and practically dissolve the different communities of converts established throughout the colonial territory, especially in the north of New Spain, where most of them were gathered (Gojman de Backal 1984).[2] At the end of the nineteenth and beginning of the twentieth centuries, the first Sephardic Jews came to Mexico mainly from Greece, Turkey, and the Balkans. Arabic-speaking Jews from Aleppo and Damascus provinces belonging to the Turkish-Ottoman Empire arrived as of 1905 (Askenazi 1982). Despite the fact that Francisco Rivas Puigcerver, a descendant of *conversos*, attempted to promote Mexico as the final destination for Jewish immigrants from the Turkish-Ottoman Empire through his publication, *El Sábado Secreto*, it is more likely that the first Sephardic Jews arrived in Mexican territory by coincidence, wishing to "make America" (*El Sábado Secreto*, May 15, 1889). They worked as merchants or peddlers and established themselves in large cities, mainly in the capital. The first attempts at community organization took place during the first decade of the twentieth century (Krause 1987). However, the MSA was only established in 1912, with participation of Jews from all backgrounds. Ashkenazim and Sephardim aimed to purchase land for a Jewish

---

2. Today, there are people who claim being descendants of converts. They confirm their Sephardi origins and aim to awaken ancestral traditions through religious conversion. Examples of these are groups in Veracruz, Monterrey, Venta Prieta in Pachuca, Hidalgo, and Vallejo, north of Mexico City.

cemetery. The initiative of Isaac Capón, a Sephardic Jew from Greece who was the first president of the MSA, was crucial in this process of community structure (Alianza Monte Sinaí 2001).

The outbreak of the Mexican Revolution in 1910 had an impact on the development of the community because of the conditions of insecurity and shortage. Some of the Jews living in Mexico at that time[3] decided to leave the country for the United States or other Latin American destinations. Those who remained suffered from poverty and dearth together with the rest of the Mexican population. Furthermore, between 1914 and 1918, contact with family members from abroad was made more complicated by the First World War, which also limited the immigration flow.[4] As a result, the second decade of the twentieth century was extremely complex, affecting the MSA's growth and endangering its existence. Nevertheless, *Halebi* and *Shami* families remained strongly united, while reproducing religious and cultural practice through kinship networks (Hamui de Halabe 1999).

The decade of the 1920s is crucial for understanding Sephardic community dynamics in Mexico. Once warfare in the old world came to an end, migration was revived. Because of its proximity to the United States,[5] Mexico received a large number of immigrants who had escaped from Europe, Asia, and North Africa when the economic, political, and cultural reconstruction of the country began. Commercial opportunities were now available, legal guarantees of freedom of worship had been confirmed by revolutionary regimes, and foreigners were allowed to get new citizenship. These were attractive offers leading to a significant increase in the number of Jews established in Mexico (Zárate 1986). The MSA was growing, and Sephardic and Ashkenazi pioneers were helping their

3. For an estimated number of Jews in Mexico during the first two decades of the twentieth century, see Seligson (1973) and Liwerant (1992).

4. An example of communication difficulties in this period is expressed in Mr. Emilio Mussali Mujaled's testimony in his 2000 book.

5. In 1921, new North American migration laws called "Quota Acts," restrained immigration. Many Jews who intended to immigrate the United States decided to remain in Mexico hoping to emigrate to the neighbor country in the future. However, throughout time, they worked, progressed, and adjusted to the community and the country and were finally established in Mexico (Zárate 1986; Gojman de Backal 1983).

co-religionists to adjust to the country. At the same time, however, differences arose between groups from different places of origin, leading to community diversity. The conflict came to a head in their common synagogue,[6] where Sephardim and Ashkenazim disagreed on the order of prayers and their pronunciations and tunes, leading to tension and anger. The Yiddish-speaking Ashkenazim decided to separate from the MSA in 1922 and organized their own liturgical services in order to create an "authentic religious life similar to the *shtetl* in Eastern Europe" (Zack de Govesensky 1993, 30).

On the other hand, in 1924, Ladino-speaking Sephardim decided to organize themselves independently in order to help each other. The MSA and the first-built synagogue were spaces mainly visited by Arabic-speaking Jews, who shared a cultural and religious heritage. Nevertheless, *Shamis* and *Halebis* would also separate by 1931, as Aleppo descendants built their own synagogue, located in Córdoba Street in the Roma neighborhood, and stopped paying their fees to the MSA. In 1935, Damascus descendants declared the MSA exclusively theirs, compelling the *Halebis* to establish their own charitable society called Sedaká u Marpé (Assistance and Health) in 1938 (Hamui de Halabe 1997a).

The Sephardic groups established in Mexico had different levels of religiosity. Of the three Sephardic communities, the most religiously observant were the *Halebis*. Even in Aleppo, they were characterized by their exaggerated ritualism and adherence to a life ruled by the *Halacha* (Jewish law). Although modernity had reached the Jewish community in Aleppo through French cultural influence, and many of its members attended the Alliance Israélite Universelle, they preserved their values and beliefs based on their view of a world rooted in the ancient tradition of rabbinical Judaism. For these Jews, religious practice was an

6. Venustiano Carranza, president of Mexico in 1918, signed the authorization to build the first synagogue in Justo Sierra St. in front of the Loreto Square, in the center of the capital. The synagogue, managed by the MSA, started functioning in 1922 and most Jews living nearby attended religious services offered. Until then, more than half of the Jewish population came from Turkey, Syria, Lebanon, and the Balkans. Eastern Europe Jews made up scarcely 200 families. Since 1921, thousands of immigrants from Russia, Poland, Romania, Lithuania, Austria, Germany, Hungary, and Czechoslovakia arrived in the country. Approximately 9,000 Ashkenazim and 6,000 Sephardi Jews came to Mexico during this decade and joined those already established, making a total of 21,000 Jews (Sutton et al. 2005; Hamui de Halabe 2005, 121–22).

integral part of their lives manifested through kinship, business relations among themselves, Jewish holidays celebrated on time, domestic space, gastronomy, and daily interactions, all molded by shared symbolic codes that provided meaning to their acts (Hamui de Halabe 1999).

Damascus immigrants remained united within informal social networks strong enough to strengthen their group identity. As opposed to the *Halebis*, the *Shamis* benefited from an early institutional network, as they inherited common community organizations such as the MSA, the cemetery management, and the first synagogue. Their cosmopolitan characteristics, as they came from the Syrian capital, allowed them to adjust rapidly to the Mexican environment, as well as to a more relaxed attitude toward religiosity.[7] Nevertheless, they preserved their religious customs while having their own rabbis, kosher food, *mohel* (performer of ritual circumcision), a group of *Gmilut Hasadim* (charity), Talmud Torah and midrashim (Torah study venues), and offices for the management of community issues.

For their part, Sephardic Jews from Greece, Turkey, and Bulgaria remained united by traditions and folklore. Ladino had been a cultural element allowing them to adjust rapidly to the country. However, their Jewish identity was a powerful unifying factor leading to the reproduction of their ideas, way of life, and traditional values. Once they separated from the MSA, their main interest was concentrated in philanthropy and mutual assistance. Women founded an organization called "The Good Will" aimed at supporting immigrants and their families in their integration to the new country. Male adults founded "The Fraternity" to take care of community and religious needs, while the youth created social spaces such as the movement "Union and Progress." The Sephardic Union was the community that put least emphasis on the religious aspects of its priorities. However, collective tradition and memory were nourished by Judaic motifs, which were continually transmitted within the family by parents to children and by common organizations.

7. For instance, Sabbath observance was much more rigid among *Halebis* than among *Shamis*. The latter carried out their commercial activities on Sabbath, which was a good day for sales. However, it should be mentioned that both groups included very religious family nuclei who faithfully preserved and reproduced the rituals practiced in their place of origin.

The energy of immigrants from all backgrounds was focused on the creation of communal institutions that structured Jewish life in the country. Immigrants who arrived when they were children, and the first generation born in Mexico, were integrated into the collective tasks developing the work of their parents. During the 1930s, Jews in Mexico confronted an important challenge: from a minority that had been invited by the government a decade earlier, they became a tolerated group considered as not being able to assimilate into the mestizo majority. The xenophobic nationalism of right-wing groups in Mexico at the beginning of the 1930s (Gojman de Backal 2000), as well as the ideological influence of Nazism, fascism, and the Spanish Franco regime, unleashed anti-Semitic expressions that caused a unified reaction from different community sectors and led to the creation of the Israelite Central Committee of Mexico in 1938 (Linder 1995). Although the division between sectors could not be avoided, the Jews relied on an organization for representation and antidefamation that contributed considerably to work on behalf of the rescue of European Jewish refugees and that negotiated with the Mexican authorities during World War II (Salzman 2000). The antifascist and pro-Allies attitude of the Mexican government favored the condemnation of right-wing anti-Semitism and, following the war, helped to found the Pro-Palestine Committee, a nongovernmental organization that supported the Jewish aim to create a national homeland in Palestine. Thus, world Jewish events, the Holocaust, and the creation of the State of Israel marked the future of the Mexican Jewish community during the 1930s and 1940s.

Meanwhile, opportunities associated with national economic reconstruction favored the economic progress of Mexican Jews in industry and commerce, as well as their rise in the socioeconomic ladder toward the business bourgeoisie. The decades of the 1940s, 1950s, and 1960s, known as the "Mexican miracle," were reflected in the construction of sumptuous synagogues, the creation of community schools whose objective was the cultural reproduction of Judaism, the purchase of land for cemeteries in each communal sector, and the moving of families to better residential areas. In 1942, The Sephardic Union built the impressive Rabbi Yehuda Halevi synagogue located on Monterrey Street, in the Roma neighborhood, which would become the core of community life for many decades. For the Jews of Damascus, it took more than ten years to build a beautiful synagogue, the Mount Sinai Temple, inaugurated in 1953 in Queretaro Street within the same neighborhood. It is a large synagogue that, in addition to the religious spaces, includes rooms for social events. The Aleppo Jews moved from the Roma neighborhood to Polanco, where they established their second religious grounds: the Maguén David Temple, a model of contemporary architecture and art (Hamui de Halabe 2005).

Within the configuration of their Jewish identity, the second generation—the first born in Mexico—found it difficult to provide coherence to diverse and sometimes contradictory codes reflected in their parents' culture and religiosity (Abou 1989). On the one hand, the intensity of the events in world Jewry required the attention of all the Jews in Israel and in the Diaspora, and on the other, they had to cope with their integration into the country in which they were born, where they experienced daily life, while internalizing symbolic codes that gave meaning to their existence. These dilemmas were dealt with through the establishment of a form of social life with centripetal and centrifugal forces, where the secularization experienced by Mexican modernism and the political commitment of Jewish Zionism acted as essential referents, displacing religion as a nucleus of collective identity (Liwerant 1991); only a few families preserved vivid beliefs and practices, transmitting them to future generations. In spite of the secularization experienced by Mexican Jews, the Orthodox rite was still dominant among Sephardic Jews, as their practices and beliefs in synagogues and worship locations continued.

Community Experience Throughout the Third and Fourth Generations of Sephardic Jews in Mexico (1970–2000).

Throughout the third and fourth generations, there was a synthesis of the different points of view in the expression of the Mexican-Jewish formula. As adults, they had to face the changes of globalization; the economic turbulences of the 1970s, 1980s, and 1990s; and the configuration of new paradigms, forms of identity, and a sociocultural space where their children would grow up "protected" from the late changes of modernity. The return to the community has been remarkable, both within the traditionalist sector, where parents choose for their children integration into the Jewish school network[8] (with schools fostering an intensive sense

---

8. According to the demographic study carried out in 1991 by Sergio DellaPergola and Susana Lerner (1995, 77–80), 70–80 percent of school-age children and adolescents attended Jewish schools

of belonging to the Jewish people in addition to the sense of national belonging), and in the rise of new religious movements, mostly fundamentalist, within the *Halebi* sector, the most ritualistic. Traditionalists[9] view Judaism as a cultural resource by which existential aspects of their personal, family, and social life develop. Conversely, those identified as religious think of Judaism as an integral social system ruling the most minimal attitudes and practices of its members. It should also be noted that although the traditionalist sector is the most dominant, a small part of Mexican Jewry (approximately 5 percent) is not affiliated with any institution and does not relate to the community context. Some of these members have assimilated, having lost their religious and cultural particularities.[10]

Religious tendencies developed in countries such as Israel, the United States, and Argentina contribute to the understanding of this phenomenon in Mexican Judaism after the decade of the 1970s. Transcultural flows depend on networks established among religious institutions in different regions. In the case of Mexico, several links are maintained with Israeli organizations, as well as with North American Judaism, especially with Ashkenazi organizations associated with Conservative Judaism. In addition, an indirect relationship is maintained with Argentine Judaism through Israeli yeshivot for Latin American rabbis, where Spanish-speaking rabbis bound for Mexico are trained.[11]

The religious responses of the three Sephardic communities analyzed in this chapter have been different. While the MDC (before Sedaká u Marpé) has been characterized by the development of several ultra-Orthodox religious movements

---

at that time. A more significant fact relates to a 10 percent increase or more during the next decade according to data appearing in the sociodemographic study of the Jewish community in Mexico carried out by Alduncin and Associates in 2000.

9. Traditionalists practice some religious rites according to standing dates in the Hebrew calendar and the Jewish life cycle as well, providing them with a social sense and cultural identity besides religious meaning. They are secular Jews who are integrated to the country economically and culturally but with a strong attachment to the Jewish community. For a description of types and scales of religiosity in the Jewish community of Mexico, see Hamui de Halabe (2005, 215–38).

10. See the sociodemographic study carried out in 1991 by Sergio DellaPergola and Susana Lerner (1995, 77–80).

11. An example of these kinds of networks are those existing between the Keter Torah Yeshiva and the Daroma Yeshiva of Bnei Brak, where Mexican Jewish youth study.

that tend toward Jewish fundamentalism, the MSA has experienced a controlled return to religious ritualism. This phenomenon has taken place less intensively in the SU, although there has also been a return expressed by an exaltation of cultural particularism.

According to the study carried out by Alduncin and Associates in the year 2000 (unpublished data), the rate of religiosity of the three Sephardi communities is presented in percentages (see table 6.1).

Religious observance is more emphasized within the MDC, where the lowest percentage of traditionalists is presented (66 percent) and similar numbers appear on the extremes, 17 percent of observant and very observant and another 17 percent of secular members. These findings indicate real and potential conflicts among exclusionist points of view, which may lead to serious confrontations in collective decisions and an eventual rupture within the congregation.

In order to offer an in-depth analysis of these religiosity-increase modes, all the synagogues, worship sites, and Torah study locations throughout the Mexican Republic were classified according to some major characteristics (Hamui de Halabe 2005). From the fifty-three worship locations available in 2002, nineteen were built before 1970 and the other thirty-four were created during the following thirty-two years, indicating both a quantitative and a qualitative change. Worship locations existing before the 1970s and belonging to the first and second generation are mainly synagogues attended by secularists and traditionalists as well as by religious Jews and therefore are ample and large structures. In contrast,

Table 6.1.
Rate of religious observance in Sephardi communities in Mexico

	MAGUÉN DAVID COMMUNITY	MOUNT SINAI ALLIANCE	SEPHARDI UNION
Very observant	9	4	2
Observant	8	8	3
Traditionalist	66	82	83
Mildly observant	15	6	4
Secular	1	0	8
Atheist	1	0	0

Source: Data from Alduncin and Associates (2000).

during the following three decades, various small worship locations were created as a result of two parallel dynamics: first, Jews moved to other residential areas and therefore new worship sites, such as synagogues and/or midrashim, were required in order to practice Jewish rites. And second, the ultra-Orthodox sector had grown, leading to the establishment of small worship centers and Torah study locations attended mainly by the very observant and observant public that excluded those who do not share their religious perspective.

These spaces have increased within the Maguén David Community and on its margins, in autonomous religious movements directed by rabbis or charismatic religious leaders and made up of a *Halebi* population. The risk of religious deinstitutionalization expressed in the loss of control of the sacred environment has led Maguén David Community authorities to protect these religious movements, most of which are of fundamentalist character. The majority of the new midrashim, yeshivot (schools for Jewish studies), and *kolelim* (advanced yeshivot) established during the last thirty years are concentrated within the *Halebi* sector.

The Mexican *Haredism* (Ultra-Orthodox Movement) in the MDC[12]

Religiosity modalities that have been observed in the MDC are the result of the synthesis of diverse cultural elements in the ultra-Orthodox environment. Since the second half of the twentieth century, the fusion of Ashkenazi and Sephardic cultural traditions[13] has brought forth a more active, purposeful kind of religiosity able to reinvent itself every day in its struggle against Western modernity in general and against Zionism in particular (Heilman and Friedman 1994), as both factors are considered serious threats to the preservation of "authentic" Judaism. This attitude of obstinacy and anti-acculturation is a characteristic of behavior and discourse of current Israeli and Mexican fundamentalist religious groups,

---

12. The data discussed in this chapter are based on research discussed in Hamui de Halabe (2005).

13. After World War II, Ashkenazi yeshivot of Hasidim and *Mitnagdim* (opponents) were established in Israel and in the United States. As Sephardi Jews emigrated from Arab countries after the creation of the State of Israel, many religious families sent their children to these yeshivot, producing a synthesis among Ashkenazi and Sephardi cultural elements that were expressed in peculiar religious movements similar to the Shas political party (Heilman and Friedman 1994).

acting as a regulating principle by which consciousness is organized, meant, and interpreted. Such an ethos[14] is expressed by the individual's subjectivity as well as by the objectivity of the acts carried out through which beliefs are materialized (d'Epinay 1990). Religion has been recovered as a cultural resource by some sectors of the Jewish community, especially by the MDC, providing a strong unifying energy that tends to reinforce particularism and searches for the return to the "real" source of Judaism in order to provide feasibility and continuity to the group. This movement relates to most hierarchical, conservative, and less sophisticated organizations, at least intellectually speaking, which base their arguments on the authority of sacred texts and rabbinic interpretations of the divine power. The reevaluation of the Jewish people's past in the current decades projects the intention to provide continuity to the millenarian heritage, ensuring religious attachment. Even though the religious homogeneity and stability of Sephardic communities have been supported by the traditionalist sector, the last decades were characterized by a subtle tendency toward the recuperation of different elements of Judaism through the reconfiguration of the religious environment.

Community structures were consolidated by the 1970s. Mexican Judaism was then led by secular members who supported rabbinic orthodoxy with respect to religious matters, as part of the community's representative organizations. These organizations have been characterized by an emphasis on unity and consensus, tending to draw social boundaries that limit the appearance of diverse religious expressions. One of the clearest examples of this trend is the intercommunity agreement rejecting institutional affiliation changes, or celebration of Jewish life-cycle rituals in a synagogue different from that to which the person belongs without an authorization letter from the original community. This measure is intended to compel members to pay their fees and to comply with community regulations. Intracommunity coordination is thus reflected in religious matters in the reinforcement of the traditionalist-orthodox trend, which supports each community and maintains certain limits.

During the 1990s, new synagogues were build within the MDC: Eliahu Fasja in Tecamachalco; another one in the Bosques de las Lomas neighborhood,

---

14. Ethos is understood as the set of beliefs, values, standards, and models leading behavior. It is the core of a culture characterizing a society, a group, or an institution.

in Lomas Anáhuac; and the large project of the Maguén David Center, which included a synagogue and a ballroom, and which was inaugurated in 2003. The religious sector, with or without the board of directors' support, opened a large number of midrashim and *kolelim*, leading to the pulverization of attendance in the existing worship locations. This decline is an interesting issue that can be explained by various factors: first, pressure from community members for the establishment of new worship places, leading to employment of religious personnel responsible for their functioning, and second, the establishment of autonomous midrashim and *kolelim* that are not economically dependent on the community and that compel the institution to respond to the demands of their members, who may otherwise find what they are looking for in other marginal groups. These midrashim and *kolelim* have risen at the initiative of rabbis who were once employed by the MDC and left for some reason, who then created their own religious organizations.

The balance between the religious and traditionalist sectors is more and more difficult to keep, as both become stronger and exclude each other, creating a difficult situation for the board of directors of the Maguén David Community. Both sectors try to influence collective morale, the former by opening it and adapting it to the changing world, and the latter by closing it with the intention of preserving Judaism, which they feel is threatened by the environment of modernity.

Control of Religiosity in the MSA

The MSA board of directors includes a Committee for Religious Affairs in charge of administrating the functioning of the synagogues, the purchase of religious items, and the employment of rabbis and *hazanim* (cantors). Each synagogue has a *guizbar* (treasurer or administrator) in charge of preparing the site for religious ceremonies and holidays as well as the daily liturgical services. This official has always been in contact with the board of directors responsible for administrating temples or midrashim (Alianza Monte Sinaí 2001). From 1982 to 2005, the Committee for Religious Affairs was directed by Isaac Kably, who, in addition to managing all synagogue matters and the employment of rabbis, was responsible for the preservation of the religious ideology of the community deriving from the customs and traditions transmitted by fathers and grandfathers and brought over from Damascus. However, members are currently facing the penetration of new and more religious movements into the *Shami* public, which is characterized by traditionalism rather than religiosity.

An event exemplifying this resistance took place when, at the onset of the 1990s, a group of religious members wanted to establish a *kolel* authorized by the institution. Their proposal was rejected, and they were told that such trends were unacceptable within the Mount Sinai Alliance. This more orthodox group had two alternatives: to adjust to the decisions made by the board of directors or to leave. Its decision was to leave, and the group founded its own organization named Or Damesek (Light of Damascus), which has functioned independently until today with a large attendance of *Halebis*. In 2002, Or Damesek established small branches in the new residential areas inhabited by Jews. These are not very crowded spaces, but the approximately thirty people attending each of these locations study and worship according to the strict orthodox standards of the *Halacha*.

Institutions and religious personnel have been closely controlled by the MSA board of directors in order to guarantee that the religious traditionalism inherited by their ancestors will be faithfully preserved by future generations. The melodies of the prayers, study methods, and religious education programs in the Talmud Torah are supervised by the Committee for Religious Affairs. The homogeneity of religious expression in the Damascene community and the social cohesion based on kinship networks and group endogamy has been remarkable throughout its history. A sign of religious homogeneity is the absence of worship locations other than the synagogues, with the midrashim only transitory spaces during passage from one residential area to another. Considering that the synagogue is the widest and most cohesive spiritual space, refusals to establish sites where a more deeply marked religiosity would be practiced exclusively for more religious sectors has been a recurrent policy of this sector. The sociocultural properties of the *Shamis* are characterized by the preservation of rituals and by the promotion of moderate religiosity. The community's traditionalist profile is based on a view that on the one hand integrates a sociocultural identity linked to a common place of origin and to a religious heritage with particular customs, and on the other to a secular and modern lifestyle allowing its members to adjust successfully to the economic, political, and cultural environment of Mexico. This acculturation formula preserves their distinction as a minority but at the same time allows them to integrate in different spheres of national life. The MSA aims to preserve the traditionalist profile of its members, while avoiding what they call extreme deviations—assimilation or extreme religiosity—that might risk the balance of this pattern.

Folkloric-Religious Traditionalism of the Sephardic Union

When the Sephardic School moved to the Tecamachalco residential area in 1985, a midrash was built inside it that actually served as a synagogue for most of the members of the community, as at that time only very few still lived in the neighborhoods of Roma and Del Valle. In 2000, a religious, social, and cultural center was established near the school, where a beautiful synagogue was built in the style of Toledo in Spain. This center revived the social dynamics of the Sephardic community and projected its cultural richness to other sectors of the Jewish community. The SU has been characterized by intercommunal openness.

Throughout its history in Mexico, the SU has not been distinguished by religious devotion. Its members managed to preserve original community traditions such as gastronomy, Ladino songs, ancestral history, family genealogical lines, and other traditions associated with domestic customs or Jewish life-cycle rituals such as circumcisions, *bar mitzvot*, weddings, and deaths that connect them with Jewish heritage. However, there are no religious movements aimed at restoring beliefs and alternative ways of life. Most rabbis who conducted services in the synagogues on Monterrey Street and in the Tecamachalco neighborhood came from Istanbul. Links with the Jewish community of Turkey have not been lost and are still maintained by kinship relations. Nevertheless, an Argentine rabbi of *Halebi* descent was employed three years ago in order to serve the Monterrey *kahal* (public), with Rabbi Abraham Palti (from Istanbul) officiating as the chief rabbi of the community in the Tecamachalco synagogue. The rabbis have adjusted to the traditionalist pattern of the community, and although they conduct all the religious activities according to the Orthodox rite—they perform weddings, do divorces, teach children how to pray in the synagogue's Talmud Torah, assist families of the deceased, lead daily religious services and on Jewish holidays according to the Hebrew calendar—they respect the secular and modern lifestyle of most of the members of that community.

Religion and Its Implications in the Life of Sephardic Communities

Religion is a basic aspect of community identity. However, the influence of religious standards in daily decisions varies from one community sector to the other. According to the pattern that prevailed prior to 1970, the boards of directors, through the Committee for Religious Affairs, administered aspects of community practices and rites and set out action guidelines for the personnel in charge, including the rabbis, that respected the policy defined by the voluntary members of this board. Nevertheless, this model has been modified during the last decades, especially within the MDC. The increasing moral influence of religious leaders on the board meetings tends to determine community public decisions, leading to reactions from secular members who are worried by the increasing regulations and prohibitions based on Jewish ultra-Orthodox parameters. There is a constant pressure to provide certain services to members, including more rigid methods and ritual prescriptions such as kashruth supervision, specific circumcision procedures, the bridal shower ritual (*hamam*) carried out by a bride before her wedding, and so on.

The Sephardic Union appears to be well balanced, without religious confrontation. As noted in the previous table, this community comprises 83 percent traditionalists, 5 percent observant and very observant, and 12 percent mildly observant and secular. These findings indicate that the dominant trend is to apply Jewish tradition within the framework of modern life. The fact that the community owns only two functioning synagogues leads to delimited and stable religious expenses, which do not represent a budget deficit. The board of directors' treasury administers donations of *aliyot* granted during religious services and the wages of rabbis and religious personnel. Unlike the MSA and the MDC, the SU does not have a kashruth department and uses the services of MDC. Rabbis have a limited influence on the decisions made by the board of directors, while community policy is determined by active members of the board of directors and enforced by the religious personnel. Rabbis are appreciated and respected. They participate in social events of members, as well as in school events related to the Hebrew calendar, are involved in community publications including religious reflections, and maintain the Talmud Torah attended by children before their *bar mitzvot*. In addition, they serve as judges for the resolution of family or business conflicts.

In the cultural field, the SU holds to pro-Zionist ideologies and is concerned about what happens in Israel. It considers the Shoah a catastrophe in recent Jewish history and participates in the annual memorial together with other community sectors. During the last two decades, the Sephardic school has reevaluated the millenarian Sephardic heritage, preserving and transmitting its cultural pride and the Ladino language and customs, characterizing the school as an inclusive factor because it admits Ashkenazi, *Shami*, and *Halebi*, students without having them lose their group uniqueness.

The *Shami* sector has shown greater participation in rites and religious customs. Although synagogues are full during *Shabat* (Sabbath), and although they became privileged social spaces for youth and adults, the return to religious practices has not been guided by a deep religious conversion or *teshuvah*. Homogeneous lifestyles have still been preserved, while the board of directors has encouraged religious expressions in inclusive spaces like the synagogues, without canceling the spiritual impulses of its members. The MSA maintains a kashruth department and employs four or five rabbis in its different sacred places. None of them participates in board meetings, but they respect their resolutions. A Talmud Torah is available, teaching a large number of children. It is also the place where religious members of the community gather daily for the study of the Torah. Family life follows modern Mexican urban life, to which they have adjusted while keeping in mind their ethnic communal belonging. This situation is expressed by an extreme awareness of endogamic marriages and in the group's rejection of conversion to Judaism. Culturally speaking, they maintain a pro-Zionist position but do not encourage *aliya* (immigration) to the State of Israel, as it would threaten extended family cohesion, a highly appreciated factor within the community context. In summary, we may state that although community religiosity has increased, the original cultural heritage, recognized and defended by community policy decisions, has not been thoroughly changed.

In contrast, the creation of new institutionally dependent synagogues, midrashim, and *kolelim* within the Maguén David Community throughout the last thirty-five years has led to increased employment of religious personnel,[15]

---

15. The issue of religious personnel employed in worship locations during the last years has to do with the presence of Argentine rabbis. Many of these rabbis were trained in yeshivot in Israel

Furthermore, large portions of the annual community budget have been used to pay the wages of the rabbi instead of designating them to charity or to the creation of inclusive and pluralistic spaces. In fact, the religious sector (members making *teshuvah* and living according to rigid *Halacha* standards dictated and supervised by recognized ultra-Orthodox rabbis) has grown since 2000. Its members aim to dedicate themselves to the study of the Torah and to bringing up many children, creating an unproductive sector, economically speaking, with increased poverty. This situation leads them to require help from community institutions in order to pay for rent, Jewish school tuitions, medical services, and other basic needs, presenting a financial burden hard to overcome.[16] Meanwhile, the economic pressure on the community may eventually lead the secular sector to refuse to pay its fees to support the religious sector, which criticizes and rejects them for not following their ideology and lifestyle.

The boards of directors find themselves in difficulties, trying to reconcile to the recurrent demands of the ultra-Orthodox religious to adjust public decisions to *Halacha* standards, such as censorship of community media and artistic expressions exhibited in different collective spaces, imposition of strict kashruth

---

and linked with ultra-Orthodox world networks (on the radicalization of Argentine Syrian sectors see Susana Brauner's chapter in this volume). Once trained, they managed to find jobs in Mexico because they spoke Spanish and were Orthodox, and often from the same ethnic background. In fact, most of the twelve rabbis employed by the Maguén David Community in 2002 were relatives who recommended each other. We might ask why they did not integrate as community rabbis if there was a yeshiva in Mexico that trained religious personnel. The answer is that during the 1980s and 1990s, there were no thoroughly trained young men. During the 1990s, the arrival of Argentine rabbis to all Sephardi communities was a phenomenon that attracted attention in promoting the religious transformation described above.

16. Many of the religious institutions depending on the MDC, as well as marginal autonomous groups attended by the *halebis*, receive economic assistance from wealthy people who practically support these organizations. However, poverty among religious families has become common. Given the fact that not all yeshiva graduates can completely dedicate themselves to the study of the Torah in the *kolel*, the MDC religious sector, supported by the board of directors, has implemented the creation of a technological institute providing students with the necessary tools and abilities to find at least a part-time job in order to make a living. This initiative, which began in 2006, had only limited results, since it was not fully supported by the leadership of the Yeshivá Keter Torá.

standards in institutional events, women's dress in sacred spaces, and the construction of precincts for the religious sector such as schools and midrashim. The great challenge faced by the MDC is to preserve the unity of two observance levels with contradicting points of view that are closely linked by kinship networks and by their identification with a common cultural heritage. Often, more strict practices are adopted because of family ties and not by conviction. The religious sector finds in the secular one the possibility of increasing the number of people willing to make *teshuvah,* aside from economic support. In turn, the secular sector sees in the religious members a way to give continuity to their Judaism from which they feel they have moved away, but, at the same time, they are concerned with the changes leading toward an increasingly strict community morality. The tensions in this public community space has overwhelmed the board of directors, and decisions are made sometimes that benefit one sector or the other.

The MDC integrates the strongest religious institutions of the whole community of Mexico. Its kashruth department is the biggest in the country, employing a large number of religious personnel as supervisors in different locations where food is prepared. It includes the largest number of clergy—more than fourteen well-paid rabbis—and manages the largest number of synagogues, worship locations, and Talmud Torahs. As in other Sephardic communities, the rabbis provide religious services in events related to the life cycle, in schools, as arbiters and judges in intra- and intercommunity conflicts, in funerary rites, and so on. Rabbis are appointed by the Committee for Religious Affairs. However, upon their arrival, they are strongly influenced by the rabbis in the religious sector and tend to apply strict *Halacha* standards, alienating them from the traditionalist sector that employed them. The influence of religion in community social and cultural life is diverse. While secular members are modern, pro-Zionists—though without encouraging *aliya*—and take an active part in the economic, political, and cultural life of the country, the religious members are anti-Zionists, against acculturation, and refuse to commemorate the Shoah. Their relationship with Israel is pragmatic and aimed at the religious sector only, through yeshivot or political and social institutions and contact with senior Sephardic rabbis connected to the Shas, the ultra-religious political party.

The daily lives of the traditionalists and the religious are also different. The former interact with the surrounding world, while the latter standardize family life; limit women's role to mother, wife, and housewife; and establish strict rules in the schools attended by their children. Furthermore, some religious leaders even control the most intimate behavior of their followers. They have their own educational spaces operating independently, such as midrashim and *kolelim*, where they support several *avrechim* dedicated to the study of the Torah as their major activity. Their mechanisms of social and cultural reproduction are aimed at the continuity of their way of life. In summary, the dynamics of religious movements in the MDC have their own specific traits, different from those of other Sephardic and Ashkenazi communities in Mexico.

During the last decades, the religious development of Sephardic communities in Mexico has gone through interesting changes in various directions. The secular model, which in the past provided a public space closed to the religious dimension, is now challenged by the appearance of multiple groups offering alternative ways of life. The particularism of the third and fourth generations is expressed by the appearance of religious fundamentalist groups, which has led to lifestyles marked by a rigid delimitation of sociocultural boundaries. These groups regard themselves as guardians of a threatened Judaism and defenders of moral values against the modern "degenerated" world.

We have noted that restricted identities have appeared in various modalities within Mexican Sephardism as follows: the restoration of cultural heritage through the reevaluation of customs linked to religious parameters; the restriction of collective expression of ritual practices; and the appearance of ultra-Orthodox movements representing important challenges for preserving the balance of a community with diverse lifestyles.

Mexican Judaism is not disconnected from the future of the Jewish people. It presents, however, interesting sociological characteristics for analysis. Sociocultural ingredients available in Mexican Sephardic communities combine, resulting in particular forms that both associate and separate themselves when compared with other Jewish experiences in America and worldwide.

The tendency toward cultural and religious particularism that we have observed leads us to reflect about the future of community space: third and fourth generations, far from losing their identity, have transformed it, adapting in the present relevant aspects of their ancestral heritage, combining them with elements of world Judaism and national reality. We can guarantee that community continuity is not in danger because the structural foundations of its institutions, family social dynamics, and Jewish values tend to reproduce fluently.

7

Transnational Identity and Miami Sephardim

HENRY A. GREEN

During the 1970s, there was a popular USA TV show called *All in the Family*. One day a friend asked Archie Bunker, the main character, about another friend, "the Hebe," whom he had not seen for a while in his New York neighborhood. Archie answered: "He's gone to the 'Promised Land.'" "Oh," the friend replied, "the Hebe's gone to Israel." "No," Archie snapped back, "the Hebe's gone to Miami Beach." Between 1960 and 1972, the Jewish population in Florida grew three times faster than the general population. In Southeast Florida (Palm Beach–Broward–Miami-Dade counties), the Jewish population grew from 52,000 in 1950 to 496,000 by 1980.

The greater Miami Jewish population comprised nearly half of that total (230,000) and close to 20 percent of the total county population. Miami Beach, a small island off the mainland, was three-quarters Jewish (Millon 1989). For those smitten with colonialism, "The Beach" was endearingly referred to as "New York South," home of the "snowbird" and "condo commando." South Florida, a peninsula encroached by malaria swamps (the Everglades), and bounded by salt water on three sides (the Atlantic, the Caribbean, and the Gulf of Mexico) and Lake Okeechobee in the north, had been transformed in three

Earlier drafts of this paper were presented at the 14th World Congress of Jewish Studies, Jerusalem, Israel, July 2005 and at the Gimelstob Symposium in Judaic Studies, Florida Atlantic University, Boca Raton, Florida, January 2007.

Table 7.1.
Persons in Jewish households in South Florida, 1950–1980

YEAR	MIAMI-DADE COUNTY	BROWARD COUNTY	PALM BEACH COUNTY	SOUTH FLORIDA
1950	47,000	2,000	3,000	52,000
1960	119,000	10,000	5,000	134,000
1970	198,000	39,000	10,000	247,000
1980	230,000	174,000	92,000	496,000

Source: Sheskin 2005a, 5.

generations: from a trace of Jews in 1900 to the third most populated area for Jewry in the Americas.

According to Ira Sheskin's 2006 demographic study of Southeast Florida Jewry, the region is home to 10 percent of the American Jewish population (table 7.2). In addition to the northerner migrating south, residents have emigrated from Cuba, Central and South America, the former Soviet Union, Israel, Canada, and during the last few years, France.

South Florida Jews are engaged in every type of local industry and professional undertaking—finance, tourism, real estate, retail and wholesale merchandising, and manufacturing. They thrive on the high-rise condominium boom and take advantage of regional, national, and international expanding markets. They have built one of the foremost Jewish economic infrastructures in North America and erected scores of synagogues, Jewish schools, and community centers.

Many Southeast Florida Jewish residents continue to view Israel as a surrogate for Judaism. Southeast Florida Jews are frequent visitors to Israel and witness the uncanny similarity between Tel Aviv and Miami Beach. Each are around 26 degrees north latitude and have prime real estate on the water's edge. Modern cities, founded in the early twentieth century and with significant international-style (Bauhaus/Art Deco) architectural districts, both have significant concentrations of Holocaust survivors. Just as Tel Aviv has blossomed into a Jewish tourist haven for North American Jewry, so has Miami Beach and Southeast Florida become the American Jewish tourist capital for Israelis. Israeli fund-raisers visiting Miami or Boca Raton comment jokingly to their close friends that they have chosen the "wrong Promised Land."

Table 7.2.
Twenty largest American Jewish communities

RANK	COMMUNITY	STATE	NUMBER OF JEWS
1	New York	NY	1,412,000
	South Florida*	FL	602,850
2	Los Angeles	CA	519,200
3	Chicago	IL	270,500
	Palm Beach County*	FL	255,550
4	Broward*	FL	234,000
5	San Francisco	CA	228,000
6	Boston	MA	227,300
7	Washington, DC		215,600
8	Philadelphia	PA	206,100
9	South Palm Beach*	FL	131,300
10	West Palm Beach*	FL	124,250
11	Miami*	FL	113,300
12	Essex-Morris	NJ	109,700
13	Detroit	MI	94,000
14	Baltimore	MD	91,400
15	Rockland County	NY	90,000
16	San Diego	CA	89,000
17	Atlanta	GA	85,900
18	Phoenix	AZ	82,900
19	Cleveland	OH	81,500
20	Las Vegas	NV	75,000

Source: Sheskin 2006, chap. 3, 19.

*Includes Jews who live in part-time households (who live 3–7 months of the year in the local community).

Historical Background

Historically, social pundits did not foresee this demographic transformation. On the eve of World War II (1940), fewer than 10,000 Jews lived between Palm Beach (eastern side of the peninsula), Sarasota (the western side of the peninsula), and Key West, the most southeastern tip of the United States. Moreover, during the 1950s there were still "gentlemen's agreements" restricting Jews from purchasing land in South Florida.

The migration of Jews to Southeast Florida mirrors the migration of northern Americans to the Sunbelt. It began in the late nineteenth century when Henry Flagler extended his East Coast Railway from Jacksonville to Miami in 1896. Flagler, John D. Rockefeller's former partner in the Standard Oil Company, capitalized on the industrial technology of his era and married transportation with hospitality and tourism. After World War II, numbers swelled in the wake of the experiences of tens of thousands of soldiers, sailors, and pilots stationed in Florida who had glimpsed the possibility of living a tropical lifestyle. Their firsthand familiarity with the tropics coincided with the introduction of the mass production of air conditioners and commercial flights to Southeast Florida. For the first time, the region became comfortable and accessible to the average American.

The phenomenal growth of the Southeast Florida Jewish community during the post-war period and its impact on American Jewry remains a researcher's delight. Social scientists and historians who have studied American Jewry did not predict its growth and with the exception of demographic studies, for the most part do not address how Southeast Florida Jewry influences postmodernity and transnational identities (see Sklare 1971; S. Cohen 1983; Goldscheider 1986; and Hertzberg 1989). Recent books celebrating the American Jewish community's 350th birthday (1654–2004) discount or snub Miami and Southeast Florida (Diner 2004; Sarna 2004). The few examples of research undertaken are ethnographies, biographies, and comparative studies such as Moore's comparative study of Los Angeles and Miami (1994) and Green's biography of rabbi, social activist, and Zionist Leon Kronish of Miami Beach (1995; see also Bettinger-Lopez 2000).

Even more telling than the lack of studies on Southeast Florida Jewry is the nearly total absence of any acknowledgment of the Sephardim. Joseph Papo's *Sephardim in Twentieth Century America: In Search of Unity* (1987) and Daniel Elazar's *The Other Jews: The Sephardim Today* (1989), mention Miami only in passing. Martin Cohen and Abraham Peck's *Sephardim in the Americas* (1993), a tribute to the Sephardim after the Inquisition, and Ilan Stavans's *Modern Sephardic Literature* (2005), do not include one reference or voice from Southeast Florida.

This absence is surprising. Sephardim were the early Jewish frontiersmen of Florida. They traveled as *conversos* (forced converts) with Columbus when he sailed to the Americas in the late fifteenth century, and may have accompanied Ponce de León when he landed near St. Augustine, Florida (1513). Green and Zerivitz have speculated that Pedro Menéndez Márquez, the third Spanish governor of Florida (1577–1589), was a *converso* (1991; see also Angel 1982 and Trigano 2004). The introduction of a Spanish Inquisition tribunal in Mexico (1570) followed by other tribunals in Peru (1570) and Columbia (1610) acutely reminded Sephardim of the consequences of visibly practicing their Judaism in the face of Catholic colonialism. Many assume, although there is still no empirical evidence, that Sephardim and *conversos* in the mercantile trade escaping the Inquisition tribunals in the sixteenth and seventeenth centuries may have passed through South Florida. The twenty-three Jews who arrived in New Amsterdam in 1654, celebrated as the "founders" of American Jewry, were also Sephardim evading Catholic persecutors.

Two centuries later, in 1845, Florida became the twenty-seventh state of the Union. Its architect was David Levy Yulee, a Sephardic Jew, son of Moses Levy, who emigrated to Florida in 1819. Yulee was the first Jew to serve in the US Senate, elected seven years before his Louisiana cousin, Judah P. Benjamin. The Yulee family is a microcosm of Sephardic Jewry following expulsion from Spain in 1492. They were intermittent "migrating Jews." In three centuries, the family had emigrated from Morocco to Gibraltar, to St. Thomas, to Cuba, and to Spanish Florida (Monaco 2005).

Hispanics and Sephardim in the United States and Southeast Florida

The invisibility of the Sephardim in the American Jewish educational system in the early twenty-first century is, in part, a reflection of those that study American Jewry and write curricula. As descendants of Eastern European Ashkenazim, their focus is on their own history and culture. It is also a clue to the disconnect between our understanding of the landscape of America at the beginning of the twentieth century and today. In 1900, the US population was 76 million; Hispanics constituted less than 1 million (1.2 percent). Entering the twenty-first century, Hispanics in America are the largest ethnic group (12.5 percent), with a population of approximately 300 million. In greater Miami, the Hispanic population was less than 5 percent at midcentury. Today it hovers around 65 percent. Nearly one in four Southeast Floridians is Hispanic.

The migration of Sephardim to the United States at the beginning of the twentieth century pales in numbers compared to the Ashkenazim but is nonetheless significant. The push of persecution and diminishing labor markets in the wake of the collapse of the Ottoman Empire and the Balkan Wars led several thousands to migrate, primarily from Greece, Rhodes, Turkey, Syria, and Palestine. Proud of their heritage and eager to maintain continuity, they established separate communities and founded Sephardic institutions to maintain their identity, culture, and language, Ladino. Often this development was driven by Ashkenazi response to their yearning to preserve Sephardic identity. Trickles of Sephardim also migrated from North Africa and other Islamic countries. Few, if any, came to Florida (Angel 1982).

After the Holocaust and the establishment of the State of Israel, small numbers of Sephardim (Mizrachim) from Iraq, Egypt, North Africa, and Lebanon migrated to the United States. Muslim response to European colonialism and the rise of Arab nationalist movements and nation-states generated a hostile environment. For many Jews it became unbearable. Reaction to the spread of Zionism led to violent attacks against Jews. Most immigrated to Israel. Many French-speaking Sephardim who were more affluent made France or Quebec, Canada, their destination of first choice. Among the few who settled in Miami were a handful of Holocaust survivors.

With the Castro communist revolution, the Cuban Jewish community, en masse, migrated to the United States, primarily to Miami. Of those, approximately one thousand families were Sephardim whose parents and grandparents had emigrated from the Balkans and the former Turkish Empire in the early twentieth century (see Levine 1993 and Bejarano 2002). Over the next three decades, Jews in Latin America would gravitate more and more to Miami and Southeast Florida, as their countries' economies went into decline and right or left governments came to power. With increasing political instability and escalating incidents of anti-Semitism, Miami appeared to be a good compromise. Many of these new immigrants are Sephardim and have maintained their identity and heritage. Originally from Islamic states, they had migrated to South America, in part, because the United States and Canada were not welcoming. By the end of the twentieth century, Jews from Colombia, Argentina, Venezuela, Peru, and Brazil were immigrating at an accelerated pace to greater Miami.

Except for Latin America, the largest proportion of foreign-born Jewish emigrants to Southeast Florida hails from Israel. These emigrants, *yordim*, are frequently students who remained in America after earning their degrees or who emigrated from Israel seeking economic opportunity. Most of the Israelis who are Sephardim emigrated after the war in Lebanon (1982), and many represent the "new bourgeois" in Israel. Their growing presence has led to the establishment of a remarkable infrastructure of schools, synagogues, bookstores, and restaurants. In the last decade, four new synagogues were launched and are supported by the community. Similar to other ethnic groups in previous migration flows (e.g., East European Jewry), Israelis are involved in chain migration. Disillusionment with Israel and perceived ethnic discrimination are significant causes of Israeli Sephardim immigration to Southeast Florida. "I am of Kurdish origin and in Israel [they] treated us as trash. Being Sephardic is associated with being primitive or being 'Chah-Chah' [riffraff]. When I came to Miami, I left all of this behind. Nobody treated me as an inferior Sephardic" (Gold and Phillips 1996, 66).

The trauma of September 11, 2001, and increasing hostility in France to Israel and the United States because of the Iraq War has led mounting numbers of Sephardic French Jews to emigrate to Israel, Canada, and the United States. Although there are no current data available, French Jews in Southeast Florida are very visible with estimates ranging from one to several thousand. Many of these emigrants were born in North Africa and migrated to France in the late 1950s and 1960s. They carry with them a vibrant Sephardic identity, one rich with Sephardic culture shaped by two generations in France.

In addition, there are Sephardim in Southeast Florida who are American born, from the Northeast (New York, New Jersey, Massachusetts, and Pennsylvania), who have migrated to the tropics with families or have chosen the area for retirement. Some are first-generation Americans. They mirror the general flow of migration to the Sunbelt in the United States (Mohl 1990). During the season, Thanksgiving (November) to Passover (April), the total number of Sephardim living in Southeast Florida increases substantially because of the "snowbird" phenomenon (Sheskin 1985).

For the overwhelming majority of the Sephardim living in Southeast Florida, immigrating to the United States was a process that involved migrating to one, two, or even three countries before perching in Miami, Fort Lauderdale, or Boca Raton. For example, many of the Sephardic Cuban Jews emigrated from Turkey to Cuba in the first quarter of the twentieth century before they and/or their children migrated to Miami in the third quarter of the century. Many of the Sephardic Jews from North Africa (Morocco, Tunisia, and Algeria) settled in France and in Quebec in the third quarter of the twentieth century before migrating to Southeast Florida in the fourth quarter. Some of the emigrants who went to Quebec from France lived in Montreal for an extended period before migrating south to Florida. There are also a significant number of examples of North African Sephardim who lived in Spanish North Africa (e.g., Tangiers, Morocco) and could not emigrate to Canada and the United States because of visa restrictions. They moved in the third quarter of the twentieth century to Latin America (e.g., Venezuela, Argentina, and Columbia) before political instability drove them to find another safe haven. In addition, there are many Sephardic Jews in Latin America who migrated from Islamic countries and Europe in the second quarter of the twentieth century, fearing Nazism and Arab nationalism, before migrating to Southeast Florida in the fourth quarter because of political instability. Although Israelis have had fewer restrictions on entering the United States in the fourth quarter of the twentieth century, many of them and/or their children were born in North Africa, Iraq, and other Islamic countries before emigrating to Israel. Some of these Israelis, unable to come directly to the United States, have selected Canada or South America as a "hotel" country to establish the appropriate legitimacy before applying and coming to Southeast Florida. Finally, the recent immigration of Sephardic French Jews in the wake of 9/11 represents a population that decided not to emigrate to Israel or the United States in the 1950s and 1960s. Only because of mounting anti-Semitism have they migrated to Southeast Florida.

Memory, Transnational Identity, and Otherness

To understand Sephardic migration to Miami and Southeast Florida, in particular, and globally, more generally, in the twentieth century is to grasp the full ramifications, personally and collectively, of a dislocated, traumatized community. Shmuel Trigano, the author of the term "Forgotten Exodus," explains in his February 22, 2004, speech why the Sephardic narrative is ignored: "An unresolved malaise encumbers the Sephardic conscience. They were not able to go through the mourning process of their uprootedness. Their trauma did not disappear." Without addressing questions regarding victim, exile, and transnational identity, appreciating the trauma of their ethnic experiences and contextualizing them within the framework of refugees and migration is bypassed. Without exploring the meaning of "otherness," "marginality," and "self," comprehending the Sephardic human experience is naïve. Albert Memmi, the novelist and sociologist, was born in Tunisia and migrated to France in 1959. His description of the Sephardic condition is most revealing: "I am ill at ease in my own land and I know of no other. My culture is borrowed and I speak my mother tongue haltingly. I have neither religious beliefs nor tradition. . . . To try to explain what I am, I would need an intelligent audience and much time. . . . I am Tunisian but Jewish, which means that I am politically and socially an outcast" (Stavans 2005, xvii).

Sephardim in Southeast Florida represent a constellation of Jewish ethnicities and transnational identities. Their numbers are growing but constitute less than 10 percent of the Jewish population. They have little influence in the decision making of Jewish community organizations. In contrast, the Sephardim play a much more significant role within the Hispanic population, although they constitute less than 1 percent of that population.

Demographic Profile of Miami Sephardim

The following section highlights several features of a demographic profile of the Sephardim in greater Miami. They are the only Sephardic community in Florida with empirical data. It provides the raw statistics for a more theoretical discussion regarding memory, transnational identity, and otherness. This modest attempt is no more than an outline of the ingredients for a comprehensive discussion and a future study. The data are from Ira Sheskin's 2004 Greater Miami Jewish Community Study (GMJCS) (2005b).

There are 113,000 Ashkenazim and Sephardim in Miami, with more than half living within three zip codes (2005b, chap. 1, 13–15; chap. 4, 3–7). More than two-thirds were born in the United States; very few were born in Miami. The greatest number of foreign-born come from Middle and South America (table 7.3). The only city in North America that has more Jews born in foreign countries is Toronto (41 percent to Miami's 30.8 percent; chap. 4, 13–15).

Respondents in the Miami study were asked if they considered themselves to be Hispanic Jews, Sephardic Jews, or Israeli. Table 7.4 provides this data. Many of the Hispanics and Israelis view themselves as having multiple Jewish identities. For example, 37.6 percent of Jewish adults who are Hispanic Jews also consider themselves to be Sephardic, and 42.5 percent of Jewish adults who are Israelis

Table 7.3.
Place of birth

Adults in Jewish households

Sample size: 3,433
Number of adults: 99,3588

US LOCATION	PERCENTAGE	FOREIGN LOCATION	PERCENTAGE
Miami	13.2	Cuba	3.3
Broward or Palm Beach	0.6	Israel	3.3
Other Florida	1.0	Russia	2.8
Total Florida	14.8	Argentina	2.2
New York	28.1	Poland	2.2
Pennsylvania	5.8	Canada	1.8
Illinois	3.2	Colombia	1.8
New Jersey	3.2	Venezuela	1.5
Ohio	2.2	Germany	1.1
Massachusetts	2.0	Other foreign	10.8
Connecticut	1.2	Total foreign-born	30.8
Other US	8.7	South America	7.3
Total US-born	69.2	Middle America	4.6
Northeast	41.3	Middle East	4.5
Midwest	8.1	Eastern Europe	4.5
South	18.7	Former Soviet Union	4.3
West	1.1	Western Europe	3.0
		Other foreign	2.6

Source: Sheskin 2005b, chap. 4, 12.

consider themselves to be Sephardic Jews.[1] The "Total Sephardic" population in Miami therefore is larger than indicated in the Sephardic column in table 7.4. Thus, the percentage of Sephardim in Miami is, in all probability, more than double the percentage of Sephardim in the United States. The 2000 National Jewish Population Study states that the Sephardic population in the United

1. Sheskin also points out that 7.8 percent of Jewish adults who are Hispanic also consider themselves to be Israeli; and 11.1 percent of Jewish adults who are Israeli also consider themselves to be Hispanic (2005b, chap. 4, 22, 24).

Table 7.4.
Sephardic Jews in Dade County (Miami)

Base: Jewish Adults

	HISPANIC JEWS		ISRAELIS		SEPHARDIM	
Geographic Area	%	Number	%	Number	%	Number
North Dade	11.6	5328	10.1	4651	15.5	7146
South Dade	7.6	2335	3.0	906	9.6	2947
The Beaches	11.8	1868	7.0	1106	12.2	1937
All	10.3	9531	7.2	6663	13.0	12,030

Source: Sheskin 2005b, chap. 4, 25.
Note: Total number of persons in Jewish households in 2004 was 113,300.

States through self-identification is 7.2 percent. Many of these Sephardim are highly concentrated in the three zip code areas noted above. Only three other cities in the United States have 10 percent or more Sephardim: Monmouth, Illinois (13.6 percent); Seattle (12.1 percent); and Los Angeles (10.0 percent) (2005b, chap. 4, 26).

Table 7.5 identifies the countries of origin of Hispanic Jews. Most countries in Latin America are listed as well as countries from North Africa (Morocco), Europe (Spain), and the Caribbean (Jamaica). Many of these Hispanics in Miami are Sephardim (see table 7.4). Memory and transnational identities are again in play.

Length of residence, like place of birth, is an indicator of attachment to community and institutions. The percentage of new households (0–4 years in Miami) is higher for Sephardic households (22) than for non-Sephardic households (10) (2005b, chap. 4, 44). The median age of persons in Sephardic households is 37.2 compared to 50.7 for the Jewish Miami population as a whole. Only 13 percent of the Sephardim are age 65 and older, compared to 30 percent for the Jewish population. In contrast, 28 percent of persons in Sephardic households are age 0–17 compared to 18 percent for the Miami Jewish population (chap. 5, 2, 3, 6, 52).

Tables 7.6–7.10 provide a cross-section of Sheskin's Jewish identification and religious behavior data based on total number of households. Table 7.6 addresses religious Jewish identification of the respondents. Sephardim are more likely to

Table 7.5.
Countries from which Hispanic Jewish adults come

Base: Hispanic Jewish Adults

Sample size 338
Number of adults: 9,531

LOCATION	PERCENTAGE	LOCATION	PERCENTAGE
Cuba	28.5	Chile	0.5
Argentina	18.0	Ecuador	0.3
Colombia	16.2	Jamaica	0.3
Venezuela	15.2	Nicaragua	0.3
Mexico	4.0	Panama	0.3
Uruguay	2.2	Bolivia	0.2
Spain	1.9	South America	1.4
Morocco	1.8	Other	2.0
Puerto Rico	1.8	Total	100.0
Peru	1.4	South America	56.7
Brazil	1.3	Middle America	34.8
United States	1.0	Other	8.5
Dominican Republic	0.7		
Guatemala	0.7		

Source: Sheskin 2005b, chap. 4, 28.

Table 7.6.
Jewish identification (religious)

Base: Jewish respondents

VARIABLE	ORTHODOX	CONSERVATIVE	RECON-STRUCTIONIST	REFORM	JUST JEWISH	SAMPLE SIZE	NUMBER OF HOUSE-HOLDS
All	9.1%	32.3%	1.1%	26.6%	30.9%	1,808	54,000
Sephardic	20.5%	31.7%	0.0%	17.4%	30.4%	271	7,938
Non-Sephardic	7.1%	32.4%	1.3%	28.2%	31.0%	1,537	46,062

Source: Sheskin 2005b, chap. 6, 11–12.

identify as Orthodox than are respondents in non-Sephardic households. They are also less likely to identify as Reform than are respondents in non-Sephardic households. Identification with the Conservative movement for both Sephardim and non-Sephardim show little difference. Similarly, there is no significant difference between those who identify as just Jewish (no religious affiliation).

Tables 7.7–7.10 present data surrounding Jewish practices (mezuzah, Passover seder, Chanukah, and Sabbath candles). More Sephardic households (table 7.7) have a mezuzah on their front door (91%) than non-Sephardic households (80%). More Sephardic households (table 7.8) always/usually participate in a seder (89%) than non-Sephardic households (77%). More Sephardic households (table 7.9) always/usually light Chanukah candles (89%) than non-Sephardic households (75%). In addition, nearly double the Sephardic households (table 7.10) always/ usually light shabbat candles (58%) than non-Sephardic households (30%).

Sheskin's data disclose several other significant differences between Sephardic households and non-Sephardic households concerning religious practice. Nearly half of Sephardic households keep a kosher home (45 percent) compared to less than one-fifth (18 percent) of non-Sephardic households (2005b, chap. 6, 68, 73). More than one-quarter of Sephardic households (27 percent) keep kosher in and out of the home, compared to one-tenth in non-Sephardic households (chap. 6, 73). Sephardim are much more likely to attend services once per month (40 percent) than those in non-Sephardic households (24 percent) (chap. 6, 98, 103). Only one in ten (11 percent) of Sephardim never attend services compared to 27 percent in non-Sephardic households (chap. 6, 103).

Table 7.7.
Have a mezuzah on the front door

Base: Jewish households

VARIABLE	HAVE A MEZUZAH ON THE FRONT DOOR	SAMPLE SIZE	NUMBER OF HOUSEHOLDS
All	81.7%	1808	54,000
Sephardic	90.9%	271	7,938
Non-Sephardic	80.1%	1537	46,062

Source: Sheskin 2005b, chap. 6, 31–32.

Table 7.8.
Participate in a Passover seder

Base: Jewish households

VARIABLE	ALWAYS + USUALLY	ALWAYS	USUALLY	SOMETIMES	NEVER	SAMPLE SIZE	NUMBER OF HOUSEHOLDS
All	78.8%	67.4%	11.4%	13.9%	7.3%	1808	54,000
Sephardic	89.1%	83.0%	6.1%	8.3%	2.6%	271	7,938
Non-Sephardic	76.9%	64.7%	12.2%	14.9%	8.2%	1537	46,062

Source: Sheskin 2005b, chap. 6, 40–41.

Table 7.9.
Light Chanukah candles

Base: Jewish households

VARIABLE	ALWAYS + USUALLY	ALWAYS	USUALLY	SOMETIMES	NEVER	SAMPLE SIZE	NUMBER OF HOUSEHOLDS
All	76.7%	68.5%	8.2%	10.7%	12.6%	1808	54,000
Sephardic	88.7%	82.2%	6.5%	5.2%	6.1%	271	7,938
Non-Sephardic	74.6%	66.0%	8.6%	11.6%	13.8%	1537	46,062

Source: Sheskin 2005b, chap. 6, 50–51.

Table 7.10.
Light Sabbath candles

Base: Jewish households

VARIABLE	ALWAYS + USUALLY	ALWAYS	USUALLY	SOMETIMES	NEVER	SAMPLE SIZE	NUMBER OF HOUSEHOLDS
All	34.1%	28.1%	6.0%	22.8%	43.1%	1808	54,000
Sephardic	58.0%	50.6%	7.4%	20.8%	21.2%	271	7,938
Non-Sephardic	30.0%	24.2%	5.8%	23.2%	46.8%	1537	46,062

Source: Sheskin 2005b, chap. 6, 69–70.

Given these findings, the assumption can be made that Jewish continuity would be stronger among Sephardim than non-Sephardim if measured by intermarriage of adult children. According to Sheskin's data, 28 percent of Sephardic households are households with intermarried adult children compared to 43 percent of non-Sephardic households (chap. 6, 142, 145).

Sheskin's data also explores the membership profile of the Miami Jewish community. Current synagogue membership of Sephardic households is 49 percent compared to 37 percent of non-Sephardic households (chap. 7, 13). Table 7.11 identifies Sephardic synagogues in Miami and the number of member households. The most revealing feature of table 7.11 is the establishment of four new synagogues since 1994 (a 57 percent increase). This institutional development mirrors more than any other variable the growth of the Sephardic community and their self-identification to perpetuate Sephardic memory and birthright. Moreover, there are abundant anecdotal data suggesting that another dozen Ashkenazic synagogues have significant Sephardic membership representation and cater to their religious and social needs.

Sephardim are less likely (42 percent) than non-Sephardim (48 percent) to become members of Jewish community centers and Jewish organizations (chap. 7, 81). They are less familiar with the Greater Miami Jewish Federation (31 percent) compared to respondents in non-Sephardic households (27 percent) (chap. 9, 52). More Sephardim are unfamiliar with the Miami Jewish Home and Hospital for the Aged (60 percent) compared to respondents in non-Sephardic households (40 percent) (chap. 9, 70). Respondents in Sephardic households are less likely to contribute to the Jewish Federation (30 percent) than respondents in non-Sephardic households (46 percent) (chap. 13, 10, 19). However, if membership in a synagogue, Jewish community center, and Jewish organization are combined as a variable called "association with the Jewish community," more Sephardic households (58 percent) than non-Sephardic households (53 percent) are associated (chap. 7, 116). In summary, Sephardim feel a part of the Jewish community in Miami, but it is highly synagogue-centric.

Among other variables presented by Sheskin's study of the Greater Miami Jewish Community were respondents' connections to formal and informal Jewish education. Sheskin found no significant difference in the percentage of born-Jewish adults who attended formal Jewish education as children between Sephardic households and non-Sephardic households. On the other hand, it was

Table 7.11.
Results of the synagogue survey: Number of member households

		NUMBER OF HOUSEHOLDS		
Sephardic synagogue	Location	1994	2004	1994–2004 Increase/ (decrease)
Beit Edmond J. Safra Synagogue	Aventura	0	100	100
Congregation Magen David Sephardic Jewish Center	North Miami Beach	50	35	(15)
Ner Yitzchak of Highland Lakes	North Miami Beach	0	25	25
Or Yaacov Orthodox Sephardic Congregation	North Miami Beach	0	25	25
Sephardic Congregation of Florida–Torat Moshe	Miami Beach	100	50	(50)
Shaare Ezra Sephardic Congregation	Miami Beach	0	25	25
Temple Benarroch Sephardic Congregation	Sunny Isles Beach	25	25	0
Total Sephardic synagogues		175	285	110

Source: Sheskin 2005b, chap. 7, 32.

more likely that children (ages 5–17) of Sephardic households attended a Jewish day school (43 percent) than children in non-Sephardic Jewish households (38 percent) (chap. 8, 59, 63). Regarding informal Jewish education, more Jewish adults in Sephardic households were active in a Jewish youth group as teenagers (54 percent) compared to Jewish adults in non-Sephardic households (41 percent) (chap. 8, 22). They also were more likely to attend adult education in the past year (35 percent) compared to the respondents in non-Sephardic households (25 percent) (chap. 8, 43).

One of the most salient facts of Sheskin's study is the connection between the Sephardim and Israel. The data reveal that nearly three in four (74 percent) of Sephardic households contain a member who visited Israel compared to 60 percent of non-Sephardic households (chap. 11, 3, 6). Nearly half (48 percent) of these Sephardim traveled to Israel on a Jewish trip (chap. 11, 3). In addition, 74 percent of Sephardic households are extremely/very attached to Israel compared to 60 percent of respondents in non-Sephardic households (chap. 11, 18, 22).

Conclusion

Southeast Florida's Jewish community is undergoing rapid ethnic change mirroring the American terrain. The Sephardic population is not monolithic and their transnational identities play out in intriguing ways. The recent waves of Sephardim and Ashkenazim from Latin America over the last quarter century have joined the "Jewbans" (Jewish Cubans) to strengthen their ethnic (Hispanic) voice. In 1989, South Floridian Hispanic/Sephardic Jews were directly responsible for sending a Catholic Cuban to Congress rather than a Jew. Ethnicity, not religious identification, was the deciding factor. Jewish Hispanics/Sephardim have served as a bridge into the non-Jewish Hispanic community and have repeatedly used their political capital to gain support for Israel and American Jewish causes.

The Hispanization of greater Miami has led to "white flight." The non-Hispanic, English-speaking white population of greater Miami has declined from 80 percent in 1960 to less than 25 percent in 2000. Consequently, a significant number of non-Hispanic Jews have left Miami and migrated to other parts of South Florida. With the decreasing Jewish population in Miami and the increasing Latinization of its community, the Jewish federation and affiliated institutions reach out to the Jewish Hispanic and Sephardic population and cater to their specific needs, often under the guidance of established organizations such as the Miami chapter of the Federation of Latin American Sephardim (FESELA). In the years ahead, more Sephardic Jews will migrate from Latin America to Miami, as will Sephardim from France who are evading Islamization. Already it is very common to hear Spanish, French, Hebrew, and English in the malls and marinas in North Miami.

The multiculturalism of Southeast Florida Jewry is creating a unique "New South." With emigrants looking for the "Promised Land," it remains to be seen how "otherness" will be transformed in the American landscape.

8

From Turkey to the United States

The Trajectory of Cuban Sephardim in Miami

MARGALIT BEJARANO

The Sephardic Congregation of Florida in Miami Beach was founded by
Sephardim who had left Cuba following the Castro revolution (1959). The community is situated at the crossroads of Latin America and the United States and is
characterized as having four collective identities: Jewish, Sephardic, Cuban, and
American. Cuban Jews in the United States are defined by scholars as "Jewish Hispanics" or "Hispanic Jews," a hybrid group that differs both from the typical Latin
immigrants and from the English-speaking Jewish "Anglos" (see Green 1995, 132).
The importance of this group has been growing because of the increasing Hispanization of South Florida as well as the constant immigration of Latin American
Jews and of different groups of Sephardim who settled in Greater Miami.

The Sephardim from Cuba share with other Sephardic groups the religious tradition and memories of a remote past, while their coreligionists from
Latin America speak the same language and have a similar social background.
The objective of this chapter is to analyze the connections between places and
memories, and their influence on the formation of the collective identity on the
Cuban-American Sephardim. The first part will deal with Miami and its Jewish
population; the second with the historical memory from the three main stations
in the history of this community: Sepharad, the Ottoman Empire, and Cuba; the

An earlier version of this article was published in 2003 in Hebrew: "Between the United
States and Latin America: On the Sephardic Cuban Community of Miami," *Pe'amim* 97 (Autumn):
107–23.

third will deal with the encounter with the United States and the processes of integration and organization that consolidated the four identities.

Miami: A Population in Transition

Miami in South Florida is the entrance gate for passengers from Latin America: it is an enormous metropolitan city, an international crossroad for commerce and finance, a lively center of entertainment and recreation, and a haven for political refugees. Greater Miami is a meeting place for different ethnic groups, including the largest group of Cubans in the United States, and is one of the largest centers of Jewish population.

The Cuban exile started to consolidate immediately after the revolution of Fidel Castro that deposed the government of Fulgencio Batista y Zaldívar. In the early years after the revolution, a large number of the economic and social elites of prerevolutionary Cuba arrived in Miami, including the owners of land properties or large business enterprises, professionals, managers, and technicians (Fagen, Brody, and O'Leary 1968, 16–23; Portes and Bach 1985, 84). The socio-economic level of the immigrants from Cuba declined gradually, but the elite groups formed the basic characteristics of the Cuban exile. They participated in the economic development of South Florida, acquiring considerable success. At the same time they integrated into local politics and became pressure groups also on a federal level. Nevertheless, they still consider their life in the United States as *el exilio*, continuing to cherish dreams of return to their homeland, while waiting for the fall of the "Antichrist"—Fidel Castro. Lisandro Pérez predicted that the "exile" would become "a minority" after the disappearance of the two basic conditions that nourish it: the power of Fidel Castro and the hostile policy of the United States toward Cuba (1990, 4–5; Rieff 1993, 26–32).[1]

The Jewish population in Southeast Florida is the third largest Jewish concentration in the United States (after New York and Los Angeles) and is the sixth largest urban center in the Jewish world.[2] Miami, which Deborah Dash Moore

---

1. The passing of power to Raúl, Fidel's brother, in 2006, did not change that conception.

2. According to the American Jewish Yearbook (2010) there were 2,007,850 Jews living in New York; 684,950 in Los Angeles; and 485,850 in South Florida—not including part time residents

described as a "Golden City," was a small and distant recreation town, full of sunny beaches and palm trees, where the "snowbirds" from northeastern United States sought refuge from the cold winter. After World War II it became a prosperous commercial and industrial center that attracted retired Jews from New York and Chicago (1994, 26–29; Lehrman and Rappaport 1956).

A study conducted by Ira Sheskin from the University of Miami demonstrated that the Jewish population in South Florida increased from about 10,000 persons in 1940 to 60,000 in 1950 and to 155,000 in 1960. During that period 90 percent of the Jews lived in Dade County (1989). The largest concentration of aged Jews was created in Miami Beach—a recreation town on a strip of land on the Atlantic Ocean, 80 percent of whose residents in 1960 were Jews.

The population of Dade County increased from 500,000 inhabitants to almost 2,500,000 in 2010. In official statistics most Jews are included among the white English speakers: the population of Anglos that amounted to 80 percent of Miami's residents in 1960 decreased to 15.4 percent in 2010. At the same time the rate of Hispanics grew from approximately 5 percent to 65 percent (see table 8.1) (Portes and Stepick 1993, 211).[3]

The trend of decline of the white population since the 1980s characterized also the aged Jewish population of Miami Beach. Owing to the growth of the Hispanic population in the area and the increase of crime, many Jews preferred to move to the northern suburbs outside the metropolitan area of Miami: Broward County and Palm Beach became the center of gravity of retired Jews: In 1989 76 percent of the Jews living in Palm Beach were over sixty years of age, as compared with 46 percent in Dade County, 18 percent in Chicago, and 3 percent in New York (Zadka, Sheskin, and Green 1989, 154).

Until the 1980s the presence of Sephardim in the Jewish population of Greater Miami was marginal. According to Sheskin's 1982 study, 92 percent of the Jews living in Dade County identified themselves as Ashkenazim and only 2

(DellaPergola 2010). Henry Green in chapter 7 of this book (see table 7.2) states that South Florida is the second largest Jewish center in the United States. Ira Sheskin's figures that he uses include part-time residents in South Florida and different calculations of regional limits.

3. Figures for 2010 are taken from: Miami-Dade County, Florida, QuickFacts from the US Census Bureau, http://quickfacts.census.gov/qfd/states/12/12086.html (accessed 1.27.2012)

Table 8.1.
Ethnic composition of Miami's population, 1960–2010

	1960	1970	1980	1990	2010*
Total	935,000	1,268,000	1,626,000	1,937,000	2,496,435
White (Anglos)	80.0%	61.4%	47.7%	30.3%	15.4%
Hispanics	5.3%	23.6%	35.7%	49.2%	65.0%
African Americans	14.7%	15.0%	17.2%	19.5%	18.9%

Source: For the data for 1960–1990: Portes and Stepick 1993, 211; for 2010 data, US Census Bureau, http://quickfacts.census.gov/qfd/states/12/12086.html.

percent as Sephardim. The first Sephardic community was founded in the 1940s by Jews from Turkey and the Balkan countries who, like their Ashkenazi brethren, had retired to Miami from the Northeast. In the 1960s they were joined by immigrants from Cuba, and later by additional Sephardim from North Africa, Israel, and Latin America (see chapter 7 in this volume).

The Historical Memory and the Community: Sepharad

The historical memory of the Sephardic Jews in Miami is related to three places: Sepharad, from where they were expelled in 1492; Turkey, from where they emigrated with the collapse of the Ottoman Empire; and Cuba, which they abandoned after the 1959 revolution. The traces of the three stations in the trajectory of the community are reflected in the *Libro de Oro* (Golden Book), published in 1979 for the inauguration of Temple Moses of the Sephardic Congregation in Miami.

The residue left by Sepharad on the memory of the Cuban Sephardic community finds expression in the article "The Jews in Sepharad (950–1492)," which focuses on the Golden Era of the Jews in Spain under Islamic rule, manifested in rabbinical writings as well as in the prosperity of philosophy, sciences, and literature. According to this article, since the "loss of their nationality" Spain became "a second homeland" of the Sephardic Jews, remaining marked in their memory through language and cultural tradition.

> This profound identification with Spain . . . was the cause that on being
> expelled they carried to the exile in foreign lands, the element that unites and

shapes a people—the language, the culture of the Peninsula, and in an absolute way, the Castillan form of the Spanish romances.

    The *coplas* of the Judeo-Spanish Romancero survived among the Sephardim and were sung during more than four centuries distant from the *madre patria*, . . . These Sephardic songs reflect the folkloric Judeo-Spanish traditions and preserve a nostalgic memory dyed by love and admiration. (Florida Sephardic Congregation 1979, 72)

The language, the liturgy, the religious laws, the customs, and other elements of the cultural heritage brought over from the Iberian Peninsula were common to the Jews of Sepharad throughout the Diaspora. The singularity of the Cuban community—like that of other Sephardic communities in Latin America—was the encounter with a country whose language, cultural sources, and historical roots stem from Spain of the period of expulsion. When they arrived in Cuba, the Jewish immigrants were frightened to discover the traces of the Inquisition in the names of the streets of Old Havana where they settled, such as Jesús María, Picota (pillory), and Inquisidor. They realized, however, that their fears had no foundations. Spain of the Catholic kings was identified by the Cubans with the forces of reaction and the enemies of Cuban independence (Franco [1942] 1988).

    The Jews from Turkey who arrived in Cuba did not meet the Spain of the sixteenth century, but that of the twentieth century. The few documents referring to the rediscovery of Spain reveal gratitude to King Alfonso XIII for his assistance to the Jews of the Ottoman Empire during World War I and appreciation of the studies of Angel Pulido (1904), author of *Españoles sin patria y la raza sefardí* (Spaniards without homeland and the Sephardic race) (Blis 1936).[4] Shortly after the establishment of the Second Republic in Spain, the Cuban Sephardic community in Havana petitioned the Spanish vice-consul for "a Spanish citizenship and a passport" because they remained stateless as a consequence of the fall of the Ottoman Empire. A representative of the community

---

4. Samuel Amon, "El papa y los judíos," September 23, 1919, manuscript of an article prepared for *La Amerika*, Papers of Marcos Matterin, Archive of the Casa de la Comunidad Hebrea de Cuba, Patronato.

explained to the vice-consul "that for ethnic reasons, the Sephardim are united to the Spaniards, and that spiritually they feel the same."[5]

The main impact of the renewed encounter of the Turkish Jews with the "Sepharad" of Cuba was on the language: the similarity between the Castilian Spanish spoken in Cuba and Ladino (Judeo-Spanish) blurred the differences between the traditional elements of the Jewish language and the Spanish spoken in the Cuban street. From a language of a Jewish minority, limited to the family and the community, Spanish became a modern language and a linguistic bridge with Cuban society as well as with the Ashkenazi immigrants.[6]

The Impact of Turkey on Havana's Sephardic Community

If the memory of Sepharad was basically cultural, the historical memory of the life in Turkey left its imprint on the social patterns and on the institutional frameworks established in Cuba, as reflected in the Golden Book of the Miami Sephardic Congregation:

> The year 1918: Arriving from Turkey, various Sephardic families settle in Havana. They rent an apartment in the street Luz and turn it into a synagogue. Later they move to Inquisidor 407 (Upstairs) that receives the name *Shevet Ahim*.

> The year 1921: Membership increases and the *Unión Hebrea Shevet Ahim* [Hebrew Union Shevet Ahim] has already large premises in Prado 551. They also have a cemetery, a *Talmud Tora* [religious school] *Teodoro Herzl* . . . to prepare all our future generation. They organized the Committee of *Bikur Holim* [visiting the sick], *Hebra Kedushá* [funerary association] and the Ladies Committee *La Buena Voluntad* [good will]. . . . In the interior of the island, Santiago de Cuba, Matanzas, Holguín, Santa Clara, Manzanillo and Artemisa other Sephardic communities are flourishing. (Florida Sephardic Congregation 1979, 4–5)[7]

5. Minutes of *Bikur Holim*, November 30, 1931, Patronato.

6. On the transmission of the Sephardic identity in a Spanish-speaking society see Cohen de Chervonagura (2001).

7. The communal organization Shevet Ahim was founded in 1914 but was officially recognized in 1918.

The Jews of the Ottoman Empire arrived from a multinational society that was divided by law and tradition between secluded ethno-religious groups. The reforms of the Tanzimat (1839–1956), which granted equality to non-Muslim minorities, did not abolish communal autonomy, and the processes of modernization and secularization did not break the frontiers between the minorities and the majority society.

Immigration to an open and secular society forced the Sephardic immigrants to found new institutional frameworks on a voluntary basis, yet the model of the Unión Hebrea Shevet Ahim in Havana was taken from the *Cal* (*kahal*= community) of the mother communities. Shevet Ahim was a centralized communal organization that provided religious, social, and educational services to all the Sephardim in Havana and served as an umbrella organization to those in the interior of the island. The presence of rabbis and teachers among the immigrants was an important factor in the consolidation of a spiritual-religious leadership that strengthened the resistance of the Sephardim against the influence of Cuban society and helped them to transmit their identity and cultural heritage.

The Sephardim in Cuba were characterized by the homogeneity of their population. Almost all of them arrived from two regions: Istanbul and the nearby town of Silivri (now a suburb of Istanbul), and Edirne—on the Bulgarian border—and the nearby town of Kirklareli. Many of them were related to the same families. Their migration was formed by chains of relatives, who created upon their arrival social enclaves of their mother community, where they reconstructed the way of living of the old home and maintained a clear social distinction from the environment, especially for girls and women: "Family life was exactly as in Turkey, there was no difference whatsoever; religious life was the same and so was social life."[8]

The impact of the communities of origin in Turkey is reflected also in the Zionist movement that developed among Sephardim in Cuba. Esther Benbassa's study *Hayahadut Haotmanit bein Hitmaarvut Lezionut 1908–1920 (The*

---

8. Interview with Cali Maya, Miami 1984. See also interviews with David and Reina Pérez, Raquel Egozi-Behar, Sol Credi, Miami 1984; interview with Manzanillo group, Miami 1993, Oral History Archive, Harman Institute of Contemporary Jewry, the Hebrew University of Jerusalem (henceforth cited as ICJ).

Ottoman Jewry between Occidentalization and Zionism, 1908–1920) deals with the period that coincides with the immigration to Cuba. Benbassa points out the impact of the Zionist movement on the Jewish masses that granted them "a sort of self esteem and at the same time respected their traditional world." She emphasizes the central role that the clubs of Macabi fulfilled among the Jewish youth: "These clubs, whose declared objective was the physical rehabilitation through training in sports . . . became important centers of popular propaganda. . . . [The youth] was now offered to take an active role in the struggle for an ideal that would awaken the soul to new life. In the same way that the sport clubs of Macabi inspired the body, Zionism was perceived as a means of self identification" (1996, 114, 246–47). In Cuba the Zionist activities of the Sephardim were an integral part of the social life in the framework of Shevet Ahim. In 1924, Rabbi Guershon Maya, the spiritual leader of the community, founded the day school Teodoro Herzl, which combined Jewish tradition with the Zionist cause (Bejarano 1985). Macabi, founded ten years later, became the major social framework for the Sephardic youth of Havana, strengthening the body with sports and inculcating Zionist conscience: "The activities of the Youth Section of *Macabi* created a continuity between the [primary] school *Teodoro Herzl* and the [public high school] *Instituto de la Habana.* Our activities in Macabi were very lively, . . . we prepared theater performances . . . we brought lecturers . . . and in addition we had many sports races in which we played against the youth clubs of the Ashkenazim."[9] The main social framework of the Sephardim in Havana was the Club Social, which centralized cultural and social activities in the Cuban capital. Several families from the interior of the island moved to Havana when their children grew up, to make sure that they would find Jewish spouses. Until the Castro revolution, the Club Social of Shevet Ahim was considered the most effective barrier against intermarriage.[10]

Even after the separation from Cuba the Sephardim sought to preserve the institutional heritage that was brought from Turkey to Cuba, and to create organizations that would protect their children from assimilation. An ex-president of

9. Interview with Salomon Garazi, Miami 1987, ICJ.

10. Interviews with José, Sol, and Eugenia Credi; Raquel Egozi-Behar; Rabbi Nissim Gambach, Miami 1984; Juan and Rebeca Matalon, Miami 1991, ICJ.

the Sephardic Cuban community explained: "Our parents . . . had two objectives: to cultivate the family and to keep our Judaism. . . . The same tradition we transmit to our children."[11] The awareness of continuity—of a chain that links between generations and between places—is reflected in the historical survey in the Golden Book of the community:

> The year 1959: With the establishment of a Communist regime in Cuba starts the "exodus" of hundreds of thousands of Cubans, and among them many of our Jewish families. . . . The majority settles in Miami; every day more and more Sephardic Cuban exiles arrive to these shores, and history repeats itself: exactly as 1918 in Havana in 1968 in Miami.
>
> A group of enthusiastic coreligionists who wish to be reunited in exile in order to remember and to pray together. The Sephardic Hebrew Congregation was born. (Cuban Sephardic Congregation 1979, 4–5)

The Memory of Havana in Miami

With the immigration to the United States after the Castro revolution, Jewish Sephardic life in Cuba passed into memory. Yet the fifty years of being the passage between Turkey and the United States had an impact on the customs and mentality of the Sephardim who had lived in Cuba that shaped their way of life. They had adopted the values of Cuban society, identified with its historical heroes, and absorbed its culture. They had consolidated their separate identity as a Cuban Jewish minority—an identity that continues to exist also in the United States.

Like other Cuban exiles, the Jews look back with nostalgia and tend to idealize life in prerevolutionary Cuba. Between the end of World War II and the Castro revolution, the economic situation of the Jews had improved considerably, and many of them had left Old Havana and moved to fancy neighborhoods. The Ashkenazim built the Patronato—an impressive building that was inaugurated in 1955 with the presence of President Batista. The rich Sephardim decided to follow them and to build a magnificent communal building that would suit their new social status. Shortly after the inauguration, however, most of the founders of the Centro Sefaradí in Havana were living in Miami.

11. Interview with Isidoro Behar, Miami 1991, ICJ.

The economic and social progress of the Jews was reflected in the buildings of the communal organizations as well as in the academic studies of the second generation. During the 1950s the three Jewish communities—Americans, Sephardim, and East Europeans—drew closer to each other. Nevertheless, the process of social integration into Cuban society was still in its beginning. There were Jews who felt rejected by their Cuban friends, who called them *polacos* (Poles), even when they were born in Cuba to parents from Turkey. Others saw it as a voluntary segregation, deriving from the desire of the Jews—Sephardim and Ashkenazim alike—to remain in a separate social framework.[12]

Social segregation of the Jewish minority was manifested in their limited presence in the revolutionary activities against the Batista dictatorship that united a large number of university students during the 1950s. Most Jewish youth were very active during that period in Zionist frameworks, and their identification with Judaism and with the State of Israel was more central to their existence than identification with the political problems of Cuba. Only a small number of Jews were active in the 26th of July (the revolutionary movement of Castro) or in the Revolutionary Directory of the Students, and almost all of them belonged to the Ashkenazi sector (Bejarano 1997).

The exodus from Cuba strengthened the Cuban factors in the identity of the Jews. Their emigration was not a Jewish process; it was an integral part of the migration of the Cuban bourgeoisie that was motivated by the rise of a communist regime, the nationalization of private business, and preoccupation for personal safety and for the children's future. Oral histories reflect the traumatic experiences connected with migration. They include testimonies on violent nationalization of business by armed militia men, stories of persons who had to fly hastily fearing arrest, and descriptions of a hectic running after exit permits and a humiliating departure, as befit the *gusanos* (worms)—as the emigrants to the United States were called.[13]

---

12. Interviews with Israel Bichachi, and Elena and David Wek, Miami 1991; Israel Luski and Max Lesnick, Miami 1987, ICJ.

13. Interviews with Alegra Finz and Raquel Egozi-Behar, Miami 1984; Dr. Isaac Cohen, Miami 1991, ICJ.

The Encounter with the United States

The double identity, as Jews and Cubans, granted the immigrants to Miami a double advantage: as Cubans they were recognized as refugees from a communist country, entitled to receive the assistance that the American government granted to all the persons who fled from Castro's regime. As Jews they arrived in a city with an established and organized Jewish population that could alleviate the process of adaptation. While the non-Jewish refugees from Cuba settled near the commercial zone of Miami, in a neighborhood that became known as Little Havana, the Jews preferred to live in Miami Beach, where most of the residents in 1960 were Jewish.

The American Jews, however, did not welcome their coreligionists from Cuba and showed little interest in their plight. Many Cuban Jews remember with bitterness their encounters with the Anglos and emphasize that they had been rejected from synagogues because they were unable to pay membership fees. Testimonies reflect their resentment, as middle-class people who have lost their property but not their pride, and their feelings of humiliation when they had to bargain for a seat in a synagogue or scholarship in a Jewish day school.

Economically, the Cuban Jews were able to settle down without the assistance of their American coreligionists. Their experience in Cuba provided connections and knowledge that facilitated their integration, and—similar to other bourgeois Cubans—they participated in the rapid development of Miami that opened new opportunities. Nevertheless, the indifferent welcome of their coreligionists and the uninviting attitude of most religious institutions have not been forgotten (Bejarano 1997; Green and Zerivitz 1991, 21; Wartenberg 1994, 191).

The first Cuban Jewish organization—Círculo Cubano Hebreo—was founded in 1961 with the objective of providing economic assistance and social support. The Círculo was a common framework for Ashkenazim and Sephardim, but the synagogue and the religious services were limited to the Ashkenazi sector. The Sephardic Cubans, who preferred their traditional rite, prayed in the Sephardic synagogue in South Miami Beach. The young and more affluent Sephardim preferred the Conservative Temple Menorah whose rabbi, Meyer Abramowitz, was the only spiritual leader who had welcomed the Cuban

Jews, granting them free religious services until they were settled.[14] According to an article by Betty Heisler-Samuels, the gratitude of the Cuban Jews toward Rabbi Abramowitz and his congregation has not been forgotten and in the long run proved beneficial to Temple Menorah, whose most devoted supporters are Cubans (*Miami Herald*, January 17, 2001).

In 1968 a new wave of Sephardim from Cuba arrived in Miami Beach, following the nationalization of small business by Castro's government. The new immigrants belonged to the lower middle class, and many of them had been peddlers and petty merchants (Lavender 1993, 119). One of the early immigrants, Alberto Behar, recalls how the newcomers were humiliated by the leaders of the old Sephardic synagogue: "When Cubans arrived and asked to be admitted the reaction was: throw him to the street, don't let him in" since they had no money to pay membership.[15] As a consequence, the Cuban Sephardim decided to leave the old synagogue and to create their own prayer house.

The first Cuban Sephardic synagogue was established in 1968 in a dark basement that belonged to a syndicate of taxi drivers and was nicknamed *la cueva* (the cave). The enthusiasm that this modest prayer house engendered strengthened the trend toward the establishment of a separate organization and the hope for renewal in Miami of the Sephardic community that had existed in Cuba. Within ten years the Cuban Sephardim had established a congregation that included a synagogue, a Talmud Torah, the youth movement Macabi, and a women's association—La Buena Voluntad—that centralized social assistance and cultural activities. Temple Moses (today Torat Moshe) was inaugurated in 1979 with the explicit purpose of continuing the communal life that had existed in Havana (Bettinger-Lopez 2000, 65–73).

Prior to the Castro revolution the communal organization Shevet Ahim functioned in a rented building in Old Havana, and only in the late 1950s were the rich of the community able to construct their own building—the Centro Sefaradí. The erection of the communal building in Miami reflected the economic success of the Cuban Jews. Many of them admitted that their migration

---

14. Interviews with Rafael Kravec, Bernardo Benes, Rabbi Meyer, and Rachel Abramowitz, Miami 1991; Alberto Yehoshua Behar, Miami 1993, ICJ. See also Benz 2005, 70.

15. Interview with Alberto Yehoshua Behar.

to the United States opened new opportunities that improved their economic conditions. The Jews participated in the "economic miracle" of the Cubans in South Florida, and a few of them achieved prominent places in the economic elite of Miami as bankers, businessmen, and professionals.

The integration of the Cuban exiles in the United States paved their way as a political pressure group, motivated primarily by the desire to throw out Castro's regime (Wartenberg 1994, 192). In addition to their electoral power, the influence of the exiles derives from their economic support of the Republican Party. Although Cuban Jews in Miami conduct their social life in separated frameworks, they are exposed to Spanish–language media, which are directed toward the general exile population, and they share hostility toward Castro and the idealization of prerevolutionary Cuba.

Abraham Lavender studied the political tendencies of the Cuban Sephardim in Miami, showing that in the 1991 elections Cuban-born Jews had a stronger tendency to vote with the Republican Party (see table 8.2). Conversations with leaders of the Sephardic Cuban community in Miami strengthen the impression that Lavender's findings are still valid, at least for the Sephardim who were born in Cuba.

The conservative tendency of the Cuban Sephardim was reflected also in the attitude toward Israeli politics that is rooted in a historical event that connected the Sephardim in Cuba with the Revisionist movement led by Menachem Begin in the State of Israel. In 1948 two groups of volunteers, members of Betar,[16] left Cuba to fight for the independence of Israel; almost all of them were Sephardim. The first group arrived in Tel Aviv onboard the ship *Altalena* and became victims of the controversial affair in which two of their members were killed in a violent confrontation.[17] The death of their friends from the bullets of fellow Jews caused a profound wound that marked their relations with the Jewish state.[18] Menachem

16. A youth movement of the Zionist Revisionist Party that was linked to the Irgun.

17. The *Altalena* Affair: the ship carried armaments and volunteers of the Irgun. The Irgun joined the newly founded Israel Defense Force but refused to submit all its arms and munition. The Provisional Government, headed by Ben-Gurion, wishing to secure the unity and sovereignty of IDF, bombed the ship and sank it.

18. Nissim Cohen, "Report on my visit to Cuba" (in Hebrew), December 12, 1948, Central Zionist Archive, KKL5/16320; Interviews with Israel Bichachi, Salomon Garazi, Jacobo Forma, and Dr. Alberto Forma, Miami 1991, ICJ.

Table 8.2.
Voting patterns according to ethnic groups

	REPUBLICANS (%)	DEMOCRATS (%)	INDIFFERENT (%)	TOTAL (n)
Sephardim born in Cuba	58.3	32.1	9.6	156
Ashkenazim born in Cuba	38.1	48.8	13.0	215
Non-Cuban Sephardim	30.5	57.1	12.3	1h54
Non-Cuban Ashkenazim	11.7	82.6	5.7	1,430

Source: Lavender 1993, 125.

Begin, who visited Cuba in 1951 was received by the Sephardic community as the real hero of Israel's independence. His election as prime minister in 1977 was hailed with enthusiasm by the Sephardic Cubans in Miami and encouraged the pro-Likud tendencies that grew during that period.[19]

The Sephardim in Cuba had been devoted Zionists throughout their history. In 1949 they established the Consejo pro Israel as the Zionist framework of the Shevet Ahim congregation. Despite the creation of a separate Zionist framework, the Sephardim took an active part in the extensive activities on behalf of the State of Israel that characterized Jewish public life in Cuba during the 1950s. Ashkenazim and Sephardim collaborated in the common frameworks of the Women's International Zionist Organization (WIZO), the Jewish National Fund, and the United Jewish Appeal. The campaigns that were destined to sustain the economy and the safety of the new Jewish state became glittering social events of the new bourgeois of the Cuban community.

Zionism in Cuba was basically a movement of campaigns and not of *aliya* (migration to Israel): of approximately 9,000 Jews who left Cuba after the revolution, only 420 migrated to Israel. Many of them used the advantageous conditions of migration to Israel as a means to proceed later to the United States. The support of Zionist campaigns proved beneficial as Cuban exiles—who were

19. The 1998 autobiography of Dr. Alberto Forma, who participated in the *Altalena* Affair, contains a historical account with the Israeli establishment and with the Zionist Cuban establishment.

forced to leave all their property in Cuba[20]—were allowed to redeem the Development Bonds of Israel that they had acquired before the revolution. When they achieved stable economic situations they became enthusiastic donors for the cause of Israel.

The Zionist activities of the Cuban Jews in Miami were organized, with no distinction between Sephardim and Ashkenazim, in a common framework that is affiliated with the Jewish Federation of Miami. The ethnic separation was preserved primarily in religious life: the Ashkenazim founded their Cuban Jewish Congregation in downtown Miami Beach (1700 Michigan Ave.) near the early settlement of the Cuban Jewish immigrants. With time, however, the younger generations moved to better neighborhoods and joined congregations that granted formal and informal Jewish education to their children, although they continued to maintain their affiliation with the community of their parents. Observation of this community reveals that the leadership is still in the hands of the Cuban-born immigrants whose parents came from Eastern Europe, who still feel connected to the Cuban social environment. Tight relations with other Cuban Jews and exposure to the large non-Jewish exile community had an impact on the pace of assimilation among the Anglos, but the community has no means to transmit the Cuban-Jewish heritage to the next generations.

Unlike the Ashkenazi Cubans, who form a very small part of the Ashkenazim in Miami, the presence of the Cubans is more salient among the Sephardim (Lavender 1993, 118). The prominent activists of the Sephardic Cuban community form part of the leadership of the American Sephardi Federation, Florida Chapter, as well as that of FESELA (Federación Sefaradí Latino Americana)—the Latin American Sephardi Federation affiliated with the World Zionist Movement.

The Sephardic Congregation of Florida aspired to gather not only the Jews from Cuba but also Jews from other Latin American countries, being the only community whose activities are conducted in Spanish. Many Jews from Latin America come to Miami for recreation or as a second home for periods of economic and political upheavals in their respective countries. When the building of the Sephardic Congregation of Florida was inaugurated in 1980, the president

---

20. Jews who flew to Israel in three chartered flights authorized by the Cuban government were allowed to take their movable possessions with them.

of the community wrote that "[the Jews of] Latin America and their Sephardic communities are observing us. We grant them security in view of political instability" (Bichachi 1980). During that period it seemed that the Sephardim who had fled from Cuba as refugees established in Miami a stable community that could serve as a bridge between the United States and Latin America as well as between the Ladino speakers and the speakers of Castilian Spanish.

Since the 1990s, however, the Sephardic Cuban community in Miami Beach has declined, as a consequence of the aging of its members and the abandoning of the community by the younger generations. This process has still to be studied, but we can point out the demographic, geographical, and religious causes that may affect it.

The number of Sephardim living in South Florida has increased considerably during the last thirty years, and new congregations were opened in North Miami Beach as well as in other residential centers of Sephardim. The Cuban Sephardim were exposed to contacts with different Sephardic groups speaking Ladino, Arabic, and French who moved to Miami from the northeast United States as well as from North Africa, Israel, and Latin America.[21]

While the immigrants from Cuba in the early 1960s encountered in Miami only one Sephardic synagogue, their children were confronted by a larger offer of Sephardic congregations with different degrees of religious observance. In addition, they were exposed to other Jewish alternatives, such as the Conservative movement, as well as to influences of assimilation.

The Sephardic tradition brought over from Turkey was formally Orthodox, but it was characterized by a liberal attitude toward religious observance. Older members of the community were brought to the synagogue on Saturday in the congregation's van with the tacit consent of the spiritual leaders. The appointment of a strictly Orthodox rabbi with an uncompromising attitude with respect to the *Halachic* law became a source of tension between ethnic and religious tendencies. The strict observance of the religious laws attracted non-Cuban Orthodox Jews who were living in the neighborhood, but it alienated many of the Cuban Sephardim.[22]

21. Interview with Herbert Ferster, Miami 2002, ICJ. See chapter 7 in this book.
22. Interview with Rabbi Abraham Ben Zaquen, Miami 2002, ICJ.

The religious difficulties of the Ladino-speaking communities in Latin America were discussed in a FESELA conference that took place in Mexico in 2004: "We, the Sephardim, have inherited a way of religious observance that in some aspects does not correspond with the existing currents. Our fathers did not know the differences between Orthodox, Ultra-Orthodox, Conservative, Reformist and secular." One of the prominent leaders of the Miami Sephardic community presented a project in order "to find rabbis of our measure, that will take care of our songs and of the Judeo Spanish customs."[23]

The Sephardic Cuban identity of the leadership that was the fundamental motive for the foundation of the (Cuban) Sephardic Congregation of Florida is still strong among the leaders who were born in Cuba. The alienation of their children from the Cuban synagogue raises the necessity of creating alternative frameworks that would transmit the Cuban Sephardic identity to future generations.

Conclusion

Jewban, the annual publication of the Círculo Cubano Hebreo of 1970, refers to the three countries that represent the identity of its members: "Our homelands, Cuba and Israel, and the country in which we live." But, in addition to these three components of national identity—Jewish, Cuban, and American—there are ethnic identities based on the historical memory that forged the cultural heritage. The passage through Cuba and the settlement in Miami added new layers to the collective memory that was consolidated and preserved in the tradition of all the Sephardic Jews.

The major cultural component that formed the Sephardic identity was the language. The linguistic similarity between Judeo-Spanish and Castilian Spanish created an intercultural mixture that was unperceived as long as the Sephardim lived in a Spanish-speaking environment. Following their immigration to the United States, the problem of preserving the Spanish language reflected the fusion of components of Sephardic identity with components of Cuban

23. From a February 5, 2004, speech by Rafael Hodara when he assumed the presidency of FESELA at the biennial meeting of "Mexico 2004 Continuity," Montevideo.

continuity. This fusion created a cultural bridge between Jews from Latin American countries ("Latino Jews") and Judeo-Spanish-speaking Sephardim.

The Sephardim in Cuba transmitted their family and communal values through segregation and separation from the general environment, continuing the patterns of behavior in their mother communities in Turkey. The community that was founded in the 1960s in Miami was not created by individual immigrants, but transmitted the social Jewish enclave to a new place. It was a process of transplantation—uprooting from the Cuban soil and planting in a landscape, climate, and social environment that facilitated the continued segregation in the margins of two large groups—non-Jewish Cubans and American Jews.

The Sephardim who arrived from Cuba as refugees from Castro's revolution established in Miami a stable community that serves as a bridge between the United States and Latin America, as well as between Ladino and Spanish speakers. Religious confrontation with new Orthodox tendencies as well as the emergence of new generations whose mother tongue is English threaten the preservation of their collective identity.

Part 3   **Culture in Transition**

Language, Literature,
and Music

9

Ladino in Latin America

An Old Language in the New World

MONIQUE R. BALBUENA

Deeply affected by the loss of most of its speakers during the Shoah, Ladino, the vernacular Judeo-Spanish, has been living its death sentence for quite a number of years. Its unavoidable disappearance has been affirmed and reaffirmed for several decades. But as fewer people speak it today, and most native speakers approach very old age, there is a movement to revitalize the language, with an increased cultural production in Ladino. Recently, even without the organic community in which it flourished as a living daily language, Ladino has been the language of choice for a series of literary works appearing in different parts of the world: in Latin America, the United States, and Israel, to name a few, there are novels, poetry books, and musical recordings being produced in Ladino.

The fact that Ladino is presently being studied at the university, rather than being spoken in the marketplace, is a clear sign that the language is now artificially maintained, but this afterlife, provided greatly by the efforts of the last generation of speakers, should be considered in its context and is not without merit. There are new journals—in Israel, Turkey, Belgium, the United States, and Argentina;[1] academic conferences, scholarly publications, and even a vir-

---

1. Respectively: *Aki Yerushalayim*, until recently the only publication entirely in Ladino; *Shalom*, from Istanbul, publishes one full page in Judeo-Spanish, and the magazine *El Amaneser*, which since March 2005 is published entirely in Ladino; *Los Muestros*, from Brussels, also offers one full page in the language; *Lettre Sépharade*, which has recently lost its French edition and is now published only in English, from the United States, and also appears online; and *Boletín*

tual community, *Ladinokomunitá*, are made possible by the modern technologi-cal resources that maintain an active Sephardic diasporic network engaged in the preservation of the language and culture of its people.

Focusing on Latin America, this chapter intends to analyze this renewed interest in Ladino in the region and situate it within a general trend in the world at large, establishing a dialogue with poets such as Franco-Bosnian Clarisse Nicoïdski and Israeli Margalit Matitiahu, to name just two. Recent treatments of multiculturalism have prompted an inner look at intra-Jewish difference and an acceptance and even an enthusiastic reclaiming of Sephardic heritage and Jewish multilingualism. While there is a tendency to limit Ladino poetry to folk-lore and medieval traditions, I will focus here on the modern appropriations of Ladino in pop culture and on the poetry that establishes formal and intertextual connections to modern/ist lyric poetry, seeking to read the authors outside the context of Sephardic nostalgia and into that of a theoretical discussion on minor literatures and issues of nationalism. In this chapter I will examine how Ladino is eventually used to carry on different poetic projects: to reclaim or reinstitute the "mother tongue," as a mark of belonging to a family and a people, with pride in one's links with the networks of the Sephardi Diaspora. Or, as in the case of Argentine Juan Gelman, as an exilic strategy: a language built not in community, but in solitude, as the stateless language of the exile who has lost his homeland and yearns to name it—and thus recuperate it—resorting to the infancy of the Castilian language.[2]

The biggest setback to two of the better-known Jewish languages, Yiddish and Ladino (or Djudezmo, Muestro Espanyol, Espanyol, Judeo-Spanish, or Spanyolit) was the destruction of the communities and murder of most of their speakers by the Nazis. In the case of Ladino, the dismemberment of the Otto-man Empire and the formation of nation-states was also a hugely important factor in the language's diminished status and strength. Other reasons, however, contributed to the loss of prestige and gradual disappearance of both Yiddish

---

eSefarad, a weekly online publication from Buenos Aires with a great number of articles and poems in Judeo-Spanish.

2. I want to thank Leonardo Senkman for reading a previous work and offering valuable commentaries and suggestions that find their way here.

and Ladino: the Zionist refusal of diasporic life and consequent suppression of other Jewish languages in favor of Hebrew, in the process of defining a national language; the process of modernization, which changed the dynamics of the relationships within the Jewish communities and of those maintained with the surrounding communities; the interest that certain immigrant communities had in assimilating and erasing obvious markers of difference. Today, Hebrew's firmly established position as the national language of the Jewish state is not threatened, and this situation allows the state and its academic institutions to fund departments and cultural events that study and promote other Jewish languages. The government of Israel, for example, invested in the creation of the National Authority for Ladino and Its Culture in 1997, and in 2002 UNESCO organized a conference on Ladino in Paris, with the purpose of safeguarding and revitalizing the language. A similar process, at a different level, occurs with Jewish groups in the Diaspora who, their social status secure, feel empowered now to claim ties with a Jewish past and are proud of their particularism in a world that increasingly speaks of "multiculturalism." Perhaps influenced by the type of ethnic and cultural politics developed in the United States, some minorities, including the Jewish ones, feel encouraged to celebrate their "difference." In the words of Ladino speaker and professor Eliezer Papo (Ben-Gurion University), "Being different is beautiful, now everybody speaks about his roots." And he adds, tongue-in-cheek, "It's antisocial activity not to have roots" (Ellingwood 2004).

Ladino is not yet as "hip" as Yiddish, as there are no cards, fridge magnets, or summer camps in Ladino,[3] but it has undoubtedly seen a rise in interest, with university professors, popular singers, writers, and poets turning to it with renewed enthusiasm. Latin America is not immune to this process. More and more groups and Jewish associations offer classes and conversation clubs, music concerts find a willing audience, and writers discover the poetic possibilities offered by the language. Argentine poet Beatriz Mazliah, for example, writes new poetry in modern genres, while Mexican writer Rosa Nissán includes long sections in Ladino

---

3. But if these objects of consumption indicate "hipness," Ladino is well on its way—as of 2011 it is possible to find cups in Ladino on the eSefarad site, and T-shirts and baby clothes in Ladino on Sarah Aroeste's personal web page.

amid her novel in Spanish *Novia que te vea*, which interrogates Jewish Sephardic identity in Mexico.

In his novel *The Strange Nation of Rafael Mendes*, in which he rewrites Brazilian history incorporating Sephardic history, Brazilian novelist Moacyr Scliar includes snippets of Ladino as marks of a dormant memory. The protagonist, Rafael Mendes, amid the Brazilian military dictatorship and financial chaos of the 1970s, discovers that he belongs to a long lineage of Crypto-Jews, whose ancestors include Maimonides and the prophet Jonah. Recovering his genealogy allows Mendes to embrace his collective memory, and in the process, also to recover his own identity. Taking into account that, in the words of Brazilian ambassador Rubens Ricupero, "The origin of the country and the fate of the Sephardic Jews in the 15th and 16th centuries are inseparable threads of the same fabric" (1997, xvii),[4] Scliar draws a parallel between Rafael Mendes's genealogical history and Brazilian history, between his Jewish history and the Jewish presence in Brazilian history. There are no conclusive indications that Ladino as a language was present in colonial Brazil, as the colonizers were Portuguese New Christians or *conversos*, whose lingua franca, like that of the Western Sephardim, was Portuguese,[5] but the protagonist's father's notebook—the main source of

---

4. Author's translation.

5. Ladino, as a language traditionally written in Hebrew characters, would not be available to the "people of the *Nation*," the Portuguese *conversos*. However, some texts in Spanish were likely available to them because Spanish had a high literary value. Discussing the Portuguese in Amsterdam, Miriam Bodian writes, "Since Portuguese was the native tongue of the overwhelming majority of émigrés, it became the language in which the communal records were kept, sermons delivered, gossip exchanged. But even among native Portuguese speakers, Spanish was the language of literary expression. Works aimed at transmitting rabbinic tradition to the émigrés were frequently published in Spanish translation, although Portuguese translations also appeared" (1997, 92). Daniel M. Swetschinski also refers to the Portuguese in Amsterdam: "Amsterdam's Portuguese Jews spoke primarily Portuguese. All the records of the Kahal Kadosh were kept in Portuguese; most notarial documents, too, were drafted in Portuguese" (2000, 278). Swetschinski comments on the Portuguese's conservatism in their continued use of Portuguese in the Diaspora: "If in the past the stigma of New Christianhood had come to define their uniqueness, the only way to preserve the sense of that uniqueness now was through the continued use of Portuguese as the language of intra-familial and intra-communal communication, through acts and decisions of active conservatism" (312). For a broad study of Portuguese Jews in Venice, Salonika, and other regions, see Israel (2002). Samuel Usque calls Portuguese "lingua

what will be Rafael Mendes's newly found Jewish identity—includes two texts in Ladino: a poem and the verses of a traditional lullaby. The knowledge of such a song seems to be atavic, as Rafael Mendes's father writes that "[t]here were sensations, forebodings, strange happenings. 'What's this song you keep singing to lull little Rafael to sleep?' Alzira asked me one day. I didn't know what to say, I didn't know where it came from: 'Duerme, duerme, mi angelico/hijico chico de tu nación'" (Scliar 1987, 227).[6]

To Rafael Mendes's son, who is learning details of his father's trip to Spain in 1936, the old and peculiar Spanish words are the link that ties his existence to an ancient Spanish (Sephardic) life, still unknown and not yet understood. "In Spanish: Meaningful to someone who went to Spain," he says, before asking: "But what kind of Spanish is this? . . . It seems to be a Spanish dialect, but where is it spoken? In which nación?" (41). The Romanized Judeo-Spanish inscribed in the Portuguese text is a marker of difference, and it provides a certain physicality to the links between contemporary Brazil and a recognizable Sephardic past, stressing, to ears and eyes, the primacy of the Jewish presence in the original formation of Latin America. Ladino, even if briefly in this work, participates in the author's project of seeing "Brazilian history through Jewish eyes" and telling such a history through a mythologized Sephardic one, as if the Sephardic account alone has a legitimate claim to a "Latin American origin" or "belonging"—the only one that allows for a fully successful inscription of the Jewish subject into the tale of the national tribe.

Also in Brazil, and with a synchronic eye to the past, poet and scholar Leonor Scliar-Cabral has translated and promoted classical Ladino romanzas and canciones,[7] a corpus that has traditionally received attention from scholars of Sephardic studies. Her 1990 book, Romances e canções Sefarditas, presents Ladino/Portuguese versions of eight romanzas and fourteen canciones, including a Balkan version of "Durme, durme." Scliar-Cabral, a linguistics professor,

---

franca," explaining that it allows him to reach his scattered brothers, and thus justifying his decision to write his 1553 Consolação as tribulações de Israel in Portuguese, in Ferrara.

6. The ending "–ico" in "angelico" and "hijico" makes it Judeo-Spanish, but the verb "duerme" is Spanish—the Judeo-Spanish form is "durmi" or "durme."

7. In Ladino, romansas and kantigas.

explains that her work was prompted by the experience of hearing Esther Lamandier (n.d.) sing the *cancionero*,[8] and that by translating these poems and bringing
them to the Portuguese-Brazilian corpus she feels she is filling a void in the Portuguese language. Scliar-Cabral reminds the reader of the connections between
this old literary collection and modern poetry, such as García Lorca's.[9] Later,
with her 1994 poetry book *Memórias de Sefarad*, there is an affirmation of the
cancionero's power to serve as intertext and source for new poetry. Even as the
poems are written in Portuguese, the poet tries, more or less successfully, to use
metric forms and assonant rhymes associated with the Judeo-Spanish romances
and popular lyric songs, as well as a lexicon that incorporates words from the
Hebrew, while developing historical themes (life in al-Andalus, the Sephardic
exile) and themes referring to Jewish rituals and holidays.

But perhaps the most novel development in the present renewal of Ladino in
Brazil can be found in the works of Fortuna, a singer who brought the *cancionero*
closer to the world of popular music. A Brazilian Jew, née Fortunée Joyce Safdié,
she had provided vocal backing for iconic composers/singers such as Chico
Buarque and Toquinho, and, as a composer, had collaborated in songwriting
with poet Paulo Leminski. Her no-longer-available web page reveals that during
a trip to Israel in 1991, while visiting the Beit ha-Tefutsot, the Museum of the
Diaspora, in Tel-Aviv, she heard a song in Ladino for the first time, "Durme mi
alma donzeya." The experience was a turning point in Fortuna's musical career,
leading her to research and interpret medieval Jewish songs, in performances
where heavy jewelry and costumes made of silk, satin, and brocade became part
of her stage trademark. Contact with this music in Ladino afforded her not only
the "difference" she was seeking to establish between herself and other Brazilian
singers[10] but also contributed, in her own words, "to a deeper contact with Jewish
culture, religion and customs" ("Fortuna" 2006).

8. The poems translated by Scliar-Cabral were all chosen from this collection.

9. Such a connection is made explicit by one of the most important contemporary Ladino
poets, Clarisse Nicoïdski, in the last poem of her 1986 Ladino-English bilingual volume *Lus Ojus,
las manus, la boca,* which she dedicates to the Spanish poet and where she writes about his death.

10. "Precisava me diferenciar," or, "I need to differentiate myself (from them)" is how Fortuna refers to her previous work with Chico Buarque and Toquinho in an interview with Apoenan
Rodrigues (*Isto É.*, April 12, 2000).

Ladino operates in Fortuna's case as a catalyst to a fuller embrace of her own ethnic origins, whose traditions she did not really know, and a way of establishing a musical specificity, or difference, in the world of Brazilian popular music where she had been treading. The singer's first CD in this new series was *La prima vez*, released in 1994, which presents twenty-one songs in Ladino and Hebrew, divided into wedding songs, love songs, liturgical and paraliturgical songs, children's songs, lullabies, and *romanzas*. With fifteen musicians playing some twenty different instruments, she experiments with rhythms and traditions in an attempt to offer new readings of traditional songs. In works that follow, such as *Cantigas* (1995), *Mediterrâneo* (1996), and *Mazal* (2000), besides combining different musical and cultural traditions in her arrangements to old songs, Fortuna also offers original compositions, putting to music texts such as the *Shemá*, *Halleluya*, a poem by Yehuda ha-Levy, and a Ladino proverb. It is particularly striking to hear "Lechá Dodi" accompanied by the sounds of a *baião*, a syncopated 2–4 northeastern rural Brazilian rhythm, in what seems to be an attempt at composing a distinctively Jewish Brazilian music.[11]

Even if the masses do not listen to her, as she is not regularly played on the radio, Fortuna has captured an audience, selling more than 100,000 copies of her first four albums in Brazil, Israel, Argentina, Spain, Taiwan, the United Kingdom, and the United States. Her works are reviewed in the most important Brazilian magazines and newspapers, her concerts attract Jews and non-Jews alike, and one of her shows was featured in a program for TV Cultura, the educational TV channel in São Paulo. She also received the prestigious Sharp Prize for best album composed in a foreign language. Perhaps because she comes from a comfortable position within Brazilian society, Fortuna did not have problems claiming an ethnic identity and coming out as publicly Jewish. Her elaborate stage costumes serve to enhance a difference that songs in foreign languages can only magnify.

---

11. Not all the critical reviews are positive. Fortuna's ecumenical musical approach and let's-embrace-the-whole-world-with-music spirit—discussed later—is perceived by George Robinson as producing a body of work that "might be charitably characterized as world-beat-meets-disco" (2000a). In another review, he refers to *Cantigas* and *Mazal* as albums "full of folky, new-agey settings that frame her voice with a lot of echo" (2000b).

But if this "exotic," heavily dressed, foreign-language-singing woman can be representative of Brazil, it is also due to her attempts, however contradictory it may seem, at being "universal." In fact, in some songs of her fourth album, *Mazal*, Fortuna performs with a choir of Benedictine monks, an experience that will lead to a collaborative album between the Jewish singer and the monks from the São Bento Monastery in São Paulo. *Cælestia* (2002), later followed by *Encontros* (2003) and *Mundo Novo* (2005), begins a new phase in her work, in which this ecumenical collaboration becomes crucial. Fortuna starts singing in Latin, too (and includes a Greek lullaby), and to the *cancionero* Ladino she adds Latin Psalms and prayers such as "Regina Cœli" and "Rorate Cœli." Besides embarking on the adventure of the Gregorian chant, a commercial success in previous years, Fortuna develops a discourse that can touch people and broaden her audience: one of a spiritual search and of peace achieved by crossing religious divides.

Without questioning the merits of a quest for inner and world peace, what interests me here is the many uses of Ladino and the Sephardic tradition. From the beginning, publicity material emphasized a certain multiculturalism represented by the Ladino repertoire, searching a possible universalism by playing up the idea of Andalusian *"convivencia"* or *"harmonia"*: "the union of Spanish feeling, Moorish rhythm and Jewish soul."[12] Reviewers and customers picked up the idea, with *Planeta* magazine describing Ladino music as "a fertile mixture of Spanish, Arabian [sic], Gypsy [sic] and Jewish melodies and rhythms."[13] A "communion between cultures" is mentioned in the blurbs for *Mazal*, which somewhat exaggerate the New Age language: "In the turn of the millennium she [Fortuna] seeks the harmony and the convergence of the forces of creation to increase Man's wellbeing in his passage through Earth."

---

12. Director Iacov Hillel, who co-produces the albums, confirms this direction by affirming that "These songs convey the different feelings of varied cultures, for they are the fruit of a unique harmonic period of peaceful interaction among the three peoples that created them—Jews, Christians and Muslims. This is why the emotion contained in this music can touch all audiences" (2006). To be fair, the *"convivencia"* tends to come up a lot in descriptions of the *cancionero* and presentations of contemporary singers of Ladino songs. In that, Fortuna is not an exception. She just goes further in incorporating the Christian tradition and the successful Gregorian chant to her repertoire.

13. Quoted on the singer's former website.

It seems that Ladino music, while giving the singer the opportunity to appear in costume and create a niche of difference and exoticism, also has elements that allow for comfort and familiarity from the audience. In other words, it is different enough to be exotic and attractive because beautiful and foreign, but general and familiar enough to be recognized and easily embraced by other Latin cultures. While playing this interestingly ambivalent role, Ladino musical and literary tradition receives more exposure, but its future, beyond concerts and monasteries, is still far from certain.

A different musical project comes from two Argentine singers: Monica Monasterio and Dina Rot. Monasterio began singing in Ladino in Argentina, where she grew up and was trained in Western music, but relocated to Spain, where she has lived for more than fourteen years. At a time when Spain reclaims the Sepharadim as their own, and there is an institutional embrace of "Sepharad"— with universities studying Ladino, "Jewish tourism" growing into a large industry, and government representatives continuously inviting Sephardic Ladino poets to official ceremonies—Monasterio's move is a true return to "Sepharad." There she has released four albums of Ladino songs: *A las orillas del Bir* (1996), *Sefarad XXI: Cantares del avenir* (1999), *Luvia* (2003), and *Almendrikas y piniones* (2005). Besides the traditional *romanzas* and *cantigas*, Monasterio has made a point of recording works by some of the most active contemporary Ladino poets, such as Beatriz Mazliah (Argentina), Flori Jagoda (Bosnia/United States), Matilda Koén Sarano (Israel), Margalit Matitiahu (Israel), and Rita Gabbay (Greece). Monasterio combines some North African, Greek, and Turkish influences in her renditions, and with composer Horacio Lovecchio she also offers new arrangements to old songs, in an effort to update tradition and reach a modern audience—not unlike, in the United States, the work of Sarah Aroeste, who, affirming herself as both a Sephardic and a modern American woman, is drawing large numbers of young people who had not been exposed to the *cancionero* before to rave at her shows with traditional Ladino songs in modern, pop, and innovative arrangements combining rock, blues, funk, and jazz.[14]

14. See Sarah Aroeste's 2003 album, *A la una/In the beginning*, and her second album *Puertas* (2007). Her website describes her music as "A funky blend of traditional ladino music mixed with rock and jazz." (http://www.saraharoeste.com). Critics point to her success in making the music

If a modern reading of traditional songs is something several singers are try-ing to do,[15] Monasterio's project is somewhat different in what concerns Ladino's promotion and preservation, inasmuch as it points to a future and addresses the viability of the language as a literary medium.[16] Deeply grounded in the musi-cal Sephardic tradition—even if her own style is not particularly traditional— and working very much within a transnational collaborative setting, Monasterio pays tribute to the past and recognizes an underlying common heritage as she actively adds to the *afterlife* of the language by creating new songs from modern poems. These poems vary in literary value, but they all contribute to the renova-tion of the language and the continuation of its life as a possible vehicle of literary expression. Rather than a perpetual and quasi-exclusive connection to the *can-cionero*, which tends to freeze Ladino in the past and adds to the public percep-tion that the language is exotic and dead, having nothing to do with living Jews of today, the new poetry not only reflects contemporary realities, but also engages with modern lyric poetry and various national poetic traditions. Monasterio and

---

sound contemporary without losing its traditional elements, since she uses original melodies and lyrics. Her upcoming 2012 album, *Gracia*, will present new songs with original lyrics and music, in an exciting departure from her previous work.

15. I should also mention Montserrat Franco, from Paraguay, whose work with Sephardic music and indigenous Guaraní songs is among the most compelling and is deserving of a more detailed analysis.

16. The *Primer Simposio de Estudios Sefardíes* (First symposium on Sephardic studies) held in Madrid in 1964 addressed, among other issues, the future of Ladino, or "the situation of Judeo-Spanish." Several talks stressed the "decadent state" of the language and its imminent death; a number of panels urged both the so-called purification of the Jewish language and its incorporation into modern Spanish—in other words, the Castilianization of Ladino as a means of guaranteeing its survival. Manuel Criado de Val, a Spanish scholar, suggested that Judeo-Spanish should be endowed with "a literary content," designed to increase the language's prestige, thereby overcoming the shame native speakers felt over their language. Criado de Val went on to say that in addition to organizing a dictionary and a grammar, the only available contemporary means to amass the needed literary content was to translate Spanish works into Judeo-Spanish: "We cannot attribute any literary content to Judeo-Spanish by means of contemporary literary works: finding a writer in Judeo-Spanish who has the luxury to publish and to offer a work of literature would not be easy" (1970, 278). The poets writing in Ladino today are trying to prove him wrong.

Lovecchio's music, then, in lyrics and arrangements, puts the past into the present, suggesting a viable future.[17]

Similar work has been done by singer and composer Dina Rot, who, more than recording "Ladino songs," records songs, or poems, in Ladino. With arranger Emilio Laguillo, Rot undertook the task of setting to music two of the most impressive bodies of work in Ladino by contemporary Ladino poets, those of Clarisse Nicoïdski and Juan Gelman. Like Monasterio, Rot has relocated to Spain. With translations[18] and notes from the poets, her album *Una manu tumó l'otra* (1999) is named after a poem by Franco-Bosnian Sephardic poet Clarisse Nicoïdski, included in her volume *Lus ojus, las manus, la boca* (1978). From a multilingual background, growing up in a house where Italian, Serbo-Croatian, German, and French were spoken, Nicoïdski, née Abinoun (1938–1996), became a French novelist. But she started writing in her parents' common language, what they called *spaniol muestro*, upon her mother's death. Then, the shame associated with the language, for its "lack of noblesse, grammar and literature,"[19] was overshadowed, and eventually transformed, by the realization that the language was dying along with her mother, who, in her mind, metonymically stood for its speakers. The language "'de la familia,' del 'secreto,' del susto y—quizas-de la vergüenza" ("of the family," of "secrecy," of fright and—perhaps—of shame)[20] became the "lost language" in which Nicoïdski could now offer her mother a literary kaddish.[21]

Nicoïdski wrote one poem in Ladino for each of the novels she wrote in French, and her 1978 volume, published in the United States as a bilingual

17. It is remarkable, however, that Monasterio has a wider audience in Spain than in Argentina, where, reportedly (pers. e-mail exchanges, July 2006), she would draw mostly members of the Jewish community to her concerts. This confirms a current tendency of Spain to appropriate the Sephardic past and heritage and to observe the development of the Spanish language through Ladino.

18. The Argentine edition offers translations to Spanish, whereas the European edition has translations into English, French, and Italian.

19. From Nicoïdski's testimonial included in the CD's booklet.

20. Also from Rot's CD booklet.

21. In the CD's booklet, Nicoïdski writes (and I use her spelling): "Quisiera que estas palabras en la lingua perdida sean para ella, mi madre, como un kadish, repetido a menudo" (I would like these words in the lost language to be for her, my mother, as a kaddish, often repeated).

English-Ladino edition, presents the characteristic sounds and spelling patterns of Balkan Judeo-Spanish—the language of the Jews of Sarajevo in the former Yugoslavia.[22] These sixteen poems, especially the last one, dedicated to the Spanish poet Federico García Lorca, are the main intertexts to Ashkenazi Argentine poet Juan Gelman's 1994 poetry collection *Dibaxu*.[23] They are also the intertextual model for Gelman's editorial decisions, as his book offers bilingual versions of the poems as well, this time with italicized Ladino on the left and Castellano (the Argentine variety of Spanish), in regular font types, on the right. Dina Rot, in her musical album, follows this pattern, combining Nicoïdski's and Gelman's poems, and adding, side by side, their translations into Spanish. Given the paucity of studies integrating Nicoïdski's work in the reading of Gelman's—a fact that only stresses the need to offer more comparative approaches of the two[24]—Rot's initiative is a representative and well-accomplished attempt in that direction. Besides revealing the rich intertextual dialogue that Gelman establishes with Nicoïdski's work, by adding music to their poems, increasing their possible audience and thus broadening their reach, Dina Rot participates in the same project on which Nicoïdski and Gelman embark for very different reasons: to create a future from a past endangered in its present form. In Rot's voice, Ladino gains life and intensity, and, in Gelman's words, her music "rescata una dimensión de tiempo—del tiempo de esa lengua—que exalta su permanencia, su presencia, su modernidad. . . . Su existir, aunque unos digan que se apaga" (recovers a dimension of time—of that language's time—which exalts its permanence, its presence, its modernity. . . . Its existence even if people say it is dying).[25]

The poetic paths of Nicoïdski and Gelman intersect in lexical and thematic ways, and the role of death and memory in the choice of language by the two

22. The distinctive traits of this variant of Judeo-Spanish can be found in Baruch (1930, 132). They have also been briefly described by H. V. Sephiha (1997). This text presents only minor variations from Sephiha's 1977 article.

23. I also see echoes and allusions from Nicoïdski's *Caminus di palavras*, a series of poems published in the Spanish journal *Poesía*. All these texts have received a beautiful bilingual, tri-textual edition in Ladino in Rashi script, Ladino in Romance letters, and a facing Hebrew translation—an admirable work of edition and translation by the also Ladino poet Avner Perez. See Nicoïdski 2006.

24. For a comparative treatment of Gelman and Nicoïdski, see Balbuena (2009).

25. In Rot's CD booklet.

poets is not a minor one. As mentioned earlier, the death of her mother prompted Nicoïdski to revert to her childhood sounds and to write in the language of her parents and grandparents, a language she heard during World War II, while hiding in Morocco and in Lyon, her birth town, during the Vichy regime. This is how she explains her decision to write in Ladino: "comprendi que con [mi madre] se iba definitivamente un poco de esta lingua de mi infancia, y que para nuestra generación, la muerte de nuestros señores significaba la muerte de un lenguaje" (I understood that [with my mother] a bit of this language from my childhood was disappearing and that for our generation, the death of our parents meant the death of a language).[26] These words resemble those of other Ladino poets who come from Sephardic families and, upon the death of their parents—especially the mother—begin to write in Ladino. One of the most significant cases is that of Israeli poet Margalit Matitiahu, author of a body of work that has garnered interest from singers and composers as well as other poets.[27] Matitiahu had already published a number of books in Hebrew when she traveled to Salonica, her parents' hometown, whose vibrant Jewish community was destroyed in the Shoah. Following her visit to Salonica, Matitiahu describes having felt the connection both with her own and with her parents' past. The impulse to write in Ladino was rekindled by an overwhelming realization that her parents' language practically died with the Shoah. For Matitiahu and Nicoïdski, as with several other contemporary poets, Ladino resurfaces in its feminine trappings, as the mother language and the language of the mother, "En esta lingua se hallaban el amor de mi madre, nuestra complicidad y nuestras risas" (My mother's love, our complicity, and our laughter were all found in this language).[28] It irrupts both as the site

26. In Rot's CD booklet.

27. Monica Monasterio sings some of her poems, and Suzy, a Turkish-Israeli singer who also started recording traditional Ladino songs after the death of her aunt and grandmother, has a 2005 album complete with poems by Matitiahu, *Aromas y memorias*. Among other examples, Leonor Scliar-Cabral (1990) cites Matitiahu in her book of translations of traditional poetry in Ladino, *Romances e canções Sefarditas*. Matitiahu, author of *Kurtijo Kemado* (1988) and *Alegrika* (1992), to name perhaps her most famous works, has been translated into several languages and is a household name in the world of contemporary Ladino poetry.

28. In Rot's CD booklet. Nicoïdski's original spelling was respected. Matitiahu, in an August 22, 1991, interview with Mario Wainstein in *Aurora*, says: "Quien quiere escribir desde lo más

of memory and as that which can save memory, and as the mother's language it marks and is marked by affection and pain. Ladino is, in their work, a language to recover the past, to claim an ethnic identity, to assert membership in a community and reaffirm the links they maintain with the Sephardi diaspora.

Juan Gelman has a rather different relationship to Ladino. His bilingual Ladino-Castellano volume *Dibaxu* appeared in 1994, as the culmination of a process, prompted by his experience of exile, of "excavation" of his own origins and the origins of the Spanish language. Gelman had already played with authorship, developing an authorial fiction accompanied by a translational poetics and practice in previous volumes such as *Traducciones I and III* and *Los poemas de Sidney West*, where he invents poets he claims to translate, and, *Com/posiciones*, where he translates or rewrites medieval Spanish Hebrew poems he claims to compose. *Dibaxu* epitomizes this trajectory, radicalizing it with the poet's departure from his own language and the inscription of another, diasporic, and markedly Jewish language: Ladino. His turn to the Sephardic language is the conclusion of a personal, spiritual, and cultural process of identity construction, which I called "Self-Sephardization" (see Balbuena 2003 and Balbuena 2012), and which begins in exile, with a rewriting of Santa Teresa de Ávila's and San Juan de la Cruz's mystical poems in *Citas y comentarios*, followed by further rewritings, this time of medieval Spanish Hebrew poets, in *Com/posiciones*. Deterritorialization, intertextuality, and multilingualism are the three central components of this process that prompts an Ashkenazi Latin American Jew to write—and translate—Sephardic poetry, pointing to a possible (or necessary, but no less controversial) permeability of ethnic borders.

Gelman's exile from Argentina pushes him to uncover the foundation of his language and of his self, peeling away layers in his downward search. He describes his work with Santa Teresa and San Juan as "a dialogue with 16th century Castellano (Castilian)," and adds, "as if searching for the substratum of this Castellano, which, in turn, is the substratum of our Castellano, had been my obsession. As if the extreme solitude of exile had pushed me to search for roots

---

profundo de su ser, hay cosas que puede decir solo en el lenguaje de su madre" (For anyone who wants to write from the innermost part of her being, there are things that can only be said in her mother's language) (quoted in Carasso 1993).

within the language, the most profound and exiled roots of the language" (1994, 7). *Dibaxu* is, to him, "the culmination or the outcome of *Citas y Comentarios.*" The direct link the poet establishes between these works reinforces the central role of language in his enterprise, as he engages in what I termed an "archaeology of the language," delving into accumulated layers of the language in reverse order: beginning with Argentine Castellano, Gelman regresses toward sixteenth-century Castellano (Castilian), to finally retrieve an even earlier version of Spanish, one which he calls—typically but erroneously[29]—"sefardí," represented by the language spoken in fifteenth-century Spain and maintained, with new additions and variations, by the Jews dispersed across different lands after 1492.

Ladino is essentially a language of exile. It is a creation of the Jewish Diaspora, after the expulsion from Spain, and exhibits the conservatism typical of languages distanced from their center (hence the retention of fifteenth-century forms), along with the dynamism and fusion resulting from the encounter with several different languages over the ages. It is also a language of exile because, with the dissolution of the Ottoman Empire, Ladino suffered additional dislocations and losses; then, following the Nazi genocide, it was further marginalized and displaced with the death of most of its speakers. Furthermore, adding to its ex-centric position, in much of mainstream Jewish culture, and certainly in Gelman's Jewish world, Ladino is seen as marginal to Hebrew and even to Yiddish. Ladino is also the unknown other for the modern Spanish speakers who are unaware of its presence in the history of their language—hence Gelman's reference to "the most profound and exiled roots *of* the language."

Gelman was attracted to the "exilic vision" of the mystical saints and tango lyricists who both speak of the absence of the loved one: in tango, a woman; in poetry, God. If Gelman saw "symbols and representations of other abandonments" in Santa Teresa and San Juan's poems and in the tango lyrics that he combines with them, he will find in Ladino, a language so marked by and representative of exile, a way to express his own abandonment (Giordano 1986). With Ladino, Gelman speaks of his country, for which he yearns and represents

---

29. The name of the language is a contentious issue, but "sefardí," referring to the language, and not the ethnicity, is usually favored by Spanish speakers, perhaps because of the negative connotations the word "ladino" has in Spanish.

as the beloved absent woman to whom his love poems are addressed. Ladino is the possible way for him to "set his tongue free" and escape the gag that prevents his speech or that of his country—the psalmist's "cleaved tongue," to which he alludes in the poem "comentario XXIII."[30]

Gelman is gradually attracted to Ladino through his own search for his roots and for those of the Spanish language, while living the experience of exile. But his encounter with Clarisse Nicoïdski's work provides him with a direct, even if textual, relationship with Ladino, a language that he does not speak. Coupled with his increased interest in Jewish sources and the history of Spanish, Gelman is captivated by the recuperative role Ladino plays in Nicoïdski's work. Her motifs, vocabulary, and metaphors will find their way in *Dibaxu*, where Gelman revisits several images and words present in his previous works and combines these with the treatment they receive in Clarisse Nicoïdski's poetry. In a way, Gelman provides here a synthesis of his work, marked by the experience of exile and the violence of the Argentine dictatorship, but also by his intense lyricism and experimentation with language. The recurrence of layering images in *Dibaxu* seems to be a poetic, metaphorical expression reproducing the process Gelman undertakes when reflecting upon the origins of the lyric, love, or the Spanish language. His investigation into what constitutes the self and, ultimately, into the Jewish strains that shape his identity, are also expressed in recurring images of sedimentation, of the physical stratification of geological layers. As in any archaeological dig, time is a crucial element. Hence, perhaps, the poet's insistence on spatializing time: it becomes more palpable, more concrete.

Indeed, "time" is one of the most recurrent themes in contemporary Ladino poetry, and central enough in Nicoïdski's work, reinforcing the recuperative role of the language that so much captivates Gelman. A quick examination of a poem from Nicoïdski's *Caminus di palavras* in relation to Gelman's *Dibaxu* reveals not only the role of time in their poetry but also the intertextual dialogue the latter establishes with the former.

---

30. "paladar \ al que mi lengua está pegada \ como lengua de vos" (palate \ to which my tongue is cleaved \ like a tongue of you). "comentario XXIII" is a poem that rewrites San Juan's "Llama de amor viva," in which Gelman (1982) introduces Psalm 137.

A la mañana dil lugar

a la mañana dil lugar
si caminarum lus dispartus
déxame tu boz
dami la color dil tiempu
para
trucar lus ojus
para pasar cerca dil ríu.
vieni il sol
si va un airi di luvia
cargada
como un velo di recordus
abáxati
toma la yerva in tus manus
estu es lu pasadu.

(In the morning of the place

in the morning of the place
the awakened departed
leave me your voice
give me the color of time
to
change the eyes
to pass by the river
the sun comes
and a hint of heavy rain
vanishes
like a veil of memories
kneel
take the grass in your hands
this is the past.)

"Time" in this poem by Clarisse Nicoïdski acquires a physical dimension: it has color, "dami la color dil tiempu" (give me the color of time), and the past is expressed as a palpable reality one can hold, "toma la yerva in tus manus /

estu es lu pasadu" (take the grass in your hands / this is the past). But the role
of time in this poem is also expressed in the atmospheric changes that occur,
in the end of the rain and the coming of the sun, even in the word "mañana,"
which points to the passage of night to morning, and which here is combined
with "place," "a la mañana dil lugar" (in the morning of the place). "Time" is
also present in the request "déxame tu boz" (leave me your voice), which implies
a future absence, and a possibility of "presence" through voice and memory, the
memory of a voice, the voice that brings memories. Memory, which is spelled out
in the poem, "como un velo di recordus" (like a veil of memories), is constructed
through orality—another one of the main themes of Ladino poetry today, as if
stressing the oral modeling of poetry as spoken word, the importance of oral
transmission for Sephardic culture, and of the oral genres, such as *cunsejas* and
baladas, in the preservation of the Ladino language itself. In this connection of
time, orality, and memory in the works of contemporary poets, Ladino takes on
a role of reconquering memory and vanquishing death; it becomes a safeguard
of the memory of a culture, and by this process it is itself safeguarded or "saved."

In Gelman's *Dibaxu* time is also one of the dominant themes. The word
"time" appears throughout the volume, often as a physical, spacialized, material
entity. Gelman speaks of "*la puarta dil tiempu*" / "la puerta del tiempo" (the door
of time), "*la caza dil tiempu*" / "la casa del tiempo" (the house of time), "*la manu
dil tiempu*" / "la mano del tiempo" (the hand of time), and "*pidazus di tiempu*"
/ "pedazos de tiempo" (pieces of time). He spatializes time even more radically
when he writes in poem XVIII, "*todu lu qui terra yaman / es tiempu*" / "todo lo
que llaman tierra / es tiempo" (all that is called land / is time); or when in poem
XIX the "here" of the poet is a "grain of sand" that is simultaneously space and a
minute in an hourglass:

> *quirinsioza:*
> *no ti vayas d'aquí*
> *di mi granu di arena*
> *desti minutu*

> querendona:
> no te vayas de aquí
> de mi grano de arena
> de este minuto

(my dear:
don't go away from here
from my grain of sand
from this minute)

Time is also thematized in the repeated use of words such as *"pasadu"* / "pasado" (past), and the unexpected employment of verb tenses (*"si sintirá in tu pasadu"* / se oirá en tu pasado / will be heard in your past), in which past and future
coexist, shaping a historical or historicized present that is also synchronic. This
simultaneity of past-present-future in Gelman establishes a difference between
his use of Ladino and that of other—and Sephardic—writers.

Language is the site par excellence of his reflection about time; it is there
that the different streams that compose time meet and engage each other. Ladino
and Spanish are in *Dibaxu* like the islands in poem IX:

tus islas comu lampas
cun una escuridad
yendu/iniendu
nil tiempu

tus islas como lámparas
con una oscuridad
yendo/viniendo
en el tiempo

(your islands like lamps
with a darkness
coming/going
in time)

It is in the layout proper, through the similarity between the Ladino and
the Spanish languages facing each other, that Gelman's project, more than
Nicoïdski's, also stresses time. The simultaneous presence of Ladino and Spanish underscores the changes of sounds, the passing of one vowel into another,
and the shifts of consonants, allowing for more than a glimpse of the passage of
time. The page itself becomes a moving screen showing, in a condensed format,

elements of two worlds—two voices that complement each other while pointing to reciprocal similarities and differences. The page turns into a physical materialization of passing time and the history of languages, as spelling and sounds form an instantaneous snapshot of this process, yet a dynamic one. And it is the tension provoked by the languages' relationship, in their simultaneous/synchronic textual presence, that constitutes the creative force, the one constructing meaning in Gelman's volume.

The dialogue between past and present that occurs on each page of *Dibaxu* and is consistent with Gelman's larger poetic project and aesthetic choices also relates to the continuity of poetry. The future of poetry lies in the constant interaction of past and present, in the recognition of that part of the past that is still operative in the present, as well as in the creative manipulation and incorporation of voices—the rewriting of texts that make up the sediments of poetry.

In Nicoïdski's work, orality is thematized by images of mouths, speaking bodies, birds that cry aloud. Likewise, orality has a crucial role in the structure of *Dibaxu*. Sounds, but especially voice and word/speech, are central themes, developed through different motifs: birds, leaves, trees. The volume opens with a mouth, site of word and voice, and origin of poetry.[31] Explicit references to "*cantu*/canto/song," "*boz*/voz/voice," "*dixera*/dijo/said" (and "*dizin*/dicen/say"), "*senti*/oye/hears," "*silenziu*/silencio/silence," "*gritus*/gritos/cries," "*avla*/palavra/word," and "*caya*/calla/quiets/silences" serve to emphasize the pervasive presence of orality throughout the book and in the poet's reflection about language and poetry. As in Nicoïdski's *Lus ojus, las manus, la boca*, the thematization of voice and speech is related to writing. Gelman's choice of Ladino as a language of writing is in large part guided by its oral qualities—the vowel sounds and the tenderness of its diminutives—and its role as a vernacular language and a language of affection. At the same time, the act of writing poetry in Ladino also reaffirms it as a literary language while contributing to its basic survival: with his text Gelman

---

31. il batideru di mis *bezus* / *quero dizer: il batideru di mis bezus* / *si sintirá in tu pasado* / *cun mí in tu vinu*/ el temblor de mis labios / quiero decir: el temblor de mis besos / se oirá en tu pasado / conmigo en tu vino/ *(the trembling of my kisses / i mean: the trembling of my kisses / will be heard in your past / with me in your wine)* (the trembling of my lips / i mean: the trembling of my kisses / will be heard in your past / with me in your wine).

pays tribute to the tradition of oral poetry in Ladino, while by writing in the language, he helps disseminate it and add to its life, to its afterlife.[32]

But Gelman does not write in Ladino because it is the language of his people, or his nation, or because it conjures up childhood memories. Ladino is for him an ideological and a stylistic choice. Exiled from his land and his language, Gelman turns to a language that counters the rules and authority of the state, while presenting the expressive, affective qualities he values. His choice of Ladino as his writing language brings Gelman one step closer to feminizing his language, when he seeks to embrace his loved ones, as the diminutives and affective words that characterize Ladino make it more intimate and endearing, even when it speaks of terrible things. By writing in Ladino he also comes one step closer to distancing himself from the traditional trappings of Argentine national identity. If he spoke of his love for the land, he also detached himself from the country's institutional apparatus. Gelman sees in Ladino the linguistic possibility of expressing the connection he establishes between the horrors done to the Jews and those done to the Argentines. Gelman uses Ladino to speak of his Argentine exile, to describe his own country. But also through the prism of his Argentine condition he better understands and comes closer to his own Jewish origins.

Through a gradual process, Gelman perceives that his exilic experience cannot be further contained by a territorial, national, and, by association with the regime it represents, oppressive language. Contrary to Gilles Deleuze and Félix Guattari's formula for minor literatures, which correlates oppositionality

32. There is an extensive tradition of written works in Ladino, comprising biblical, rabbinical, and secular texts (see Molho 1960; Lazar 1999). However, among them, the *romancero judeo-español* acquired unsurpassed fame. A vast body of oral literature, it has been transcribed and studied by numerous scholars, who acknowledge their own role in documenting and preserving Sephardic traditional narrative poetry. Samuel Armistead writes about his and his colleague's investigation on Sephardic balladry: "This research has a single objective: to save from oblivion the last living echos of those multisecular, medieval voices, which today are in immediate danger of disappearing forever" (1978, 40). Armistead also touches upon a subject that is pertinent to Ladino and its relation between oral and written text, the "concept of oral literature." He writes that "The very concept of oral literature has been—and continues to be—rather difficult to comprehend for some of us who are part of now basically literate cultures" (45).

and deterritorialization only with minor writing in a major language,[33] in his revolutionary project Gelman abandons his native Spanish (Castellano) and radically assumes a new language. To write his exile and express his deterritorialized, decentered identity, Gelman instead writes in a minor language, one of a culture created "without a State behind it to support or foment this process" (Montanaro and Ture 1998, 44). In order to speak, fighting back the imposed "cleaved tongue," Gelman forges a new poetic voice in Ladino. The Sephardic language provides Gelman with the means not only to speak of his suffering in exile, but also productively to regain a powerful position, finding a singing, poetic voice. It is indeed through Ladino that, amid all the horror, he can sing again and share a renewed optimism.

Despite the oft announced demise of Ladino, this Sephardic language has seen a revival in the past years, with a growing number of university classes devoted to it all over the world, as well as an explosion of books and music CDs that make use of it. This increased activity, which cannot replace the fundamental role Ladino had in the lives of organic communities now disappeared, at least prevents the total erasure of the language and maintains it as a cultural language, in which it is still possible to sing and write poetry. It also provokes what Ken Ellingwood (2004) termed "an incongruity": "[Ladino] is surging even as it is fading." Surprising as it is, more than fifty years after the death of most of its speakers, this renewed enthusiasm and productivity in Ladino is in sync with a stage in identity politics when "the celebration of differences" is valued, and several minority communities, for social and economic reasons, feel now integrated to their societies and comfortable accepting and even flaunting their ethnic and cultural specificities.

33. In chapter 3 of *Kafka: Toward a Minor Literature* (1986), Deleuze and Guattari give a positive value to "minor," equating it with "oppositional" and "revolutionary" (26). To them, in a "minor literature," "language is affected with a high coefficient of deterritorialization" (16). They also claim that "a minor literature doesn't come from a minor language; it is rather that which a minority constructs within a major language" (16). In so doing they valorize a monolingual production, which does not take into account the multilingualism of minority cultures, and, by favoring only the major, even if unwillingly, Deleuze and Guattari end up reproducing a Eurocentric and colonialist stance. See Kronfeld (1996) and Balbuena (2003), "Introduction."

Ladino, perhaps because of its similarities to Spanish and Portuguese, has found fertile ground in Latin America and has enjoyed something of a renaissance on the continent. Sephardic artists turn to the collection of Ladino sayings and songs as a gateway to their own culture, which is often only vestigial (Brazilian Fortuna, for example), or use the language as a vehicle to express their childhood memories and maintain the legacy of their families, thus affirming their identity and links to the great Sephardic "nation" (Argentine Matilde Gini de Barnatán[34] and Mexican Rosa Nissán, among others). Some combine that with the discovery of Ladino's poetic properties and choose it as a language of creation (Argentine Beatriz Mazliah, for instance).

Ashkenazi artists have a different relationship with the language. Ladino can serve as an element in the representation of "Sepharad"—in the mythic recreation of the historical past in which some Jewish authors engage as a means to claim a presence in the continent and a part in the national narrative (Brazilian Moacyr Scliar, for example). On the other hand, Ladino can play the opposite role: it can be a poetic device to detach oneself from a limited national identity and instead privilege a diasporic positioning. In the case of Argentine Juan Gelman, Ladino irrupts as a poetic strategy to build an exilic discourse that enhances its essential ambiguity when it calls into question notions of "inside" and "outside," "original" and "translation," "homeland" and "diaspora." Written in the solitude of exile, without a community supporting it, Gelman's *Dibaxu* engages in issues such as the unreliability of origins, the unstable distinction between original and translation, and the instability of ethnic and linguistic identity *tout court*, while it breaks the monoglossia of the Argentine national idiom and begins a heteroglossic poetics in Ladino and Castellano.

---

34. "El djudeo-espanyol fue la lingua ke sintio de kriatura i, enmientres ke la esckrive i avla, esta arrebiviendo el mundo ke la enturava, los kantes kon los kualos la endurmesieron, i sus seres keridos estan ansi kaminando kon eya kada dia" (Judeo-Spanish was the language she heard as a child, and when she writes in it or speaks it, she is reliving the world that used to surround her, the songs with which she fell asleep, and her loved ones walk alongside her every day). (Santa Puche 1999, 61).

10

A Taste of *Sepharad* from the Mexican Suburbs

Rosa Nissán's Stylized Ladino in
Novia que te vea *and* Hisho que te nazca

YAEL HALEVI-WISE

When Rosa Nissán's fictional autobiography *Novia que te vea* burst onto the Mexican literary scene in 1992, followed by its sequel *Hisho que te nazca* (1996), it was immediately recognized as a groundbreaking introduction of the Sephardic voice into Mexican literature, and, more importantly, as an unusual interweaving of a historically marked Judeo-Spanish dialect into a modern Spanish narrative. Encouraged by the renowned novelist and journalist Elena Poniatowska, and entering the literary scene at a time when women writers, many of them Jewish, began to contribute in larger numbers to Mexican letters, Nissán's deliberate juxtaposition of the quaint melody of the Ladino language and the chatty contemporary vernacular of a feminist bildungsroman struck her readers as an extraordinarily fresh and original technique.

In a suggestive metafictional scene that takes place in *Hisho que te nazca*, Oshinica, the novel's protagonist, brings an autobiographical text to a creative writing workshop led by Poniatowska. As she finishes reading, her peers convey

Parts of this essay appeared in *Hispania* in 1998 under the title, "Puente entre naciones: Idioma e identidad sefardí en *Novia que te vea* e *Hisho que te nazca* de Rosa Nissán." *Hispania* 81, no. 2 (May): 269–77. I wish to thank Victoria Wolff and Brett Hooton for their valuable assistance in updating and translating this article, and to acknowledge the Memorial Foundation for Jewish Culture and the Social Sciences and Humanities Council of Canada for their support of this project.

their delight in the Ladino expressions that fill Oshinica's story.[1] Realizing that the mixture of old and new pleases her audience, she decides, "For the next meeting I'll compose something with lots of little words in *yudesmo*, so they'll have a good time."[2] Nissán's original sentence itself—"La próxima clase voy a escribir algo y le *vo* a meter muchas *palabricas* en *yudesmo* para que se divier-tan"—demonstrates how her narrative style complicates conventional ideas of language (1996, 138–39). Its modern Spanish is liberally sprinkled with Ladino: *vo* instead of the modern *voy*, *palabricas* instead of *palabras*, *yudesmo* instead of *Judeo-Español*.

While Nissán's playful linguistic hybridity adds a charming ethnic ring to her narrative, its real significance lies in the embodiment of the protagonist's (and author's) Sephardic heritage as a bridge between the past and the present, with complex roots in medieval Spain through the experiences of a young woman in modern-day Mexico. Not only does Nissán's work usher in an autobiographical Sephardic perspective that had never been presented in Mexican letters, but also the very texture of her language evokes a sense of historical depth that creates a healing link between disparate nations and generations. Although history itself is rarely discussed in these novels, Nissán's dual linguistic register (Ladino/modern Spanish) evokes a conflicted Judeo-Spanish past that transcends the confines of Oshinica's individual saga. It reminds us of both the encounter between Old and New Worlds and the expulsion of the Jews from Spain, which were simultaneously commemorated during the 1992 quincentennial ceremonies that coincided with the publication of Nissán's first novel. Nissán's linguistic hybridity, along with the historical implications of its authentic Sephardic background, distinguishes her writing from Jewish literary productions that draw on an Eastern-European Yiddish heritage, as well as from those that "borrow" a

1. Because Nissán refers to her ancestral language as "Ladino," I have decided to maintain her terminology in this article. Nevertheless, academically, it is more common to refer to this language as Judeo-Spanish. The Sephardic language is also known as *judesmo*, *spanyolit*, *muestro espanyol*, *espanyolico* and other variants of these terms. See note 14 for a brief explanation of the language's history.

2. Unless otherwise noted, the English translations are mine. Given the focus of this paper, I will also include the original citations whenever relevant, italicizing Ladino terms to point them out.

Judeo-Spanish heritage to create strategic links between an Iberian past and a contemporary Jewish presence in Latin America.[3]

The importance of Ladino in Nissán's novels cannot be over-emphasized, especially after the translation of *Novia que te vea* and *Hisho que te nazca* into English (2002). Dick Gerdes's translation, commissioned by Ilan Stavans for the prestigious Jewish Latin America Series, unites the two books into a single volume, as Nissán originally intended, though when the first part was ready, Poniatowska encouraged the aspiring writer to publish it separately. A reference to this suggestion appears near the end of *Hisho que te nazca* when the mentor advises her protégé to "Divide your novel right here, so that Oshinica's married life can appear later" (285).[4] The single-volume version recuperates a sense of continuity that at the same time highlights the thematic and stylistic differences between the two parts, which differ in two main points: thematically, through the portrayals of childhood in *Novia que te vea* and maturity in *Hisho que te nasca*, and stylistically, through the former's use of a child narrator and the latter's metafictional references to the process of producing the text that the audience is simultaneously reading.

Yet in spite of these benefits, the English version considerably limits the ability of a non-Spanish-speaking audience to understand and appreciate Nissán's key use of Ladino. Indeed, Stavans's introduction to the volume opens with an admission that the interspersed Ladino phrases, which add such verve and vivacity to the original text, become flat and mundane in translation (2002, xi). The main purpose of this chapter, then, is to clarify and illuminate for an English audience what makes Nissán's texts unique as a stylized linguistic bridge between nations and generations across a wide Judeo-Spanish historical experience culminating in modern Mexico.

Although Jewish literature in Mexico can be traced back to the Spanish colonial period, a substantial body of work did not emerge until the twentieth century, when mass immigration of Ashkanazi Jews fleeing the Russian Revolution

---

3. On the strategic deployment of Sephardic motifs in Latin American literature, see Aizenberg (1992; 2002, 49–67) as well as Senkman (1983). For an analysis of the representation of Spanish-Jewish history in the modern literary imagination from the eighteenth century to the present, see Halevi-Wise (2012).

4. Nissán details this process in her interview with Emily Hind (2003, 138).

and World War I created a local tradition of Mexican Yiddish literature in the 1920s (Lockhart 1997, 159). However, it was especially when the children of these immigrants began to write in Spanish in the 1970s that Jewish Mexican literature started to attract readers outside the Jewish community and beyond the borders of Mexico. As evinced by numerous studies comparing her with other Mexican, Latin American, and Sephardic authors, Nissán's work forms part of an extraordinary boom in ethnic-oriented and autobiographical fiction by women.[5] According to Ilan Stavans's literary history of Mexican Jewish writing, Nissán and such writers as Gloria Gervitz and Sara Levi-Calderón belong to a second literary generation building on the foundations laid by Margo Glantz, Angelina Muñiz-Huberman, and Esther Seligson (1999, 12–13). Nissán's work also overlaps with what Stavans regards as a third generation of Mexican Jewish writers, spearheaded by Sabina Berman, Sara Sefchovich, Ethel Krauze, and Miriam Moscona.[6]

Among modern Jewish novels written in Mexico, it was Glantz who introduced the autobiographical sensibility that soon became an extraordinarily popular literary form.[7] After the appearance of her *Genealogies* (1981), other Mexican Jewish authors such as Berman, Levi-Calderón, and Nissán turned to fictionalized autobiographies as a way of expressing their own multivalenced Jewish, Mexican, and female sense of identity. The result is a strongly feminist point of view that challenges conventional attitudes toward gender within both Mexican society and Jewish culture. After Nissán introduced a Sephardic perspective into this milieu, other Sephardic Mexican women, notably Vicky Nizri with *Vida Propria* (2000), began to create autobiographical works that showcase this ethnic

5. Emphasizing its autobiographic and Sephardic dimensions, Nissán's work has been compared at length to that of other contemporary Mexican women writers, such as Sabina Berman, (Lockhart 1997); Elena Poniatowska and Silvia Molina (Gardner 2003); Angelina Muñiz-Huberman and Sara Levi Calderón (Loyola 2004). Other studies have placed Nissán within the wider context of contemporary Latin American Jewish writers, such as Alicia Steimberg from Argentina (Schneider 1999) and Teresa Porzecanski from Uruguay (Scott 1998). Tracing an even wider scope, Jonathan Schorsch (2007) situates Nissán's work within an international proliferation of Sephardic autobiographies at the end of the twentieth century.

6. An excellent discussion of contemporary feminist Mexican writing can be found in Castillo (1992); see also Ibsen (1997) and Valdés (1998).

7. For more on Glantz's contributions to Mexican literature, see Cortina (2000, 35–60); Glickman and DiAntonio (1993, 19); and Stavans (1999, 9).

dimension. In Nissán's case, the Sephardic dimension enriches and complicates her artistic expression, conveying the worldview of a minority within a minority.

Rosa Nissán's multivalenced identity as a Sephardic-Mexican-female author is anchored principally in her special use of the Ladino language, which differentiates her from Ashkenazi and Middle Eastern coreligionists as well as from the Christian Spanish speakers who surround her in Mexico. The degree of her familiarity with the ancestral language also constitutes, as we shall see, an additional barrier between the generation that immigrated to the New World and those who, like herself, were born there.[8] But by rendering testimony to an almost extinct language, Nissán's novels also create a symbolic bridge between the Spain that in 1492 expelled its Jews and conquered Mexico and the Jews who, five hundred years later, come to find a new home in modern Mexico. Nissán's use of Ladino in *Novia que te vea* (1992) and *Hisho que te nazca* (1996) is, therefore, much more than a little folkloric spice so that her audience will have a good time, "para que se diviertan." It is rather a key ingredient in the complex historical and sociological identity of Oshinica, the protagonist, who reflects on her childhood, adolescence, motherhood, and independence in the suburbs of Mexico City.

Unfortunately, the translation of Nissán's novels erases her wonderful use of Mexican slang along with the bilingual toggling between Ladino and modern Spanish. As Lockhart points out, "Oshinica's social heteroglossia, a literary refraction of Nissán's own, is evident in the two different types of social language she manipulates." In the first volume, her vocabulary is typical of Mexican youth in her time, filled with slang terms such as *retefeo, hijoles,* and *qué padres* (Lockhart 1997, 168). This popular usage tends to be translated literally in the English version, losing the author's implied commentary on race and social status. It is also worth noting that while the original edition of *Novia que te vea* presents a uniform text, from a visual point of view, the sequel *Hisho que te nazca* exhibits a keener awareness of the importance of its Ladino terms by italicizing them all.

---

8. A useful summary of the sociohistorical background of the modern Sephardic presence in Mexico City is given by Medina (2000).

While Nissán's work presents a unique set of problems for the translator, Spanish-speaking audiences, especially those located outside of Mexico, face their own challenges when reading these novels. A contemporary Argentinean or Chicana, for example, would presumably not have the same understanding of Nissán's discourse, because they might not necessarily differentiate between her Jewish-Mexican slang, Capitalino slang (specific to Mexico's capital), the 1950s slang of Nissán's childhood, and the 1960s slang of her adolescence, though the historical significance of the Ladino language tying it all together would be evident. When fully understood, the heteroglossic vitality of these novels paints a fresh portrait of Mexico City's diversity, re-creating the sense of separate neighborhoods that characterized this city before it became the busier metropolis it is today. "The cadence of speech is captured astonishingly well," notes Stavans, "and equally astonishing and vivid, too, are the various Spanish dialects recorded in the novel, each used by a different type of people" (2002, xiv). Lockhart extends this idea further, noting that Nissán's texts constitute "a valuable socio-historic record" of Jewish life in the capital during the 1950s and 1960s (1997, 164). These two scholars provide testimony that, while Nissán's use of language may seem quaint, it is in fact an integral and deliberate component of her writing.

Yet the success of Nissán's contribution to Mexican literature, which led to her work's translation as well as its transportation to the big screen, has paradoxically obscured her wonderful integration of cultural-linguistic registers, and especially her use of Ladino, which made her work stand out in the first place. The most striking example of a depreciation of Nissán's original text is Guita Schyfter's cinematic version of *Novia que te vea* (1993). In this feature, the filmmaker grafts onto Nissán's story a parallel plotline about an Ashkenazi girl who marries a Christian Mexican youth. While the film maintains some of the novel's ethnic flavor, and does indeed employ Ladino as the language spoken by Oshinica's relatives, it neglects all aspects of Nissán's text that do not contribute to Schyfter's supplementary storyline. The filmmaker acknowledges that the majority of her screenplay was written before she read Nissán's novel, and that she adapted elements and episodes from Nissán's text to her own (Grandis and Mennell 2003). However, by repeating Nissán's title (initially with the author's blessing), Schyfter sought to capitalize on the novel's best-selling success. Indeed, although the film brought even more attention to Nissán's work, its extreme departure from the original text forced the novelist to disassociate herself from the filmmaker.[9]

Even more problematic, however, is the confusion that the film's plotline has created among scholars interested in Nissán's novels. The film received considerable attention in its own right,[10] and this attention has in turn contributed to blurring the differences between Nissán's text and Schyfter's screenplay. As a result, there is now a need to strip away some misleading and contradictory readings of Nissán's original work so that readers can again appreciate her contribution to Mexican fiction through the lens of the Sephardic experience and the use of Ladino with its attendant historical implications.

During the Middle Ages, and until the seventeenth century, Sephardic Jews constituted a majority among Jews. However, beginning with the emancipation of Central European Jewry, through the breakdown of the Ottoman Empire, and then the Holocaust, their population and importance weakened (Zimmels 1976, 75–76). Presently, of the tens of thousands of Jews who still speak Ladino throughout the world, few are under sixty years of age and none are monolingual (Lazar 1972, 29). Today, Ladino is spoken at home and among old friends in the synagogue, heard on an infrequent radio program, or perhaps read in an ethnic newspaper.[11] Yet outside of the home, the contemporary Ladino speaker generally communicates in the language of the country where he or she lives and must master at least one additional language (Sephiha 1986, 10). This eclectic mix of cultural registers is not itself new; indeed, it has characterized the Judeo-Spanish experience throughout the course of its history as Hebrew, Greek, Turkish, Arabic,

9. Rosa Nissán, personal interview, Mexico City, July 1997.

10. See, for example, Mennell (2000) and Hershfiel (1997).

11. Although several new Sephardic publications have appeared in recent years in the United States, Israel, Latin America, and France, very few of the multitude of Ladino newspapers and magazines that were launched during the nineteenth century survived the Holocaust. A bibliographic summary of previous journalistic production in Ladino can be found in Gaon (1965). With respect to a *bellelettrista* production in Ladino, Elena Romero affirms that "from the twentieth century, an uninterrupted decline in Judeo-Spanish literature set in" (1992, 459). In opposition to this pessimistic appraisal of current literary Sephardism, various sources predict that at least some type of *resefardización* or *neosefardismo* will appear in Latin America. Edna Aizenberg presents a summary of the origins and development of the neo-*sefardización* concept in her article, "Sephardim and Neo-Sephardim in Latin-American Literature" (1979–82). See also chapter 9 in this volume.

French, Portuguese, and Italian terms were incorporated into the medieval Castilian dialects that form the foundation of this language. Nissán's work reflects not only a multilingualism that was once typical to the diasporic Jew, but also a more recent syncretism of Ladino with modern Spanish. This metamorphosis represents an additional phase in the development of a language whose origin and very reason for being are situated at the intersection of languages and cultures.

The linguistic and cultural influences that surround Ladino speakers tend to infiltrate their ethnic tongue, transforming it constantly. In Nissán's two novels, even the character most strongly identified with Sephardic culture, Oshinica's mother, speaks a Ladino mixed with the Turkish from her childhood and influenced by the modern Spanish she learned in Mexico.[12] As these novels indeed demonstrate, the cultural threat to a Ladino speaker who settles in a Hispanic environment is especially dire, for although one might assume that the Ladino spoken by a Latin American Sephardic Jew would be more stable because it is reinforced by the contemporary Spanish that surrounds it, linguistic assimilation among Ladino-speaking Jews in Spanish-speaking countries tends to be *greater* and swifter than that of Sephardic Jews in non-Hispanic environments (Marcus 1965, 75).[13] Modern Spanish apparently absorbs and modernizes the older vernacular, eroding it to a greater extent.

In reality, the very notion of a "pure" Ladino is misleading, as this language was originally sanctioned to facilitate the comprehension of religious texts written in Hebrew or Aramaic for Jews who lived in Spain under Muslim and Christian rule. Only after the group's expulsion from Spain did the language become a specifically Jewish language.[14] But because it was never subjected to strict grammatical and orthographic rules, Ladino reflects the temporal and geographical

12. The influence of Turkish on Ladino has been studied by Benbassat (1987) and Danon (1913).

13. On the diminishing demographics of Ladino speakers see also Bunis (1981, 412–14) and Harris (1994).

14. Although before 1492 Jews from Spain integrated many Hebrew words and expressions into their respective Iberian dialects, it is now generally accepted that in medieval Spain, Jews communicated in the vernacular languages of their Catholic neighbors, even among themselves. Therefore, Ladino, as a specifically Jewish language, developed only after their expulsion from Spain (Lazar 1972, 28; Sephiha 1986, 11; Harris 1994, 53–65).

vicissitudes of the Sephardic diaspora. The word Ladino, for example, derives from "latino," a term that was applied to Moors or Jews who spoke a Romance language in medieval Spain.[15] In their daily lives, Spanish Jews communicated in local dialects, utilizing, when necessary, religious and cultural expressions that they had preserved in spite of having lost Israel, their original homeland. When the Sephardic Jews were exiled from Spain as well, they continued to maintain the fifteenth-century Castilian dialects current at the time of their departure, which then became a distinct Judeo-Spanish dialect or *judezmo: jud* from the Hebrew *yehudi* conjugated with *ezmo*, a Spanish grammatical suffix. This Sephardic language, which initially served to fill a void left by the loss of an independent Zion, became after the expulsion from Spain a reminder of the loss of the second homeland.[16] As a result, these twice-exiled Jews carry an intricate set of identities distilled into the history of their language.

In an illuminating way, Ladino usage is similar to the archaic usages of Spanish found even today among some indigenous Mexicans, whose ancestors had learned Spanish from the conquistadors, but whose isolation prevented that language from developing in the same manner as it did in other regions of Mexico. Illustrating this point, Oshinica recounts the astonishment of a waiter at a restaurant who realizes that Sephardic Jews recently arrived from Turkey speak just like "Indians" ("Hablan como inditos") (Nissán 1996, 168).

For Nissán's new and growing English audience, the difference between Ladino and modern Spanish could be compared to the distance between Shakespearean and contemporary English, especially if we also take into account differences in pronunciation. Perhaps one way that a translation might preserve the historicized layering of Nissán's language would be to employ Shakespearean English where Nissán uses Ladino, though this solution still lacks a historical link to the experience of the Jews from Spain, and therefore does not drive home the importance of the group's resettlement in modern Hispanic lands after an

---

15. In Spain during the Middle Ages the word "Ladino" referred to romance languages (Latin and its derivatives, for example, Castilian) as opposed to Arabic (see *Diccionario crítico etimológico castellano e hispánico*). Today, in some Latin American countries such as Guatemala, this designation is still used by indigenous peoples to refer to Spanish speakers.

16. Greatly moved by his discovery of this process, and hoping to capitalize on it, the philosemitic Spanish senator Angel Pulido romanticized it in his *Españoles sin patria y la raza sefardí* (1905).

intervening period of five hundred years. Such a proposal also makes it harder to preserve the chatty tone of Oshinica's discourse.

In Nissán's novels, Oshinica, a Sephardic Jew born in Mexico to a Turkish mother and a Persian father, must learn to differentiate among her multiple identities in order to balance conflicting cultural elements in her life. But simply noting the various components of Oshinica's ethnicity (Jewish, Sephardic, Mexican, Turkish, Persian) does not capture the full richness of her roots. Although her paternal grandparents hail from Iran, Oshinica's father was born in Israel, or rather Palestine as it was called under Ottoman rule. Oshinica's parents and grandparents immigrate to Mexico from Turkey and the Middle East after World War I, in the wake of the demographic upheavals that resulted from the collapse of the Ottoman Empire, under whose domain lived the largest number of Sephardic Jews (Beinart 1970; Díaz-Mas 1986, 232–33).[17]

This complex background does not prevent Oshinica from considering herself Mexican. Indeed, she belongs to a generation of Jews born in Mexico who fully identify themselves with this country. Even though her parents initially enroll her in a Catholic school, presuming that she will not participate in the Christian prayers, Oshinica chooses to pray with the nuns—otherwise "they will wonder why I'm leaving the room" (Nissán 1992, 10–11), and in any case, she enjoys it. The result is that during part of her childhood, Oshinica functions as a crypto-Christian, happy that at least the Ten Commandments remain the same for both Jews and Christians. Ironically, this crypto-Christianity represents an inversion of historical events in Spain when, during the Inquisition, thousands of Jews feigned conversion to Catholicism while continuing to practice Judaism in secret.[18]

Although Oshinica states with relief that, "fortunately you can't notice so easily who is Jewish," her ancestry is far from an enigma (Nissán 1992, 13–14). When she accidentally steps on a classmate's sand castle, Oshinica's companions descend upon her, calling her a Jew and accusing her of killing Christ (10). Soon after this incident, Oshinica's parents transfer her to a Jewish school, which

17. Yosef Kaplan (1992) describes the migratory flows of Sephardic Jews to the New World; see also Muñiz-Huberman (1989, 261–63, 265–67).

18. On representations of crypto-Judaism and Marranism in the modern literary imagination, see Halevi-Wise (2012, 22–23, 27–29).

according to Renée Scott is an attempt to resolve "the problem of discrimination by marginalizing themselves from Mexican society" (1995, 606). However, as Nissán repeatedly demonstrates, segregation is never impermeable. In fact, when she repeatedly encounters anti-Semitic stereotypes after having grown more comfortable with her own identity, Oshinica is able to respond, "I am Jewish, but what you say about killing Christ isn't true. The Romans did it, and it was a long time ago, anyway" (1992, 46). Nissán's technique for combating such bigotry is worth noting. She tends to present these scenes of crude anti-Semitism with humor,[19] and eventually her protagonist concludes, flippantly, that "it's hard to be a Jew, at least where one's a minority" (1996, 271).

Once married, Oshinica chooses to live in a building rented principally by Mexican Jews from a variety of backgrounds. Though they share a religious affiliation, they do not follow the same customs and linguistic mannerisms. Nonetheless, there is a mutual sense of common responsibility, best exemplified when Oshinica's grandparents arrive in Mexico and another Jew takes them into his home for an entire month without asking where they are from or what language they speak (1992, 81).[20]

In general, Oshinica cultivates relationships with Ashkenazim and Middle Eastern Jews; despite the conflicts occasionally punctuating her school days, she especially relishes her interactions with Gentile Mexicans. Still, she develops a self-protective mechanism that deliberately bolsters her ethnic identity, though at times she seeks to escape from that, too. The best example of this self-alienation appears when she flaunts her Sephardic nickname in social settings outside of her autochthonous community. Rather than introducing herself as Eugenia, her official Mexican name, she uses Oshinica, which inevitably invites the question, "Are you Mexican?" This allows her to clarify, "My parents aren't. But I am. I was born here" (1992, 97). In this manner, Oshinica creates a cultural barrier, which she must consciously and continuously cross. As Elizabeth Coonrod Martínez notes, "Nissan has shown the *Sefardita* to be second-generation Mexican, Jewish, and speaker of both modern Spanish and archaic Ladino . . . therefore a

---

19. César Ferreira observes that Nissán's humor balances the young narrator's innocence and sentimentality (1998–99, 66).

20. See Zimmels (1976) for an analysis of the historical relationship between these groups.

'mediator' and 'creator' of culture" (2004, 115). In other words, the author creates a character who educates the novel's audience about Sephardic culture, using it as a foundation for a compelling narrative about modern Mexico.

On the other hand, Oshinica's Sephardic heritage limits her social and professional opportunities to a greater extent than does her minority status as a Jew within a predominantly Catholic society. Although she longs to study, work, and travel, her family and its Sephardic community push her toward marriage. Sephardic bachelors are encouraged to pursue a career and are sometimes permitted to travel, but the young women of Oshinica's generation can aspire only to work as secretaries or cashiers in order to earn a little money before getting married. Upon finishing high school, Oshinica dreams of visiting Israel like her Ashkenazi friends. But her parents inform her bluntly that "a woman leaves her home only with her husband; with him you'll go wherever you want!" (1992, 70).

Oshinica characterizes the Ashkenazim according to the language they speak, calling them "Jews from the Yiddish neighborhood," instead of categorizing them according to the geographical regions from which they migrated, as customary (1992, 69). To convey to a Catholic friend the differences between Jewish ethnicities, Oshinica divides the Jews of Mexico City into three communities, highlighting education and mother tongue as principal markers of identity:

[I]n the Sephardic school half of the students are from the [Judeo] Arab community. . . .

They usually pull out their girls right after sixth grade just to help their mothers at home, and their boys right after secondary school, to work. The Turkish girls like me [and here Oshinica identifies herself with her mother] . . . used to all go to the same temple, and we were all friends *because our mothers speak Ladino and they think alike:* they give us the same permissions and non permissions. The *Yiddish* girls are stuck up . . . but I'm jealous because they get to study. . . . And they're allowed to go out with guys. Their mothers couldn't care less if they get a bad reputation. They're kind of loose girls; so the Sephardic guys go out with them a while, but when it comes to marriage, they choose one of us, rather than a *Yiddishe,* as they say. (100–101)[21]

---

21. "[E]n el colegio Sefardí, la mitad de los alumnos son de la colonia árabe. . . . Rara es la mujer que no sacan después de sexto sólo para que ayude a su mamá en la casa, y a la mayoría de

In Nissán's novels, a mixed marriage occurs between a Catholic woman and a Jewish man, but no union takes place between Ashkenazim and Sephardim (1992, 47). Given that secularization and mutual dealings between these two communities has become increasingly common and acceptable throughout the twentieth century, this is an interesting omission from a sociological perspective (Zimmels 1976, 74–75). But even Oshinica's own marriage within the wider Sephardic group is considered somewhat exogamous, though with the exception of Oshinica's paternal grandparents, all of the principal marriages in these works do seem to occur between Sephardic and Middle Eastern Jews. As previously noted, Oshinica's mother comes from Turkey while her father's family emigrated from Iran via Palestine. Oshinica herself marries a young man whose mother is Syrian and whose father is Sephardic. And although Nissán continually illustrates and endorses a complex mix between the various communities, she is always careful to distinguish among them. Even within the Sephardic community, those who speak Ladino are differentiated from the Middle Eastern Jews who do not. Oshinica and her peers are keenly aware of these distinctions, while their Ashkenazi counterparts tend to consider the entire group to be Sephardic because they follow liturgical customs that differentiate them from Ashkenazim at large.[22] This nuanced ethnic awareness is offered also to Nissán's Gentile readers, who from a distance might have viewed the entire Jewish community as a cohesive entity.

As the above passages demonstrates, Oshinica envies the freedom enjoyed by the young women of Mexico City's Ashkenazi community and flees the restrictions and lack of decorum that she observes in the youth of the Middle Eastern group. Having witnessed her aunt's humiliation after the collapse of a highly anticipated engagement to an "Arab Jew," Oshinica decides that she will never

---

los niños después de la secundaria, a trabajar. Las turcas . . . íbamos al mismo templo, y éramos amigas *porque nuestras madres hablan en ladino y piensan igualito:* nos dan los mismos permisos y no permisos. Estas cuatas son *idish* y se creen mucho . . . pero lo que me da envidia es que las dejen estudiar más . . . Y las dejan tener novios; a sus mamás no les importa si se queman. Pero son más locas; por eso los sefarditas salen con ellas, pero a la hora de casarse prefieren una de las nuestras que una *idishá*, así dicen" (100–101; my emphasis).

22. An excellent article on the differences between Sephardic Jews and Jews from North Africa is by Jacob Barnai (1992). Díaz-Mas explains this difference briefly (1986, 72–73). See also Bensoussan (1993).

get involved with a member of this group (Nissán 1992, 26–27). Nonetheless, she eventually marries Lalo, whom she classifies as "Arab," though his father is Sephardic and his mother is a Syrian Jew. Here it is evident that the mother considers herself of higher status because of her Syrian background. Upon meeting Oshinica, the relatives of the future mother-in-law immediately ask whether the bride is "jálabi or shami," that is, from the Syrian city of Aleppo or Damascus. A comical silence descends when the mother-in-law answers that Oshinica is just Turkish (174). Among her in-laws, then, Oshinica is nobody; she lacks status and her history is unknown.[23]

By contrast, when the elder Turkish women ask, "Sweetheart, whose are you?" ("¿Ishica, de quién sos?"), Oshinica courteously responds that she is the daughter of Sarica, the one from "Estambul." Here the recognition is strident, "Of course I know her! We were neighbors with your grandma in Istanbul; we were brought up together, your uncle was a tailor; she was ye' small, I'm already sick, before you know it, you get old. Give her my regards, sweetie . . ." ("¡[C]laro que la conozco!, me *acodro* que éramos *vicinos* con tu abuelita en *Estambul, mos criímos yuntas,* tu tío laboraba *fraguas,* ella era *chiquitica,* yo ya estoy *jasina,* cuando *avoltas* la cara, ya te hiciste *viesha.* Salúdamela, chula . . .") (38). Here, the Ladino language represents a primary means of identification between members of this Sephardic group. It is assumed that Oshinica, the descendent of her Ladino-speaking mother, knows the ethnic language.

Although Ladino figures so prominently in Oshinica's sense of identity, and in Nissán's texts, in *Novia que te vea* and *Hisho que te nazca* the protagonist/ narrator rarely speaks this language herself. The author reserves its use for Oshinica's mother, maternal aunt, and the mother's friends, chiefly Rashel la Puntuda, whose gastronomic whims are accompanied by an incessant chatter in a Mexicanized Ladino. Furthermore, the only allusion to a literary Ladino occurs when Oshinica's aunt gives her a traditional *romancero,* a book of medieval ballads.[24] Perhaps because Oshinica's mother and her circle are so closely identified with

23. For a description of various Syrian communities in Mexico, see Hamui de Halabe (1989 and 1999) and chapter 6 in this volume.

24. Armistead and Silverman's classic 1982 study sheds light on these medieval ballads as an expression of Sephardic culture in Spain and emphasizes their influence on Spanish literature at large.

the language, the father is rarely quoted speaking Ladino, though it is mentioned that he learned this language from his wife. In the home of Oshinica's paternal grandparents, Persian is spoken, laced with Hebrew for biblical citations and religious events (1992, 16). In one salient instance, Nissán's kaleidoscopic discourse includes the Hebrew idiom of a popular Jewish youth group, as Oshinica reports, "Andrés's friend from the *Shomer* came to my house with her *tilvoshet,* her *anivah* and a big smile" (123).[25]

The only occasion in which Lalo, Oshinica's husband, appears speaking Ladino (without any explanation of how he learned it) coincides with his hysterical attempts to extinguish his wife's artistic aspirations. Oshinica has been busy studying, writing and taking photographs, and Lalo feels that these creative pursuits are causing her to neglect her responsibilities as a housewife. Here, the use of Ladino marks a conflict between traditional expectations and modern options: "Why are you wasting your time instead of organizing these closets a little better before they fall apart, for God's sake! Why don't you sew a little? What's this mess of clothing over here? A man wants an organized wife in his house." ("¡*Cuálo* haces ahí *pedriendo* el tiempo en lugar de arreglar un poco más esos clósets que se están *caiendo,* señor! De que no *cuses* un poco, ¿qué es esta *angusina* de tiradero de ropa, un hombre *quere* en su *caza* una *musher nicocherá?*") (Nissán 1996, 80).

Similarly, when the elder Sephardic women try to keep the younger generation in line, they employ choice Ladino expressions that encapsulate their community's expectations. The figure of Señora Magrisó personifies this generational influence. Each Saturday on the stairs of the synagogue, she asks Oshinica about her family, and before parting ways, she wishes her "todo lo bueno" and "mazal bueno," good luck. However, her blessings are not as innocuous as they may seem, for in this cultural context, good luck simply means a good marriage— though the opposite condition of a *desmazalada* (constructed from the Hebrew *mazal,* luck, and the negative Spanish prefix, *des*) may encompass all kinds of misfortunes, from becoming an invalid to having only daughters. Therefore,

---

25. "Vino una amiga de Andrés de la *Shomer* a mi casa, llegó con su *tilvoshet* puesto, su *anivá* y una gran sonrisa," (123; my emphasis).

Señora Magrisó's well-wishes invoke the community's belief that a young woman faces no worse fate than spinsterhood and bareness. More than anything, the Sephardic tribe yearns to see its daughters dressed as brides: "¡Novia que te vea!" they exclaim, "as a bride may I see you!" Remarkably, they never say, "Novia que te *veas*," (may you see *yourself* as a bride), but rather, may *I* see you as such: "Novia que te *vea*." This construction places the desire and delight on the person who observes the wedding, as if both the bride and the onlooker are identical in their needs and pleasures.

From an early age, Oshinica rebels against many of her community's demands. Instead of marrying the wealthier but stingier doctor favored by her mother, she selects her own spouse. After her marriage, she hopes to continue studying. Yet she can only resist so long before the weight of the community's collective desire proves overwhelming with its impatient: "Are you expecting yet?" ("¿Ya estas pre-ñada?"), and especially, "A son may you have!" ("¡Hisho que te nazca!"). Ultimately, Oshinica puts aside her studies and travel plans to start a family, but eventually the keen sense of personal loss and frustration bursts out with such force that she gives up husband, children, and home to realize the artistic aspirations that both her family and society had discouraged her from exploring.

Paradoxically, as soon as Oshinica is free from her traditional role as house-wife, she gains an increased appreciation for the aesthetic and historical value of the rites, languages, and ethnicities that make up her identity. In the company of her parents and children, she cries nostalgically when she hears a touring Turkish-Sephardic group sing Ladino ballads. Now the traditional Ladino stories about Uncle Yojá begin to amuse her. These same tales bothered her as a child because they emphasized her difference from Mexicans who never heard of "ese tal Yojá" (Nissán 1996, 89). Even Middle Eastern music, an aspect of her patri-mony from which she disassociated herself as an adolescent, now inspires in her a sense of pride—but all this happens only after she seizes control of her own des-tiny (226–27). As she breaks away from her former circle of housewives, Oshinica rediscovers and affirms a heritage she was not able to appreciate during the more sheltered periods of her life. What Poniatowska observes in reference to Nissán's *Las tierras prometidas* (a love story and travelogue of a trip to Israel, which I do not examine in this article because its use of Ladino is almost nonexistent) is equally applicable to the autobiographical novels explored here: "Rosa's journey was an introspective voyage, a path as effective for self-knowledge as any psycho-analysis" (Poniatowska 1997).[26]

When Oshinica dares to present her writing in Poniatowska's workshop, the latter wonders why Oshinica's sentences are constructed backwards ("al revés") (Nissán 1996, 152). This prompts the budding author to realize, "I write like this because this is the way I've heard it at home: 'Muddled you are?' 'A tourist you are?' Ladino is like that, 'that's the way it must be,' says my mother, that's why I write like this. What a bother to try and change it" (234).[27] Actually, this unusual syntactical order, which give Nissán's novels a wonderful vitality, derives from non-Hispanic influences that affected Ladino throughout its existence (Lazar 1972, 4) and therefore sound particularly quaint to the ear of a modern Spanish speaker.

Combined with its fresh glimpse into Mexico City's Jewish communities, Nissán's use of Ladino terms and syntactical constructions extends beyond a simple folkloric element that lends a unique flare to her style. Just as Ladino, in and of itself, represents a historic intersection between Jews and Hispanics, its use in *Novia que te vea* and *Hisho que te nazca* shapes the ideological impetus of these works, anchoring them both within a traditional Jewish world and a contemporary Hispanic environment not always compatible with each other. Although the members of Oshinica's own generation communicate among themselves primarily in modern Spanish, after Oshinica's divorce her Sephardic friends are kept at arm's length through a strategic representation of Ladino. This linguistic mimicry of the elder generation allows Nissán to accentuate the differences between Oshinica's traditional circle of friends and her new social niche, composed mainly of Mexican artists and writers. Yet compared to the language used by Oshinica's mother and her mother's friends, the Ladino spoken by the Mexican-born Sephardic women of Nissán's generation appears far more diluted: "Did you know that I married all my *hishas* and now I'm a grandmother?" (1996, 248). In this sentence only one Ladino word is used, but it brings along an entire baggage of social pressures. Uncomfortable with Oshinica's new status, her old

---

26. For an analysis of Nissán's multivalenced ethnic identity, as presented in her third novel, see Schneider (2001).

27. "[A]sí lo escribo porque así lo he oído en mi casa. Digo: '¿Atavanada estás? ¿Turista eres?' Así es el ladino, 'ansina tiene que ser,' dice mi madre, por eso escribo así, qué lata y qué difícil cambiar" (234).

friends ask, "Aren't you planning to rebuild your life?" ("¿No *pensás* rehacer tu vida?"), implying that she should get married again (248–49). But now the conventional formulas have lost their power over Oshinica. Indeed, she intends to rebuild her life, but as an independent individual and writer. The visit by her Sephardic friends thus becomes another occasion to observe, from an ideological and aesthetic distance, the behaviors and customs to which she is expected to subscribe.

Over the course of these novels, Oshinica gathers and exhibits fragments of her artistic work three times. The first instance appears before her marriage when her mother finally gives her permission to assemble the knitted squares that will form the quilt for her wedding bed. The second event occurs when Elena Poniatowska informs her that the moment has arrived to order and unite the disparate scenes that will form her first novel. Finally, encompassing these two unions, Oshinica creates a new identity from the fortuitous mixture of her Sephardic Jewish roots and her talents as a Mexican writer. In order to accept and understand this complex knot of identities, Oshinica measures each component of her cultural heritage against the others as she produces her first literary work.

Linking continents and generations, Nissán's writing functions much like the Sephardic troupe that travels from Turkey to sing in Ladino for multiple ethnicities and generations now gathered together in Mexico. This becomes a cultural event enjoyed by all, from those who had immigrated to Mexico ("*abasharon* de los barcos")— whose own ancestors traveled on boats sent by the sultan of Turkey to rescue Spain's exiled Jews—to those, like Oshinica, born in Mexico but raised according to the old traditions, and, finally, their assimilated and secularized children and grandchildren. From a historical and symbolic perspective, the presentation of Sephardic culture and its language in a contemporary Latin American novel represents a cultural bridge that links and filters five hundred years of history through an ancestral heritage now transmitted, in the form of a modern novel, to the generation of Nissán's children (and her readers). Thus, although Nissán dwells much on difference, by doing so she ultimately enables individuals from different nations and generations to subtly breach the historical ruptures within the various geographic, religious, ethnic, and linguistic identities that can be encompassed by a Jewish and Ibero-American heritage.

11

The Role of Music in the Quebec Sephardic Community

JUDITH R. COHEN

The history of the Canadian Sephardic community constitutes a relatively little-known chapter of the Sephardic Diaspora. The Sephardic community of the Province of Quebec, Canada, located mostly in Montreal, occupies a unique position: it is a French, Judeo-Spanish, and Arabic-speaking Jewish group within primarily francophone and at least nominally Catholic Quebec, and, at the same time, has had to fit into a predominantly English- and Yiddish-speaking, long-established Ashkenazi community. Judeo-Spanish speakers are a small minority among Canadian Sephardim, who tend to use the term "Sephardic" in its broadest, if not very accurate sense: basically, as non-Ashkenazi. The focus here is on the Sephardim in the stricter sense, that is, descended from or culturally identified with descendants of those Jews expelled from Sepharad, the Iberian peninsula and islands, in the final decade of the fifteenth century, or who left later on as Christians, regaining their Jewish identity when they reached a place where it was safe to do so.

A Brief Historical Context

Before discussing those Sephardim identified with Judeo-Spanish culture, a brief overview of the history of general Sephardic settlement in Canada is in order. Canada's population of over 32 million, spread over a vast territory, includes about 350,000 Jews according to the last census (Statistics Canada 2006), of whom Ashkenazim constitute a majority.

Sephardic Jews in the United States emigrated there from former Ottoman lands, many in the early twentieth century, but in Canada the vast majority of Sephardic Jews arrived several decades later, and many more came from North Africa and the Near East than from the former Ottoman lands. In the Quebec Sephardic community of approximately twenty thousand, Judeo-Spanish speakers are a minority of only a few hundred families. Their numbers are similar in Toronto, where, however, they constitute the majority of the Moroccan Sephardic population. The few Ottoman region Sephardim in Canada also emigrated here, for the most part, much later than did their counterparts in the United States, and many of them lived in Israel or elsewhere before coming to Canada. The first wave of Moroccan Jewish migration to Canada took place between 1957 and 1964. Of those who came between 1966 and 1970, 40 percent had previously lived in France and 10 percent in Israel (Lasry 1982, 119). In some ways these migrations also reflected social and class differences: the tendency was for community leaders to choose France, the middle class and merchants America, and the working class Israel (Fillion 1978, 11).

As early as 1627, non-Catholics, including Huguenots as well as Jews, had been forbidden to settle in the new French colony, and until the British took full control of New France in 1763, Jews still could not legally settle in what was to become Quebec. By 1832, Canadian Jews had full rights as British subjects (American-Israeli Cooperative Enterprise 2006). The Jewish population grew slowly, and until the mid–twentieth century was largely Ashkenazi.

However, the man who appears to have been the first Jew to arrive in what would become Canada arrived much earlier, during the time Jews were not allowed in New France. Joseph de la Penha was from a Portuguese Sephardic family who had settled in Holland after the Inquisition. In 1677, de la Penha claimed Labrador (a cold, rocky part of eastern Canada) for England; when he saved the life of William III about a decade later, the latter granted him most of the territory. De la Penha's family attempted, vainly, to reclaim the land in the early twentieth century, and again as late as 1982, as Janice Arnold noted in a *Canadian Jewish News* article on December 11, 1986, entitled, "De la Penha's Labrador Claim Hits the Rocks" (see also American-Israeli Cooperative Enterprise 2006).

The young Esther Brandeau, the first Jewish woman in Canada, was from a Sephardic family in southern France; she arrived disguised as a boy in 1738 and was eventually deported back to France (American-Israeli Cooperative Enterprise 2006; Jewish Women's Archive n.d.). Another French Sephardic Jew, Abraham Gradis, founded the Society of Canada to encourage trade with France. Although he put all his family's money into a (vain) attempt to save New France from British rule, as a non-Catholic he was never permitted to set foot in the colony he had helped to finance (American-Israeli Cooperative Enterprise 2006). Several Jews arrived in Canada with the British army under General Wolfe, as well as from the Shearith Israel congregation in New York City. These early Canadian Jews were Ashkenazi but followed the Sephardic rites of London and New York (Anctil 1984, 173); others were descendants of New Christians. Some years later 10 percent of Montreal's merchants were Jewish (Rosenberg 1970, 28). In 1831, twenty years sooner than their coreligionists in England, Canadian Jews received political rights and began to play important roles in the development of the country (American-Israeli Cooperative Enterprise 2006). Some of their descendants are still active in the "Spanish and Portuguese" Synagogue, and two, Aaron Hart (eighteenth century) and Abraham de Sola (nineteenth century) had Montreal streets renamed for them (Canadian Jewish Congress 2006). In 1768, the She'arit Israel Synagogue was founded in Montreal. It followed the Sephardic rites of its namesake in New York City, established in 1654, which in turn followed the London rite (Rosenberg 1970, 42). It was Canada's first synagogue and remained its only one for seventy-five years. In 1876 it was incorporated under the name "Spanish and Portuguese She'arit Israel Congregation" and today is usually spoken of as the "Spanish and Portuguese" (or, in French, simply "La Spanish"). Today its members are from many different Jewish backgrounds and cultures. Judeo-Spanish is not used except, occasionally, for the sung blessing "Bendigamos."[1]

The Communauté Sépharade Unifiée du Québec (CSUQ) and the Moroccan synagogues use mostly French, while the main Sephardic synagogue in Toronto uses more Spanish and English. Within the Judeo-Spanish group, those in Montreal come from all the main centers of Judeo-Spanish Morocco (Tangier, Tetuan, Arzila, Larache, Alcazarquivir, Ouezzane), while most of those in Toronto were from Tangier. In both cities, there are a small number of

---

1. Esther Blaustein, untaped interview with the author, Montreal, ca. 1982.

Ottoman-area Sephardim, who tend to associate with non-Orthodox Ashkenazi groups rather than with Sephardic communities.

Sephardim in Quebec

Most Moroccan Jews speak French, including those from the former Spanish Zone of Morocco. Montreal, with its established Jewish population and French-speaking environment, was a logical choice for them. Almost immediately on arrival in Canada, Moroccan Sephardim began to set up their community structure. They formed a series of short-lived associations, struggling to define their identity and their relationship to the Ashkenazim.

The title Communauté Sépharade Unifiée du Québec (the word *unifiée* is a recent addition) may be a little misleading: Quebec is a very large province, but there are few Jews outside the Montreal region. The new "Jewish campus" is located in the area known as Côte des Neiges, a fairly quiet area near the Université de Montréal with easy access to schools, shopping, and transportation. The Sephardic component of the campus includes the CSUQ, the Grand Rabbinat Sépharade du Québec (GRSQ), and the Institut de la Culture Sépharade. The Institut runs frequent cultural and educational events, and the CSUQ, among other activities, produces *La Voix Sépharade*, a quarterly magazine mostly in French, with occasional articles in English or Spanish. The *Canadian Jewish News*, a weekly newspaper, occasionally devotes a small section to Sephardic life and culture.

The Centre Communautaire Juif (CCJ), a constituent of the CSUQ, began its existence in the originally Ashkenazi Young Men's and Young Women's Hebrew Association (YM-YWHA, often referred to among Montreal Sephardim as "le Y", "Y" pronounced as in English). The École Maimonide filled a crucial gap in the Quebec educational system, where, until recently, all government-supported schools were officially either Catholic or Protestant. As this division also broadly corresponded to a division between French- and English-language schools, many Moroccan Sephardic parents either chose a French but non-Catholic system or had to enroll their children in the Catholic system. Almost all Protestant schools, functionally more or less nondenominational, and the private Jewish schools at the time operated in English. École Maimonide, founded in 1968, uses French as the main language of instruction. English is taught as a second language, and Jewish and Sephardic traditions and values are emphasized.

While Toronto's Sephardim had to plunge into an English-speaking world, Montreal's had the advantage of being at home in the language of the province's majority. However, that did not mean there were no problems associated with becoming part of Quebec society; the difficulties they encountered in Montreal are probably unique in North America. One informant summed up the situation: "Pour les Juifs anglophones nous n'étions pas juifs, pour les Canadiens français, rigoureusement chauvins á l'époque, nous étions juifs." (Benaim-Ouaknine 1980, 361; For the English-speaking Jews we were not considered Jews; for the French Canadians, rigorously chauvinistic at the time, we were Jews). Before many years had passed, the Sephardim were well integrated into the business and professional world. They often indicated a preference for socializing with French Canadians over Ashkenazim, including mixed marriages, in which the French-Canadian partner was almost always a woman, who converted to Judaism (Lasry 1982, 120). Since that time, Sephardim and Ashkenazim in Montreal understand each other better, and marriages among them have become common.

Social Organization and Material Culture of Music

Because of the dramatic changes undergone by Sephardic society in this century, many song contexts have disappeared or have been significantly altered, in Canada as in other places.

Centre Communautaire Juif (Montreal) and affiliated performers

The Centre Communautaire Juif of the CSQ is actively involved in promoting aspects of Sephardic culture. Two main musical groups have been affiliated with it, the Chorale Kinor and Gerineldo (1981–1994). Kinor has an eclectic repertoire that includes, but is not restricted to, Sephardic songs. Gerineldo, affiliated with the CCJ but autonomous, is described below in a separate section.

The Synagogue

Judeo-Spanish speakers in both Montreal and Toronto may belong to Sephardic synagogues, or elect to join Ashkenazi congregations, or the mixed "Spanish and Portuguese." In Sephardic synagogues, the traditional music of the liturgy is used and taught to the younger generation, but, as has been the case throughout Jewish history, local melodies may also be used.

Peculiar to the Moroccan Sephardim is the *hilulá*, a Moroccan Jewish pilgrimage to the tomb of a revered rabbi, which in Canada takes a necessarily adapted form (see Voinot 1948; Elbaz 1982). The most popular one takes place in the spring, for Rabbi Shimon Bar Yohai, the legendary scholar of Mishna of the second century. In Morocco, the *hilulá* was a large community affair, with processions, singing, torches, and bonfires. In Canada, some pilgrimages to the original sites in Morocco are offered, on a rather grand scale, as organized charter trips with a package deal including air fare, pilgrimage to the tomb, and multistar accommodation. Usually, however, the celebration takes place at a synagogue or community center in Montreal or Toronto and is often used as an effective means of fund-raising for the community or for a charity.

The Home

The contexts of daily life were already changing dramatically before the large waves of emigration from what ethnomusicologist Mark Slobin has called "the Mythic Old World." This change has naturally affected the role and the practice of traditional music.

Liturgical singing in the Sephardic synagogues is strong, and it traditionally is the domain of men. Both men and women may participate in paraliturgical singing, which may be in Hebrew, in Judeo-Spanish, or in a combination of both, that is, "macaronic."

Aspects of religious and ceremonial singing do take place in the home, as explained above. However, a marked change in lifestyle, which began well before emigration and, of course, was further altered upon arrival in Canada, severely reduced the traditional contexts for many ballads and recreational songs. Among the many changes is the absence of the *matesha*, the outdoor courtyard swing, on which girls would take turns, singing as they swung back and forth: *cantares de matesha*, often ballads (*romances*) or light songs. Montreal Moroccan informants often referred to a song as *de matesha* or not *de matesha*. In fact, the association between swinging and singing was so close that a study of Montreal

Sephardim cited the following remark by an elderly woman without seeming to find an explanation necessary: "[mon mari] me faisait un balançoire, mais m'interdisait de chanter" (Berdugo-Cohen and Levy 1987, 102; [my husband] made me a swing, but he didn't allow me to sing). Jumol Edéry of Montreal provided a glimpse into adolescent life, which is rarely encountered in the literature, when she recounted how the boys took advantage of the opportunity to push a girl in the swing as she sang a ballad: "Ya lo sabían todas las muchachas, que este cantar es de mateshas, . . . tiraban la matesha para que fuera fuerte los mansebos tocaban aquí en el pecho—las muchachas a propósito lo hazían para tocar a las muchachas . . ." (laughs) (All the girls already knew, that this singing was the *mateshas*, . . . they threw the *matesha* so that it was strong the boys touched here in the bosom—the girls they did it on purpose to touch the girls . . .) (J. Cohen 1980–82, field tapes; 2007a, 135.)

Senior Citizens' Associations and Youth Clubs

Senior Citizens' clubs have become an important context for collecting, and to some extent transmitting, Judeo-Spanish songs and lore. Unlike similar clubs in Paris and Israel, though, Judeo-Spanish is usually a minority language, and French (Montreal) or English (Toronto) are commonly heard. The songs I have recorded in "groupes d'age d'or," especially in Montreal, often are heard against the sonic backdrop of rather boisterous bingo games. Tapes from these sessions include ballads, wedding songs, stories, *pasodobles*, popular Israeli songs, multilingual versions of "Happy Birthday," and a memorable, if somewhat incongruous, rendition of the popular Christmas song "Deck the Halls," intoned in a rather absent-minded and grumpy fashion by a lady intent on her bingo card. The presence of the group is conducive to eliciting songs in a relatively spontaneous way. It also affords some insight into performance practice; for example, *romances* that an informant might sing alone in a slow, almost unmeasured style might be sung by the group with a regular rhythm at accelerating tempo, as the excitement of the bingo game mounts, even with accompanying drumming on tabletops. Both styles may be heard; for example, women recognized by the group as good singers are sometimes asked to perform solos. Finally, the clubs foster song transmission: women may learn versions from each other or pass around scraps of paper with new or long-forgotten words jotted down by a faraway friend or relative. By and large, the youth clubs show little interest in working with Judeo-Spanish songs, preferring popular Israeli songs or other contemporary Jewish music.

Soirées Orientales

The soirée Orientale is a semiformal event, often put on as a gala benefit for the synagogue or community center. Live Moroccan-Andalusian or popular Middle Eastern music may be featured. The "Oriental" atmosphere is enhanced by the women's embroidered kaftans. The refreshments often echo the music and dress codes in their juxtaposition of East and West: the publicity flyer circulated for the community's 1983 gala advertised "cigares . . . [a Moroccan delicacy], egg-rolls miniatures . . . kefta [ground meat] sur roseaux . . . [and] steak-sauce Browny." The soirée Orientale is more a French and Arabic Moroccan than a Judeo-Spanish event, though a performer might include a few songs from the Eastern Judeo-Spanish lyric repertoire.

Quinzaine Sépharade and Judeo-Spanish Week

The Quinzaine Sépharade is a biennial "pan-Sephardic" event in Montreal that has existed for over twenty years. It may include theater, music, dance, lectures, discussion groups, art exhibits, and films. It hosts an international roster of artists and speakers. Specifically Judeo-Spanish content in the festival is usually limited. The 2000 Quinzaine's musical events included the Israel Andalusian Orchestra; the Moroccan-Israeli cantor Emile Zrihan, who began to appear in World Music festivals in the late 1990s; Russian Jewish immigrant musicians; and a local flamenco guitarist, as well as a musical version of Oliver Twist adapted to a Moroccan Sephardic context and concerts of Western music by several of the community's "jeunes virtuoses." Originally known as the Festival Sépharade, after several years as the Quinzaine Sépharade the event is now being reconfigured. As reported in the Canadian Jewish News (March 9, 2006), the 2006 event, in planning at the time of writing, was presented as Sépharade 2006: Méditerranéenne de Montréal, with a theme of "convivencia—convivialité," and will include aspects of Muslim and Christian culture, echoing the "three cultures" festivals that have been proliferating in Spain and elsewhere over the past several years.

The Singers: Groups and Individuals Who Perform in Public

Many of the best performers of Sephardic music in Montreal and Toronto focus on liturgical and paraliturgical singing and do not see themselves as performing musicians. Few performing artists from the Sephardic community focus specifically on Judeo-Spanish song. Synagogue choirs and *hazzanim* often include a few selections, but many performers from within the community work in non-Judeo-Spanish repertoires. The Moroccan *hazzan* Salomon Amzallag has been well-known for decades to audiences in Morocco, France, Israel, and Canada as "Samy el-Maghribi" ("Samy of the Maghreb"), performing Hebrew and Judeo-Spanish songs, Arab-Andalusian music, and his own compositions (see Benbaruk et al. 1984). Many younger Sephardim are involved in contemporary classic and popular musical forms.

Gerineldo

The ensemble Gerineldo, which focused on traditional Moroccan Judeo-Spanish repertoire based on systematic research and fieldwork of its director and members, was a noteworthy exception to the tendency of Sephardic community members to perform other repertoire rather than Judeo-Spanish songs as a specialty. The group was formed in Montreal in 1980 by its director, Oro Anahory-Librowicz, a native of Tetuan, Morocco, who had recently completed her doctorate with a dissertation on Sephardic ballads. Solly Lévy, of Tangier, Morocco, is a multitalented singer, teacher, translator, playwright, and theater director who also plays a key role in the liturgical music of his own synagogue. Kelly Sultan Amar, from Melilla and Casablanca, was already active as a much-appreciated soloist in Montreal's Sephardic choir, Kinor. I was the fourth member, the only non-Sephardic member of the ensemble. At the time I was actively working on my dissertation on Sephardic music and was delighted at this opportunity for participant observation. Virtuoso Moroccan-Israeli violinist and 'ud player Charly Edry joined the group during its later years, until it informally disbanded in 1994, initially because of the terminal illness of Amar's husband. The name Gerineldo was taken from the Sephardic version of a Carolingian ballad in which a royal page sleeps with the king's daughter; his good luck gave rise to the uniquely Moroccan Sephardic expression "el mazal de Gerineldo."

The group worked on primarily—indeed for the first years, exclusively—Moroccan Judeo-Spanish material, from members' own family and fieldwork collections, especially from Anahory-Librowicz's substantial corpus, and performed the songs very traditionally, using a couple of traditional string instruments or singing a capella or with percussion only. They also performed original theater in Moroccan Judeo-Spanish (*khaketía*), created and produced by Lévy (1992), and issued three CDs and a video. Although Gerineldo as a group is no longer active, each member continues to work with Sephardic music. Amar sings with the Kinor choir; Anahory-Librowicz has become widely recognized for her performances of Jewish, especially Sephardic, folk tales; I lecture on and perform Judeo-Spanish songs; and Lévy, now based in Toronto, has taken his ingenious one-man shows combining music and theater to appreciative audiences in Spain, Israel, Turkey, France, his native Morocco, and elsewhere.

Some Key Community Singers in Montreal

I have worked with some forty informants, the majority both in numbers and in repertoire from Montreal. Most were Moroccans, of whom I interviewed twice as many in Montreal as in Toronto; I interviewed about the same small number of ex-Ottoman-area Sephardim in both cities. The Toronto Moroccan informants are mostly from Tangiers, and in Montreal from Tangiers, Tetuan, Alcazarquivir, and Larache. Eastern informants are from Salonica, Istanbul, Izmir, Sarajevo, and Edirne. Members of Gerineldo also acted as informants for both repertoire and performance style. Some informants contributed only fragments of songs, but also valuable oral history and commentary.

Hannah Pimienta (b. ca. 1905). A native of Tangier, Hannah Pimienta trained as a seamstress and lived in Casablanca for several years before coming to Canada, where Sephardic community groups quickly recognized her knowledge of traditional repertoire. She recorded for me some two dozen *romances* in fairly complete versions, wedding and calendrical cycle songs, a few Arabic songs, and a couple of zarzuela excerpts.

Julia (Jumol) Edéry (b. ca 1905). At the Sephardic Senior Citizens Club, Mrs. Edéry picked up the small *derbukka* (goblet drum) I had brought and led the group in singing cheerfully noisy renditions of wedding songs and *romances*, playing my *derbukka* while other women drummed the tabletop. In later sessions in her one-room apartment across from the CCJ, she sang *romances* and wedding songs, accompanying herself on a small, plastic-skinned tambourine. She also recorded for me descriptions of life and customs in her native town of Larache, as well as several "miracle" stories that she related as having happened to her personally. At a community Hanukkah party Mrs. Edéry sang and danced energetically, afterwards grumbling that those "non-Spaniards" didn't know how to have fun: "Nous sommes espagnols, nous sommes vivants, nous chantons, nous dansons . . ." (We are Spanish, we are lively, we sing, we dance . . .) (J. Cohen 1980–82, field notes). Mrs. Edéry comes from a family of singers. Her father was a *paytan*, and, she added, "mi madre le ayudaba mucho. Cuando quería descansar un poco, dezía, 'Esther, me vas a ayudar, mi güeno, a cantar'" (My mother helped him a lot. When he wanted to rest a little, he would say, "Esther, please help me, my dear, with the singing") (J. Cohen 1980–82, field notes).

Mrs. Edéry identified her songs very firmly with her home town: "estos son cantares de Larache: 'Los de Tánger, de Tetuán no lo saben . . . los copiaron de nosotros'" (These are songs from Larache: those from Tangier, from Tetuan don't know them . . . they copied them from us) (see J. Cohen 2007a, 129). Her narratives ranged from her pilgrimages to the tomb of Rabbi Ben Amram to a detailed and colorful description of her own wedding. This description merits at least a partial transcription of her inimitable mixture of French, Spanish, and *khaketía*.

Announcing the wedding: "Y venían muzheres . . . para escrivir en la puerta de la calle . . . no había pinturas, habían como polvos, polvos verdes y polvos colorados y polvos rosas, y hacían tres clases de pintura . . . casamiento de tal y tal, con fulana de tal, que sea mucho más para bien." (And women would come . . . to write on the street door . . . there was no paint, rather a type of powder, green powders and red powders and pink powders, and they made three types of paintings . . . the wedding of so-and-so, with such-and-such [a girl], and wishing them all the best.)

After the *mikve*, and on the night of the henna: "Papa había traído dos troupes . . . tocando oriental . . . et las bailarinas bailando . . . este día nada más que dulces . . . de licores fechas en la casa . . . no existía 'comprar' . . . licor de uva, licor de fresa, licor de manzana . . . des amandes, marronchinos, roscitas de almendra, mazapan . . . y echaron al-henya a la novia." (Papa had brought two bands . . . playing Oriental music . . . and the women dancing . . . that day

[we ate] only sweet things . . . homemade liquors . . . you couldn't buy those
. . . grape liquor, strawberry liquor, apple liquor . . . almonds, candied almonds,
almond biscuits, marzipan . . . and they painted the bride's [hands] with henna.)

The procession to the groom's house: "Todo' los piyyutim, los paytanim
de pueblo van a venir a casa para hacer piyyutim desde mi casa hasta casa de
mi novio . . . yo estaba ya cansada . . . con mi voile . . . no había électricité . . . il
y a du moins deux cents personnes derrière moi, et tout le monde allume avec
des bougies, et todo el mundo paytineando todos, piyyutim, piyyutim hasta
casa del." (All the *piyyutim* [Hebrew hymns], the *paytanim* [singers of *piyyut*]
of the town would come to the house to sing *piyyutim*, from my house to the
groom's house . . . I was already tired . . . with my veil . . . there was no electricity
. . . there were at least two hundred people behind me, and everyone lighting
up [the way] with candles, and everyone singing *piyyutim, piyyutim*, up to the
groom's house.)

On the day the bride and groom are officially betrothed, the cow to be
slaughtered is decked in finery: "Papa compró una vaca grande . . . no podía
entrar por la puerta, empezaron a empujar . . . y la vistieron con ropas de oro,
no oro de este, oy, fantaisie, oro de dix-huit karates, bordado todo, y vistieron a
la vaca . . . ahora la saquen y todas ahora ya estan haciendo youyouyouyou . . .
y ya están cantando sobre la novia y el novio, piyyutim también . . . bueno, y a
van a quitar todo eso y el hazan ya va a matar la vaca." (Papa bought a big cow
. . . it couldn't get through the door, they started to push . . . and they dressed
it in cloth with gold, not gold that was, oy, fake, but eighteen-karat gold, all
embroidered, and they dressed the cow . . . now they lead it out and all [the
women] now are ululating . . . and now they're singing about the bride and
groom, *piyyutim* too . . . OK, now they're going to take all this away and the
cantor is going to kill the cow.)

Alegría and Rafael Benamron (b. ca. 1925). Algería and Rafael, a married
couple from Alcazarquivir, from the same extended family of generations of good
singers, both know and sing a large repertoire of *romances*, religious songs, flamenco, and popular Spanish songs, with subtle and complex ornamentation.[2]

Bouena Sarfaty Garfinkle (b. ca. 1920). Bouena Sarfaty Garfinkle (the
Ashkenazi surname was her husband's) was born and raised in Thessaloniki

2. See J. Cohen (2007a) for a fuller discussion of their repertoire and perspectives.

(Salonica). She worked with the Red Cross and eventually went to Israel before emigrating to Canada with her husband. Mrs. Garfinkle put together elaborate scrapbooks documenting life in Salonica. During our sessions she recorded over 150 songs, nearly 500 proverbs, and a collection of rhymed toasts in honor of various members of the Salonican community. Mrs. Garfinkle came from a musical family and had studied the 'ud for a while in her youth. She continually emphasized the importance of music in everyday life: "Our people, if we're happy, we sing. If we're sad, we sing . . . and we sing even in the bathroom!" Mrs. Garfinkle knew a few *romances*, and life and calendar-cycle songs, but much of her repertoire consisted of local twentieth-century compositions in Judeo-Spanish, with tunes based on foxtrots, tangos, operettas, and other popular genres. She also described musical personages such as "Bona la tanyedera" (Bona the wedding singer), who composed and sang songs for all occasions, especially weddings, and the Salonican duo León Botón and Sadik el Ciego ("Sadik i Gozós"). Mrs. Garfinkle's songs, stories, and proverbs form a vibrant and moving picture of a lost community.[3]

Nina Vučković (b. ca. 1905). Mrs. Vučković, from Bosnia, did not sing any Judeo-Spanish songs for me, but she talked about singing style and performed several Bosnian "sevdalinke." She accompanied herself on the piano, explaining that the accordion had become too heavy for her. Her life as a young woman in Sarajevo is described, albeit with errors and romanticized exaggeration, by Rebecca West in *Black Lamb and Grey Falcon*, in which she immortalizes Nina as the beautiful "*bulbul* [nightingale] of Sarajevo." She related to me her escape from the occupation and life in refugee camps and explained that on their arrival in Canada, her husband accepted a position as the (at that time only) physician on the Mohawk reserve Kahnawake near Montreal. She lived on the reserve for thirty years, including twelve years after his death. Her house was opposite "Chief Poking Fire's House," now a small museum, and was a startling but harmonious mixture of books, art and artifacts from the Balkans, and Mohawk souvenirs. The "Bulbul," about whose voice West wrote "listening to her, one might believe humanity to be in its first unspoiled morning hour" (1941, 323), died in 1987 (see J. Cohen 2007b).

---

3. See J. Cohen (forthcoming) for a fuller discussion of her repertoire.

Repertoire and Contexts

Anahory-Librowicz and I have each, working separately, recorded roughly one thousand items. Her collection focuses on Moroccans and is especially rich in *romances*, though it also includes life-cycle and other songs. My field collection includes similar material but, largely because of the Eastern Mediterranean informants (Salonica, Turkey, Sarajevo), includes more of the relatively recent genres such as lyric, satirical, and topical songs. I also recorded a number of songs in Spanish, Hebrew, French, Greek, and Bosnian, as well as oral histories, proverbs, and stories. Most, though not all, of my Eastern informants were younger than the Moroccan ones. They had left their homes at a younger age, and many had lived in Israel before coming to Canada. The Moroccan informants had spent much of their adult lives in Morocco. Several of the informants from the Eastern Mediterranean had attended school in Greek or Turkish, depending on where they had been raised. Many Moroccan and Eastern Mediterranean informants had been schooled in French. So, even before emigrating, the Eastern informants knew fewer *romances* than the Moroccans for a number of reasons. Those who had lived in Israel sometimes sang popularized versions of Judeo-Spanish lyric songs learned from prominent recording artists. "Mi generación no canta ya" (my generation no longer sings) was a poignant remark by an Izmirli grandmother, echoed by several other informants. The "flip side" of the lack of Eastern *romances* is the predominance of lyric and topical/recreational songs recorded among Eastern informants. The percentage of calendar-cycle songs in the Moroccan and Eastern repertoires is similar, while life-cycle songs were more popular in the Moroccan repertoire. Lyric songs and Zionist songs are essentially Eastern Mediterranean repertoires, which explains their quasi-absence in the Moroccan corpus.

In general, the Moroccan Sephardim sang older repertoires—*romances* and wedding songs—while the Ottoman-area Sephardim sang much more recent songs: lyric songs, topical songs, by and large the songs heard most often on recordings of Sephardic music.

Romances

Informants generally referred to *romances*, Hispanic narrative ballads, as, simply, *cantares* (songs), or sometimes *cantares antiguos* (old songs). More specific terms referred to the songs' functions. Certain *romances*, for example, are used as calendrical or life-cycle songs, while many were identified as *de cuna* (for the cradle, i.e., lullabies) or *de matesha* (for swinging) (Pimienta 1982). The Carolingian ballad *Melisenda insomne*, with its amorous opening (Melisenda, the emperor's daughter, cannot sleep for thoughts of her lover) and gory climax (she beheads her father's palace sentry with his own dagger when he wants to stop her leaving the palace late at night), seemed an unlikely candidate for a cradle song. However, isolated lines often suggest a specific function, and in this case it was the opening "todas las aves durmieran" (all the birds were sleeping): Jumol Edéry of Larache, who sang it for me in Montreal, said her son always asked for it at bedtime, as "la de las aves" (the one about the birds).

From the Eastern Mediterranean, the only *romances* I recorded in Canada were a few fragments sung by Bouena Sarfaty Garfinkle.

Calendrical Cycle Songs; Coplas

Songs for the Jewish calendar year may be the Judeo-Spanish song genre with the best chance of survival in a traditional style within the community, as many of its contexts remain more or less intact, and some conscious effort is made for transmission to the younger generations. Many of the songs in this group were recorded from male informants in both Montreal and Toronto; I also heard, but could not, because of informants' religious observances, record strong singing at events such as the family Passover *seder*. Several song texts are macaronic—a mixture of Hebrew and Judeo-Spanish.

An intriguing aspect of calendar-cycle songs is their use of *contrafactum* (usually, setting a text to a known tune), which, as noted earlier, goes back a long time. Cantors are expected to find new melodies for the Hebrew words. Interestingly enough, some Judeo-Spanish song texts associated with melodies chosen for liturgical texts may appear inappropriate, as they are not only secular, but may be decidedly bawdy. However, as in the Hasidic tradition, a melody adapted for sacred use loses its profane associations. Melodic sources from texts in Hebrew varied from *romances* to lyric songs or songs from outside the tradition altogether. The *piyyut* "Az yashir Moshe" (So sang Moses) was sung by two different male informants to the tune for the bawdy ballad "Fray Pedro." One informant felt this was inappropriate; the other, equally observant, shrugged and said tunes came from all over. The *piyyut* "Eshet ne'urim" was sung to the tune for the ballad "La Blancaniña." The Sabbath hymn "Lekha dodi" was recorded sung to several melodies: a short, bawdy ditty in *khaketía* ("Jacób y Mazaltóv"), "Scarborough Fair," and a tune identified by the singer only as "moruna—árabe." In a musical skit for a Sephardic audience, Gerineldo sang the same text to a Spanish *pasodoble* and, winning the hearts of both native and new Québecois, Solly Lévy set it to the emblematic "Gens du Pays" by Québecois songwriters Gilles Vigneault and Gaston Rochon (See J. Cohen 1990; I. Katz 1989; Seroussi and Weich-Shahak 1990–91).

Life-Cycle Songs

Wedding songs. Wedding songs are the most numerous of the life-cycle songs. They include a mixture of sacred and erotic, wistful and practical motifs: "the bride lets her hair down and the groom faints, clouds float in the sky and the groom gets wet"; "in my father's house I looked at my reflection, in my new husband's house, I look at his wallet. . . . God and his Law are the highest . . ."; "mother-in-law, you can't criticize my trousseau!"

Birth songs. "El nacimiento de Avraham," familiar to aficionados of Ladino song as "Cuando el Rey Nimrod," is the birth song par excellence. In the Moroccan tradition, there are few birth songs in Judeo-Spanish. They are somewhat more frequent in the Eastern tradition, and I recorded the well-known "O qué mueve mezes" (Oh, such nine months!) from Bouena Sarfaty Garfinkle in Montreal.

Circumcision and Bar Mitzvah songs. Most circumcision and Bar Mitzvah songs are in Hebrew rather than Judeo-Spanish. Gerineldo's repertoire included one Bar Mitzvah song, "Yo indo por un bustán" (As I passed by an orchard) where the name of the boy celebrating his Bar Mitzvah is inserted into the text.

Death and mourning. Endechas (laments) are particularly difficult to record, as the women most likely to know them were also the women most likely to observe the tradition of not singing them out of the mourning context—and not recording them in the mourning context. Out of politeness, most of them said they didn't remember any, rather than refusing outright to sing them. Most Moroccan women interviewed knew "Don Gato" (Sir Cat), a popular children's song in Spain, both as a children's song and, with a different melody, as a *qiná* (lament) sung on *Tisha Be'Av*: they say that whoever laughs while singing it on *Tisha Be'Av* will weep on Rosh Hashanah.

Lyric, Topical, and Recreational Songs

Lyric songs are largely an Eastern Mediterranean repertoire and are mostly relatively recent, often from the late nineteenth century on, sometimes by identifiable composers. The love songs are often the ones most commonly sung by popular artists and heard on commercial recordings—the ones the general public, if asked, would identify as Ladino songs or, erroneously, as "medieval." While some are also sung in Spain, others are adapted from Greek or Turkish folk songs, or newer compositions. Most of the ones I recorded are heard on commercial recordings; in some cases the informants learned them through the process of secondary orality, that is, from media recordings rather than from person-to-person transmission.

Until recently, few scholars paid much attention to the rich genre of topical and recreational songs—these may lack the *romance*'s historical exoticism, the religious/ritual song's immediacy, and the lyric song's graceful melodies and emotional appeal; nevertheless, they are a testimony to day-to-day creativity and interaction with the sociocultural environment. Full of humor, vitality and, at times, tragedy, the texts have much to reveal about twentieth-century Sephardic daily life before immigration to the "New World," while the choice of melodies borrowed from popular songs tells us about the musical climate and preferences current at the time.

Morocco. Lyric, topical, and recreational songs from the Moroccan Judeo-Spanish repertoire do not occupy the central place they do in the ex-Ottoman lands, where songs in these categories, especially lyric and love songs, have ended up forming the basis of most people's knowledge and assumptions about "Ladino music." Still, there are many songs, especially topical and recreational, in the Moroccan repertoire that deserve attention.

"Me vaya kappará" pokes fun at "current" (1930s–40s) fashions in dress and behavior, and Solly Lévy added a verse about the icy climate of Canada (see J. Cohen 1989, 183–84). The theme of being cold in Canada is echoed in several songs by Tangiers-born Jack Benlolo in Toronto. "Avramico y Davico" is set to the delightfully incongruous tune "Dominique" by Soeur Sourire, the "Singing

Nun" of the 1960s. It tells of two Moroccan Sephardi immigrants whose despair at Canada's "fríos y nevadas" (cold and snow) is somewhat mitigated by the accessibility of central heating and warm blankets. The hero of "El emigrante," based on the song of that name by Juanito Valderramas, returns to Tangiers, having braved "mucho frío" to bring back "dolares calentitos" (hot little dollars). The Spanish song "Cinta negra, pelo negro" is transformed by Mr. Benlolo into "Djellabías y tarbushes" (traditional clothing) made of "esas lanas marroquíes" (these Moroccan woolens,) which, along with spicy "hariras," are called upon to help the immigrants battle the Canadian climate, with a final despairing note: "judíos, vamonos de aquí / esto no es para un tangerouí—olé!" (Jews, let's get out of here / this is no place for someone from Tangier—ole!). Consciously or not, these references to cold weather may also reflect the differences felt by the immigrants between the emotional climates of the Mediterranean and Canada (see J. Cohen 1989, 56, lxxiii).

Other Moroccan satirical and topical songs I have recorded in Montreal, especially from the repertoire of Solly Lévy, include parodies—the tune of the popular wedding song/*romance* "Rahél lastimosa" is adjusted to fit the story of a famous Spanish bullfighter, and the devotional "Coplas de las flores" loans its graceful melody to a parody about Roosevelt and Churchill (see J. Cohen 1998).

The Eastern Mediterranean.   Salonican and Turkish Sephardim borrowed melodies from French, Latin American, Italian, Serbian, and other popular songs. Various languages might appear in the same song. Buena Sarfaty Garfinkle knew dozens of topical songs (see J. Cohen 1989). One multilingual one was sung to the melody of "La Madelón": "se fué con su musiu . . . à la plage . . . una vez cada el Shabbat . . . si . . . vos azen amotzi, dezilde en francés 'au revoir et merci'" (She went with her boyfriend [monsieur] . . . to the beach . . . once a week on Shabbat . . . if . . . they make the blessing, tell him in French "good-bye and thanks"). Abandonment of a young girl by her boyfriend, sometimes leaving her pregnant, was a common theme, and topical songs include the story of the Great Fire of Salonica, an account of life at the Alliance Israèlite Universelle schools ("A la Eskola de la Aliança"), or sly innuendos about "El vendedor de frutas" (the fruit vendor). One song was an adaptation of "Yes Sir, That's My Baby" into Judeo-Spanish and another, "La muzher que cale tomar," was sung to the tune of Maurice Chevalier's "Valentine." A composition by "Sadik i Gozós," it features a young man who sighs for a woman "de famiya," who can play violin and piano, hold her own at a "salon"—and "que tenga sex appeal . . . como flama en la cama" (who should have sex appeal . . . like a flame in bed). His friend accuses him of wanting a "kukla de vitrina" (a window mannequin).

Conclusion

The Judeo-Spanish repertoire collected in Canadian Sephardic communities corresponds in most ways to those collected elsewhere. However, the Moroccan repertoire is more important in Canada, reflecting the immigration patterns of the Sephardim in this country. As well, some compositions or adaptations of songs reflect aspects of life in their new home, Canada. It may be increasingly rare to find the older Judeo-Spanish repertoire as an active daily presence in Montreal's Sephardic community, as in others worldwide, but the Sephardic presence itself there is a flourishing, vital one. It remains to be seen whether the Sephardic revival currently gaining momentum in the "world music scene" will be echoed in Canada within the Sephardic community itself.

Works Cited   Index

Works Cited

Archives

Archive of the Casa de la Comunidad Hebrea de Cuba, Patronato, Havana.
Archives of Vaad Haeda Hasfradit, Jerusalem.
Central Archives for the History of the Jewish People, Jerusalem.
Central Zionist Archive, Jerusalem.
Oral History Archive, Avraham Harman Institute of Contemporary Jewry [ICJ], Hebrew University of Jerusalem.
Richter Library Special Collection, University of Miami, Miami.
Walter P. Zenner Archives, American Sephardi Federation, Center for Jewish History, New York.
YIVO Archives, New York.

Published Sources

Abou, Selim. 1989. "Los aportes culturales de los inmigrados: metodología y conceptualización." In *Europa, Asia y África en América Latina y el Caribe*, coordinated by Brigitta Leander, edited by Siglo XXI, 38–56. Mexico City: UNESCO, Siglo XXI.

Aguinis, Marcos. 1991. *La gesta del marrano*. Buenos Aires: Planeta.

AISA. 1960. *Actas de la Asamblea General* [Records of the General Regular Meeting] 43, November 30.

Aizenberg, Edna. 1979–82. "Sephardim and Neo-Sephardim in Latin-American Literature." *The Sephardic Scholar* 4:125–32.

———. 1992. "Las peripecias de una metáfora: el sefaradismo literario judeoargentino." *Noaj* 7–8 (December): 54–59.

———. 2002. *Books and Bombs in Buenos Aires: Borges, Gerchunoff, and Argentine Jewish Writing*. Hanover: Univ. Press of New England.

———. 2005. "Latin American Jewish Literature Began Onboard Ships." *Review* 70:48–50.

Akmir, Abdelouahed. 1997. "La inmigración árabe en Argentina" in *El Mundo árabe y América Latina*, edited by Raymundo Kabchi, 57–122. Madrid UNESCO.

Alcalay, Ammiel. 1999. *Memories of Our Future: Selected Essays 1982–1999*. San Francisco: City Lights.

Alduncin and Associates. 2000. *Estudio sociodemográfico de la comunidad judía en México. A solicitud del Comité Central de la Comunidad Judía de México*. [Sociodemographic study of the Jewish community of Mexico]. Ordered by the Central Committee of the Jewish Committee of Mexico.

Alianza Monte Sinaí. 2001. *Historia de una Alianza*. Mexico City: Alianza Monte Sinaí.

American-Israeli Cooperative Enterprise. 2006. "The Virtual Jewish History Tour: Canada." Jewish Virtual Library. http://www.jewishvirtuallibrary.org/jsource/vjw/canada toc.html. Accessed February 27, 2011.

Anctil, Pierre, ed. 1984. *Juifs et réalités juives au Québec*. Québec: Institut Québecois de Recherches sur la Culture.

Anderson, Benedict. 1991. *Imagined Communities*. London: Verso.

Angel, Marc D. 1973. "The Sephardim of the United States: An Exploratory Study." *American Jewish Year Book* 74:77–138.

———. 1982. *La America: The Sephardic Experience in the United States*. Philadelphia: Jewish Publication Society.

Arbell, Mordechai. 1998. *Comfortable Disappearance: Lessons from the Caribbean Jewish Experience*. Jerusalem: Institute of the World Jewish Congress.

———. 1999. *Spanish and Portuguese Jews in the Caribbean and the Guianas: A Bibliography*. Providence and New York: John Carter Brown Library and Interamericans.

———. 2002. *The Jewish Nation of the Caribbean: The Spanish-Portuguese Jewish Settlement in the Caribbean and the Guianas*. Jerusalem and New York: Gefen.

Armistead, Samuel G. 1978. *El romancero judeo-español en el archivo Menéndez Pidal*. Madrid: Cátedra Seminário Menéndez Pidal.

Armistead, Samuel G., and J. H. Silverman. 1982. *En torno al romancero sefardí*. Madrid: Seminario Menéndez Pidal.

Aroeste, Sarah. 2003. *A la una/In the beginning*. Aroeste Music, compact disc.

Askenazi, Isaac Dabbah. 1982. *Esperanza y realidad: raíces de la comunidad judía de Alepo en México*. Mexico City: Libros de México.

Auerbach, Samuel M. 1916. "The Levantine Jew." *Jewish Immigration Bulletin*, August and September, 10–13.

Avigur-Rotem, Gabriela. 1992. *Motsart lo haya Yehudi*. Jerusalem: Keter.

Avni, Haim. 1985. "Territorialismo, colonialismo, y sionismo." *Rumbos en el judaísmo, el sionismo e Israel* 13:57–80.

———. 1987a. "Latin America and the Jewish Refugees: Two Encounters, 1935 and 1948." In *Jewish Presence in Latin America*, edited by Judith Laikin Elkin and Gilbert W. Merks, 45–68. Boston: Allen and Unwin.

———. 1987b. "The Origins of Zionism in Latin America." In *The Jewish Presence in Latin America*, edited by Judith Laikin Elkin and Gilbert W. Merks, 135–55. Boston: Allen and Unwin.

———. 1991. *Argentina and the Jews: A History of Jewish Immigration*. Translated by Gila Brand. Tuscaloosa: Univ. of Alabama Press.

———. 1992. *Judíos en América: cinco siglos de historia*. Madrid: Editorial Mapfre.

———. 2005. "El sionismo en la Argentina: el aspecto ideológico." In *Judaica Latino-americana: estudios histórico-sociales 5*, edited by AMILAT, 145–68. Jerusalem: Magnes Press.

———. 2009. *Clients, Prostitutes, and White Slavers* [in Hebrew]. Tel Aviv: Yedioth Sfarim.

Baily, Samuel, and Eduardo José Miguez. 2003. "Introduction: Foreign Mass Migration to Latin America in the Nineteenth and Twentieth Centuries—An Overview." In *Mass Migration to Modern Latin America*, edited by Samuel Baily and Eduardo José Miguez, xiii–xxv. Wilmington, DE: Scholarly Resources.

Balbuena, Monique. 2003. "Diasporic Sephardic Identities: A Transnational Poetics of Jewish Languages." PhD diss., Univ. of California, Berkeley.

———. 2009. "*Dibaxu*: A Comparative Analysis of Clarisse Nicoïdski's and Juan Gelman's Bilingual Poetry." *Romance Studies* 27, no. 4: 296–310.

———. 2012. *Homeless Tongues: Poetry and Languages of the Sephardic Diaspora*. Palo Alto: Stanford Univ. Press.

Barnai, Jacob. 1992. "The Jews of Spain in North Africa." In *Moreshet Sepharad: The Sephardic Legacy*, vol. 2, edited by Haim Beinart, 68–71. Jerusalem: Hebrew Univ.

Baruch, Kalmi. 1930. "El judeo-español de Bosnia." *Revista de Filología Española* 17:113–54.

Beinart, Haim. 1970. "La formación del mundo sefardí." In *Actas del primer simposio de estudios sefardíes*, edited by Iacob M. Hassán, 43–48. Madrid: Instituto Arias Montano.

Bejarano, Margalit. 1978. "Sephardic Jews in Argentina" [in Hebrew]. *Bitfuzoth Hagola* 85/86:124–42.

———. 1982. "The History of the Spanish-Speaking Community of Buenos Aires (1930–1945)" [in Hebrew]. In *The Sephardi and Oriental Jewish Heritage*, edited by Issachar Ben-Ami, 161–70. Jerusalem: Magnes Press.

———. 1984. "Los Sefardíes de la Argentina." *Sefárdica* 1, no. 2:37–42.

———. 1985. "Los Sefaradíes, pioneros de la inmigración judía a Cuba." *Rumbos en el judaísmo, el sionismo e Israel* 14:107–22.

———. 1986. "Los Sefaradíes en la Argentina: particularismo étnico frente a tendencias de unificación." *Rumbos en el judaísmo, el sionismo e Israel* 17–18:143–60.

———. 1992. "The Jewish Community of Cuba 1898–1939: Communal Consolidation and Trends of Integration under the Impact of Changes in World Jewry and Cuban Society." PhD diss.[in Hebrew], Hebrew Univ., Jerusalem.

———. 1996a. *La comunidad hebrea de Cuba—la memoria y la historia*. Jerusalem: Instituto Avraham Harman de Judaísmo Contemporáneo, Universidad Hebrea de Jerusalem.

———. 1996b. "Constitutional Documents of Jewish Sephardic Organizations in Latin America." *Jewish Political Studies Review* 8, nos. 3–4 (Fall): 127–48.

———. 1997. "From Havana to Miami: The Cuban Jewish Community." In *Judaica Latinoamericana* 3, edited by AMILAT, 113–30. Jerusalem: Magnes Press.

———. 1998. "The Place of the Sephardim in the Jewish Communities of Latin America: The Cases of Havana and Buenos Aires" [in Hebrew]. *Pe'amim* 76 (Summer): 30–51.

———. 2002. "Sephardic Jews in Cuba." *Judaism* 51, no. 1 (Winter): 123–38.

———. 2005. "Sephardic Communities in Latin America—Past and Present." In *Judaica Latinoamericana: Estudios Históricos, Sociales y Literarios* 5, edited by AMILAT, 9–26. Jerusalem: Magnes Press.

Bell, Daniel. 1977. "The Return of the Sacred." *British Journal of Sociology*, no. 4:419–48.

Benaïm-Ouaknine, Esther. 1980. "Judaïcite québécoise: une intégration réussie ou une communauté désintégrée?" In *Juifs du Maroc, Identité et Dialogue*, edited by Albert Ifrah, 359–71. Grenoble: La Pensée sauvage.

Benbaruk, Salomon, Solly Levy, Dina Sabbah, and Charles Lugassy. 1984. *Samy El Maghribí*. Programme booklet. Montreal: Rabbinat Sépharade du Québec.

Benbassa, Esther. 1996. *Hayahadut Haotmanit bein Hitmaarvut Lezionut 1908–1920*. Translated by Meir Israel. Jerusalem: Shazar Center.

Benbassat, David. 1987. "Quelques exemple de l'influence de la langue turque sur le judéo-espagnol." *Vidas largas* 6:49–53.

Benchimol, Itzjak. 1999. *Contra viento y marea. Una aproximación a la obra del ʾRibbiʾZeev Grimberg*. Buenos Aires: Benchimol.

Benchimol, Samuel. 1998. *Eretz Amazônia: os judeus na Amazônia*. Manaus: Editora Valer.

ben Israel, Menasseh. 1987. *The Hope of Israel*. Edited by Henry Méchoulan and Gérard Nahon. Oxford: Littman Library, Oxford Univ. Press.

Bensignor, Isaac. 1929. "En busca de la verdad." *El Estudiante Hebreo*. August 15.

Bensión, Ariel. 1926. *Los sefaradim y el sionismo*. Buenos Aires.

Bensoussan, Albert. 1993. *L'Echelle Séfarade*. Paris: L'Harmattan.

Bentes, Abraham Ramiro. 1987. *Das ruínas de Jerusalém à verdejante Amazônia*. Rio de Janeiro: Edições Bloch.

Ben-Ur, Aviva. 2009. *Where Diasporas Met: A History of Sephardi Jews in the United States, 1654–2000*. New York: New York Univ. Press.

Benz, Stephen. 2005. "Cuban Jews in Miami." In *Jews of South Florida*, edited by Andrea Greenbaum, 66–76. Waltham, MA: Brandeis Univ. Press.

Berdugo-Cohen, Yolande, and Joseph Levy. 1987. *Juifs Marocains à Montréal*. Montreal: VLB.

Berger, Peter. 1999. "The Desecularization of the World: A Global Overview." In *The Desecularization of the World*, edited by Peter Berger, 1–18. Washington: Ethics and Public Policy Center.

Bernardini, Paolo, and Norman Fiering, eds. 2001. *The Jews and the Expansion of Europe to the West 1450–1800*. New York and Oxford: Berghahn Books.

Bettinger-Lopez, Caroline. 2000. *Cuban-Jewish Journeys: Searching for Identity, Home, and History in Miami*. Knoxville: Univ. of Tennessee Press.

Bezalel, Itzhak. 2007. "Categorizing Jewish Communities: Methods, Changes, and Characteristics" [in Hebrew]. *Pe'amim* 111–12 (Spring–Summer): 5–34.

Bichachi, Israel. 1980. "De la Presidencia." *Boletín Informativo* (September). Miami Beach: Cuban Sephardi Hebrew Congregation.

Bilsky, Edgardo, Gabriel Trajtenberg, and Ana Weinstein, eds. 1987. *Bibliografía temática sobre judaísmo argentino: el movimiento obrero judío en la Argentina (4)* [Thematic bibliography of Argentine Judaism: the Jewish labor movement in Argentina (4)]. Vol. 1. Buenos Aires: AMIA/Centro de Documentación e Información sobre Judaísmo Argentino "Mark Turkow."

Blank, Lily. 1993. "The Integration of Ashkenazi and Sephardi Jews in Venezuela Through the Decision-Making Process in the Educational System." *Jewish Political Studies Review* 5, no. 3–4 (Fall): 209–45.

Blis, David. 1936. "Memories from the Jewish Life in Cuba" [in Yiddish]. *Havaner Lebn*, March 6.

Bodian, Miriam. 1997. *Hebrews of the Portuguese Nation*. Bloomington: Indiana Univ. Press.

Bra, Gerardo. 1982. *La organización negra: la increíble historia de la Zvi Migdal*. Buenos Aires: Corregidor.

Brailovsky, Antonio Elio. 1980. *Identidad*. Buenos Aires: Sudamericana.

Brauner Rodgers, Susana. 1999. "The Jews of Aleppo in Buenos Aires, 1920–1960" [in Hebrew]. *Pe'amim* 80 (Summer): 129–42.

———. 2000. "La comunidad alepina en Buenos Aires: de la ortodoxia religiosa a la apertura y de la apertura a la ortodoxia religiosa, 1930–1953." *EIAL* 11, no. 1:45–64.

———. 2005. "Los judíos sirios en Buenos Aires: frente al sionismo y al Estado de Israel." In *Judaica Latinoamericana: Estudios Histórico-Sociales 5*, edited by AMILAT, 170–84. Jerusalem: Magnes Press.

———. 2009. *Ortodoxia religiosa y pragmatismo político: los judíos de origen sirio.* Buenos Aires: Lumiere.

Brauner, Susana, Patricio Fraga, and Cristian Shuckman. 2004. "El cooperativismo de crédito en Buenos Aires: entre la neutralidad política y la religiosa, 1950–1966." *Gecla* 1 (October): 31–36.

Brodsky, Adriana M. 2003. "The Contours of Identity: Sephardic Jews and the Construction of Jewish Communities in Argentina, 1880 to the Present." PhD diss., Duke Univ., Durham, NC.

Bunis, David M. 1981. *Sephardic Studies: A Research Bibliography.* New York: Hispanic Institute in the United States.

Carasso, Elie. 1993. "Une poétesse israélienne." *Los Muestros* 10 (April). http://www.sefarad.org/publication/lm/010/carasso.html; http://184.173.197.201/~sefarad/lm/010/carasso.html. Accessed January 16, 2012.

Casanova, J. 1996. "El revival político de lo religioso." In *Formas modernas de religión*, edited by R. Díaz Salazar, S. Ginner, and F. Velazco, 265–67. Madrid: Alianza.

Castillo, Debra. 1992. *Talking Back: Toward a Latin American Feminist Literary Criticism.* Ithaca: Cornell Univ. Press.

Cesarani, David, ed. 2006. *Port Jews: Jewish Communities in Cosmopolitan Trading Centres 1550–1950.* London and Portland, OR: Frank Cass.

Cesarani, David, and Gemma Romain, eds. 2006. *Jews and Port Cities 1590–1990.* London and Portland, OR: Vallentine Mitchell.

Círculo Cubano Hebreo. 1970. *JewBan, Anuario.* Miami: Cuban Hebrew Congregation.

Chocrón, Isaac. 1975. *Rómpase en caso de incendio.* Caracas: Monte Avila.

Chocrón, Sonia. 1990. *Toledana.* Caracas: Monte Avila.

Cohen, Haim. 1972. *Haiehudim Beartzot Hamizrach Hatichon Beyameinu* [The Jews in the Middle Eastern countries]. Tel Aviv: Hakibutz Hameuchad.

Cohen, Judith R. 1980–82. Field collection, Sephardic songs and traditions. Tapes, photographs. Montreal and Toronto.

———. 1989. "Le Rôle de la Chanson Judeo-Espagnole dans les communautés sépharades de Montréal et Toronto." PhD diss., Université de Montréal.

———. 1990. "Musical Bridges: The Contrafact Tradition in Judeo-Spanish Song." In *Cultural Marginality in the Western Mediterranean*, edited by Frederick Gerson and Anthony Percival, 121–28. Toronto: New Aurora Editions.

———. 1998. "Humour and Satire in Judeo-Spanish Song." In *Studies in Socio-Musical Sciences*, edited by Joachim Braun and Uri Sharvit, 233–44. Ramat-Gan: Bar-Ilan Univ. Press.

———. 2007a. "Je chante en bas esperando el taxi: Les Romances d'Alcazarquivir vus par les femmes qui les chantent." In *Romances de Alcácer Quibir*, edited by Kelly Basilio, 125–39. Lisbon: Univ. of Lisbon, Arts Faculty / Fundação para a Ciência e a Tecnología.

———. 2007b. "Three Canadian Sephardic Women and Their Transplanted Repertoire: From Salonica, Larache, and Sarajevo to Montreal and Kahnawá:ke." In *Folk Music, Traditional Music, Ethnomusicology: Canadian Perspectives, Past and Present*, edited by Anna Hoefnagels and Gordon Smith, 150–62. Newcastle: Cambridge Scholars Press.

———. 2011. "Selanikli Humour in Montreal: The Repertoire of Bouena Sarfatty Garfinkle." In *Judeo-Espaniol: Satirical Texts in Judeo-Spanish by and about the Jews in Thessaloniki*, edited by Rena Molho, H. Pomeroy, and E. Romero, 220–42. Thessaloniki: Ets Ahaim Foundation.

Cohen, Mario. 1980. "Los sefardíes en América Latina contemporánea." *Coloquio* 3:87–95.

Cohen, Martin A. 1971. *The Jewish Experience in Latin America*. 2 vols. New York: Ktav.

Cohen, Martin A., and Abraham Peck, eds. 1993. *Sephardim in the Americas: Studies in Culture and History*. Tuscaloosa and London: Univ. of Alabama Press.

Cohen, Robert, ed. 1982. *The Jewish Nation in Surinam: Historical Essays*. Amsterdam: S. Emmering.

Cohen, Steven. 1983. *American Modernity and Jewish Identity*. New York: Tavistock.

Cohen de Chervonagura, Elisa. 2001. "Lengua y perpetuación en una comunidad judía." In *Judaica Latinoamericana 4*, edited by AMILAT, 79–88. Jerusalem: Magnes Press.

———. 2010. *La comunidad judía de Tucumán: hombres y mujeres, historias y discursos, 1910–2010*. Tucumán: Kehilá de Tucumán, Universidad Nacional de Tucumán.

Columbus, Christopher. 1991. *The Libro de las profecías of Christopher Columbus*. Translated and edited by Delno C. West and August King. Gainesville: Univ. of Florida Press.

Congregación Sefaradí. 1995. *Rabbi Itzjak Chehebar—un visionario*. Buenos Aires: Congregación Sefaradí.

Congregation Kol Shearith Israel. 1977. *Cien años de vida judía en Panamá, 1876–1976: A Hundred Years of Jewish Life in Panama*. Panama: Congregation Kol Shearith Israel.

Cortina, Guadalupe. 2000. *Invenciones multitudinarias: escritoras judíomexicanas contem-poráneas*. Newark, DE: Juan de la Cuesta.

Costantini, Humberto. 1989. "Eli, eli, lamma sabactani." In *Panorama de la poesía judía contemporánea*, edited by Eliahu Toker, 160–62. Buenos Aires: Milá.

Criado de Val, Manuel. 1970. "Conservación del judeo-español por medio de versiones literarias." In *Actas del Primer Simposio de Estudios Sefardíes*, edited by Iacob M. Hassán, 277–79. Madrid: Instituto Arias Montano.

Cuban Sephardic Congregation. 1979. *Libro de Oro Temple Moses*. Miami Beach: Cuban Sephardic Congregation.

Dalven, Rachel. 1990. *The Jews of Ioannina*. Philadelphia: Cadmus Press.

Danon, Abraham. 1913. "Le turc dans le judéo-espagnol." *Revue Historique* 29:5–12.

Davidow, Ari. 2003. Review of *A la una*, by Sarah Aroeste. KlezmerShack. November 23. http://www.klezmershack.com/bands/aroeste/alauna/aroeste.alauna.html. Accessed January 16, 2012.

Dayán de Mizrachi, Selly, and Nadhji Arjona. 1986. *La saga de los sefarditas: del Medio Oriente a Panamá*. Panamá: Sociedad Israelita de Beneficencia Shevet Ahim.

Deleuze, Gilles, and Félix Guattari. 1986. *Kafka: Toward a Minor Literature*. Minneapolis: Univ. of Minnesota Press.

DellaPergola, Sergio. 2002. "Comments on the Socio-Demographic Study of the 'Jewish Communities in the East'" [in Hebrew]. *Pe'amim* 93 (Autumn): 149–56.

———. 2010. "World Jewish Population." *Current Jewish Population Report*, no. 2:21. http://www.jewishdatabank.org/Reports/World_Jewish_Population_2010.pdf. Accessed January 19, 2012.

DellaPergola, Sergio, and Susana Lerner. 1995. *La población judía de México: perfil demográfico, social y cultural*. Mexico and Jerusalem: Asociación Mexicana de Amigos de la Universidad Hebrea de Jerusalén.

d'Epinay, Christian Lalive. 1990. "Récit de vie, ethos et comportement: pour une exégése sociologique." In *Methodes d'Analyses de Contenu et Sociologie, Col. Sociologie*, edited by Jean Rémy et Danielle Ruquoy, 37–68. Brussels: Publications des Facultés Universitaires Saint-Louise.

de Sola Pool, David. 1913. "The Levantine Jews in the United States." *American Jewish Year Book* 56:207–20.

———. 1914. "The Immigration of Levantine Jews into the United States." *Jewish Charities* 4, no. 11:12–27.

Deutsch, Sandra McGee. 2004. "Changing the Landscape: The Study of Argentine Jewish Women and New Historical Vistas." *Jewish History* 18, no. 1:49–73.

———. 2010. *Crossing Borders, Claiming a Nation: A History of Argentine Jewish Women, 1880–1955*. Durham, NC: Duke Univ. Press.

Díaz-Mas, Paloma. 1986. *Los sefardíes: historia, lengua y cultura*. Barcelona: Riopiedras.

Diner, Hasia R. 2003. *A New Promised Land: A History of the Jews in America*. Oxford and New York: Oxford Univ. Press.

———. 2004. *The Jews of the United States*. Berkeley: Univ. of California Press.

Dines, Rabbi Efraim. 1988. "Prólogo." In *Retorno a las fuentes*, 9. Buenos Aires: Editorial Yehuda.

Elazar, Daniel J. 1989. *The Other Jews: The Sephardim Today*. New York: Basic Books.

Elazar, Daniel J., and Peter Medding. 1983. *Jewish Communities in Frontier Societies: Argentina, Australia, and South Africa*. New York: Holmes and Meier.

Elbaz, André. 1982. *Folktales of the Canadian Sephardim*. Toronto: Fitzhenry and Whiteside.

Elkin, Judith Laikin, and Ana Lya Sater. 1990. *Latin American Jewish Studies: An Annotated Guide to the Literature*. Westport, CT: Greenwood Press.

Ellingwood, Ken. 2004. "Israelis Hoping They Won't Hear the Last Word on Ancient Dialect: Ladino, derived from Spanish and spoken by Sephardic Jews, is being preserved in academia as well as song, story." *Los Angeles Times*, June 13.

Elnecavé (Sefa'tah), Nissim. 1981. *Los hijos de Ibero-Franconia: breviario del mundo sefaradí desde los orígenes hasta nuestros días*. Buenos Aires: La Luz.

Emmanuel, Isaac, and Suzanne A. Emmanuel. 1970. *History of the Jews of the Netherland Antilles*. 2 vols. Cincinnati: American Jewish Archives.

Epstein, Diana. 1993. "Aspectos generales de la inmigración judeo-marroquí, 1875–1930." In *Temas de Africa y Asia*, vol. 2, 151–70. Buenos Aires: Universidad de Buenos Aires.

———. 2008. "Instituciones y liderazgo comunitario de los judíos de origen marroquí en Buenos Aires." In *Árabes y judíos en Iberoamérica: similitudes, diferencias y tensiones*, edited by Raanan Rein, 135–58. Sevilla: Tres Culturas.

Fagen, Richard R., Richard A. Brody, and Thomas J. O'Leary. 1968. *Cubans in Exile: Disaffection and the Revolution*. Stanford, CA: Stanford Univ. Press.

Fainstein, Daniel. 1990. "Al gran pueblo argentino, Shalom: el proyecto integracionista de 'Judaica' frente al nacionalismo argentino, 1933–1943." In *Ensayos sobre Judaísmo Latinoamericano*, 59–83. Buenos Aires: Editorial Mila.

Feierstein, Ricardo. 1988. *Mestizo*. Buenos Aires: Milá.

———. 2003. "Historia y literatura de los sefardíes argentinos." In *El legado de Sefarad*, edited by Norbert Rehrmann, 59–84. Salamanca: Amarú.

Ferreira, César. 1998–99. "Una nueva versión de la infancia en México: *Novia que te vea* de Rosa Nissán." *Revista de literatura mexicana contemporánea* 4, no. 9:66–70.

Fillion, François. 1978. "La communauté sépharade de Montréal: analyse ethnohistorique des structures communautaires." MA thesis, Université Laval, Quebec.

Flanzer, Vivian. 1997. "Judeus de Rodes no Rio de Janeiro." In *Judaísmo—Memória e identidade*, edited by Helena Lewin and Diane Kuperman, 81–90. Rio de Janeiro: Universidade do Estado do Rio de Janeiro.

Florida Sephardic Congregation. 1979. *Libro de Oro*. Miami: Temple Moses.

Forma, Alberto. 1998. *"Altalena": Memorias de Israel*. Miami.

Fortuna. 1993. *La prima vez: kantes djudeos espanyoles*. Fortuna Artistic Productions, compact disc.

———. 1994. *Cantigas*. Fortuna Produções Artísticas, compact disc.

———. 1996. *Mediterrâneo*. Fortuna Produções Artísticas, compact disc.

———. 1999. *Mazal*. MCD World Music, compact disc.

———. 2001. *Cælestia*. MCD World Music, compact disc.

———. 2003. *Encontros*. MCD World Music, compact disc.

———. 2005. *Novo Mundo*. MCD World Music, compact disc.

"Fortuna." 2006. http://fortuna.uol.com.br/english/bio.htm. Accessed May 23, 2011.

Franco, José Luciano. (1942) 1988. *La reacción española contra la libertad*. Havana: Editorial de Ciencias Sociales.

Freilich, Alicia. 1991. *Colombina descubierta*. Caracas: Planeta.

Freindenson, Marilia, and Gaby Becker, eds. 2003. *Passagem para a América: Relatos da imigração judaica em São Paulo*. São Paulo: Arquivo do Estado, Imprensa Oficial.

Friedman, Menachem. 1988. *Society and Religion: The Non-Zionist Orthodox in Eretz Israel, 1918–1936* [in Hebrew]. Jerusalem: Ben Zvi Publications.

Friesel, Sigue. 1956. *Bror Chail: História do Movimento e do Kibutz Brasileiro*. Jerusalem: Departamento da Juventude e do Chalutz da Organização Sionista Mundial.

Gaon, M. D. 1965. *A Bibliography of the Judeo-Spanish (Ladino) Press*. Jerusalem: Ben Zvi Institute.

Gardner, Nathanial Eli. 2003. "'Como te ven, te tratan': The Projection of the Subaltern Character in Three Contemporary Mexican Novels." *Neophilologus* 87:63–78.

Gelman, Juan. 1969. *Traducciones III: los poemas de Sidney West (1968–1969)*. Buenos Aires: Editorial Galerna.

———. 1982. *Citas y comentarios*. Madrid: Visor.

———. 1986. *Com/posiciones*. Barcelona: Edicions del Mall.

———. 1994. *Dibaxu*. Buenos Aires: Seix Barral.

Gerchunoff, Alberto. 1910. *Los gauchos judíos*. La Plata: J. Sesé.

Gerineldo. 1989. *Ya Hasrá—que tiempos aquellos*. Original play by Solly Lévy. Produced by Claude Beaulieu. Montreal: Université du Québec à Montréal.

————. 1994a. *Cantos judeo-españoles: de Fiestas y alegrías + Me vaya kappará*. Tecnosaga, 2–compact disk set.

————. 1994b. *En medio de aquel camino*. Montreal: Gerineldo, compact disc.

Gershoni, Israel. 2006. *Pyramid for the Nation: Commemoration, Memory, and Nationalism in Twentieth-Century Egypt* [in Hebrew]. Tel Aviv: Am Oved Publishers.

Ginio, Alisa Meyuhas. 2007. Review of *Le monde sépharade*, by Shmuel Trigano, ed. [in Hebrew]. *Zmanim* 100 (Autumn): 158–60.

Giordano, Eduardo. 1986. "Conversación con Juan Gelman." *El porteño* 57:74–77.

Glickman, Nora. 2000. *The Jewish White Slave Trade and the Untold Story of Raquel Liberman*. New York: Garland.

Glickman, Nora, and Roberto DiAntonio. 1993. *Tradition and Innovation: Reflections on Latin American Jewish Writing*. Albany: SUNY Press.

Gojman de Backal, Alicia. 1983. "Los judíos en México." *WIZO* 31, no. 237 (September): 19–23.

————. 1984. *Los conversos en la Nueva España*. México: ENEP-Acatlán, UNAM.

————. 1993. *De un minyan a una comunidad, Generaciones Judías en México: La Kehila Ashkenazi, 1922–1992*. Mexico City: Kehila Nidhei Isroel.

————. 2000. *Camisas, escudos y desfiles militares: Los Dorados y el antisemitismo en México (1934–1940)*. Mexico: Fondo de Cultura Económica.

Gold, Steven, and Bruce Phillips. 1996. "Israelis in the United States." In *American Jewish Yearbook*, edited by the American Jewish Committee, 51–101. New York: American Jewish Committee.

Goldberg, Harvey, ed. 1996. *Sephardi and Middle Eastern Jewries*. Indianapolis: Indiana Univ. Press.

Goldscheider, Calvin. 1986. *Jewish Continuity and Change*. Bloomington: Indiana Univ. Press.

Goslinga, Cornelius Ch. 1971. *The Dutch in the Caribbean*. Gainesville: Univ. of Florida Press.

Grandis, Rita de, and Jan Mennell. 2003. "Making *Novia que te vea*: Interview with Guita Schyfter." In *Women Filmmakers: Refocusing*, edited by Jacqueline Levitin, Judith Plessis, and Valerie Raoul, 342–47. Vancouver: UBC Press.

Green, Henry. 1995. *Gesher Vakesher, Bridges and Bonds: The Life of Leon Kronish*. Atlanta: Scholars Press.

Green, Henry, and Marcia Kerstein Zerivitz. 1991. *Mosaic: Jewish Life in Florida*. Gainesville: Univ. Press of Florida.

Grünberg, Carlos M. 1940. *Mester de judería.* Prologue by Jorge Luis Borges. Buenos Aires: Argirópolis.

Guy, Donna J. 1991. *Sex and Danger in Buenos Aires: Prostitution, Family, and Nation in Argentina.* Lincoln: Univ. of Nebraska Press.

Halac, Ricardo. 1993. "Mil años, un día." In *Teatro III.* Buenos Aires: Corregidor.

Halevi-Wise, Yael. 1998. "Puente entre naciones: idioma e identidad sefardí en *Novia que te vea* e *Hisho que te nazca* de Rosa Nissán." *Hispania* 81, no. 2 (May): 269–77.

———. 2012. "Through the Prism of Sepharad: Modern Nationalism, Literary History, and the Impact of the Sephardic Experience." In *Sephardism: Spanish Jewish History and the Modern Literary Imagination,* edited by Yael Halevi-Wise, 1–33. Palo Alto, CA: Stanford Univ. Press.

Hamui de Halabe, Liz. 1989. *Los judíos de Alepo en México.* Mexico City: Maguén David.

———. 1997a. *Identidad colectiva: Rasgos culturales de los inmigrantes judeo alepinos en México.* Mexico City: JGH Editores.

———. 1997b. "Re-creating Community: Christians from Lebanon and Jews from Syria in Mexico, 1900–1938." In *Arabs and Jewish Immigrants in Latin America,* edited by Ignacio Klich and Jeffrey Lesser, 125–45. London and Portland: Frank Cass.

———. 1999. "Las redes de parentesco en la reconstrucción comunitaria: los judíos de Alepo en México." In *Encuentro y Alteridad: Vida y Cultura Judía en América Latina,* coordinated by Judit Bokser Liwerant and Alicia Gojman de Backal, 397–404. Mexico City: Fondo de Cultura Económica.

———. 2005. *Transformaciones en la religiosidad de los judíos en México: tradición, ortodoxia y fundamentalismo en la modernidad tardía.* Mexico City: Noriega Editors.

Harel, Yaron. 2003. *By Ships of Fire to the West: Changes in Syrian Jewry during the Period of the Ottoman Reform (1840–1880)* [in Hebrew]. Jerusalem: Zalman Shazar Center for Jewish History.

Harris, Tracy K. 1994. *Death of a Language: The History of Judeo-Spanish.* Newark: Univ. of Delaware.

Heilman, Samuel C., and Menachem Friedman. 1994. "Religious Fundamentalism and Religious Jews: The Case of the Haredim." In *Fundamentalism Observed,* edited by Martin E. Marty and R. Scott Appleby, 197–264. Chicago: Univ. of Chicago Press.

Hershfiel, Joanne. 1997. "Women's Pictures: Identity and Representation in Recent Mexican Cinema." *Canadian Journal of Film Studies / Revue canadienne d'études cinématographiques* 6, no. 1:61–77.

Hertzberg, Arthur. 1989. *The Jews in America.* New York: Simon and Schuster.

Hillel, Hagar. 1995. "Jewish-National Reform Put to the Test: The Newspaper *L'Avenir Illustrée,* Casablanca 1926–1936." In *The Jews of Casablanca: Studies of the Modernization of Jewish Leadership in a Fragmenting Colony* [in Hebrew], edited by Yaron Tsur and Hagar Hillel, 119–239. Tel Aviv: Am Oved Publishers.

———. 2004. Israel *in Cairo: A Zionist Newspaper in Egypt in the National Period, 1920–1939* [in Hebrew]. Tel Aviv: Am Oved Publishers.

Hillel, Iacov. 2006. "Fortuna." World Music Central.org. http://worldmusiccentral.org/artists/artist_page.php?id=648. Accessed July 15, 2011.

Hind, Emily. 2003. *Entrevistas con quince autoras mexicanas.* Madrid: Iberoamericana.

Horowitz, Neri. 2000. "Shas y el sionismo: análisis histórico" [in Hebrew]. *Nuevos Rumbos* 2 (April): 30–59.

Ibsen, Kristine. 1997. *The Other Mirror: Women's Narrative in Mexico, 1980–1995.* Westport, CT: Greenwood Press.

Isaacson, José. 1977. *Cuaderno Spinoza.* Buenos Aires: Marymar.

Israel, Jonathan I. 2002. *Diasporas Within a Diaspora: Jews, Crypto-Jews and the World Maritime Empires (1540–1740).* Leiden: Brill.

Jabad Lubavitch. 1997. *Veinte años: encendiendo el corazón judío.* Buenos Aires: Jabad Lubavitch.

Jewish Women's Archive. n.d. Jewish Women on the Map—Port of Quebec, 1738—Esther Brandeau. http://jwa.org/onthemap/port-of-quebec-1738. Accessed January 12, 2012.

Kabchi, Raymundo, coord. 1997. *El mundo árabe en América Latina.* Madrid: Ediciones UNESCO.

Kaplan, Yosef. 1992. "The Sephardim in North-Western Europe and the New World." In *Moreshet Sepharad: The Sephardic Legacy,* vol. 2, edited by Haim Beinart, 240–87. Jerusalem: Hebrew Univ., Magnes Press.

———. 2003. *Minozrim Chadashim Lihudim Chadashim* [From New Christians to New Jews]. Jerusalem: Zalman Shazar Center for Jewish History.

Katz, Israel J. 1989. "Contrafact and the Judeo-Spanish *Romancero:* A Musicological View." In *Hispanic Studies in Honour of Joseph A. Silverman,* edited by Joseph V. Ricapito, 169–87. Newark, DE: Juan de la Cuesta Hispanic Monographs.

Katz, Jacov. 1984. *Halakhah and Kabbalah: Studies in the History of Jewish Religion, Its Various Faces and Social Relevance* [in Hebrew]. Jerusalem: Magnes Hebrew Univ.

Katz, Samy. 1992. "De terre d'islam en terre chretienne: les juifs marocains au nouveau monde." Paper presented at the *Colloque internacional Mémoires juives d'Espagne et du Portugal,* CNRS, Paris.

Kepel, Gilles. 1995. *La revancha de Dios.* Madrid: Anaya and Mario Muchnik.

Kerpat, Kemal H. 1985. "The Ottoman Emigration to America, 1960–1914." *International Journal of Middle East Studies* 17:175–209.

Klich, Ignacio, comp. 2006. *Árabes y judíos en América Latina, historia, representaciones y desafíos*. Buenos Aires: Siglo XXI.

Klich, Ignacio, and Jeffrey Lesser. 1996. "Introduction: 'Turco' Immigrants in Latin America." *The Americas* 5, no. 1 (July): 1–14.

———, eds. 1998. *Arab and Jewish Immigrants in Latin America: Images and Realities*. London and Portland: Frank Cass.

Krause, Corinne. 1987. *Los judíos en México. Una historia con énfasis especial en el período 1857 a 1930*. Mexico City: Universidad Iberoamericana.

Kronfeld, Chana. 1996. *On the Margins of Modernism: Decentering Literary Dynamics*. Berkeley: Univ. of California Press.

Kuznets, Simon. 1960. "Economic Structure and Life of the Jews." In *The Jews, Their History, Culture, and Religion*, 3rd ed., vol. 2, edited by Louis Finkelstein, 1597–1666. New York: Harper and Brothers.

———. 1972. *Hamivne Hakalkali shel Yahadut Artzot Habrit: Megamot Baet Haacharona* [Economic structure of US Jewry: recent trends]. Jerusalem: Institute of Contemporary Jewry.

Lamandier, Esther. n.d. *Romances I and II*. Preface by Daniele Becker. Paris: Alienor.

Lasry, Jean-Claude. 1982. "Une diaspora francophone au Québec: les Juifs sépharades." *Questions de Culture* 2:113–38.

Lavender, Abraham D. 1993. "Sephardic Political Identity: Jewish and Cuban Interaction in Miami Beach." *Contemporary Jewry* 14:116–32.

Lazar, Moshe. 1972. *The Sephardic Tradition: Ladino and Spanish-Jewish Literature*. New York: Norton.

———, ed. 1999. *Sefarad in My Heart*. Lancaster, CA: Labyrinthos.

Leftel, Ruth. 1990. "Os sefaraditas egípcios de São Paulo: O renascimento de uma comunidade." In *Ensayos sobre judaísmo latinoamericano*, 45–56. Buenos Aires: Milá.

———. 1993. "A politica inmigratoria brasileira—A carácter da imigraçao dos judeus egipcios au Brasil." Paper presented at the Eleventh World Congress of Jewish Studies, Jerusalem.

Lehrman, Irving, and Joseph Rappaport. 1956. *The Jewish Community of Miami*. Miami Beach: Jewish Theological Seminary.

Lesser, Jeffrey. 1992. "From Pedlars to Proprietors: Lebanese, Syrian, and Jewish Immigrants in Brazil." In *The Lebanese and the World*, edited by Albert Hourani and Nadim Shehadi, 393–410. London: Centre for Lebanese Studies.

———. 1995. *Welcoming the Undesirables: Brazil and the Jewish Question*. Berkeley: Univ. of California Press.

Lesser, Jeffrey, and Raanan Rein. 2006. "Challenging Particularity: Jews as a Lens on Latin American Ethnicity." *Latin American and Caribbean Ethnic Studies* 1, no. 2:249–63.

———, eds. 2008. *Rethinking Jewish-Latin Americans.* Albuquerque: Univ. of New Mexico Press.

Levine, Robert. 1993. *Tropical Diaspora: The Jewish Experience in Cuba.* Gainesville: Univ. Press of Florida.

Levy, Avigdor. 1992. *The Sephardim in the Ottoman Empire.* Princeton: Darwin Press.

Lévy, Isaac Jack. 1989. *And the World Stood Silent: Sephardic Poetry of the Holocaust.* Urbana: Univ. of Illinois Press.

Lévy, Solly. 1984. "Le monde musical des Séphardim Montréalais." In *Samy El Maghribi, Programme Booklet,* edited by Solomon Benbaruk, 12–14. Montreal: Rabbinat Sépharade du Québec.

———. 1992. *Ya Hasrá, Escenas haquetiescas.* Montreal: Communauté Sépharade du Québec.

Lewin, Boleslao. 1983. *Cómo fue la inmigración judía en la Argentina.* 2nd ed. Buenos Aires: Editorial Plus Ultra.

Lewis, Mollie. 2008. "Con Men, Crooks, and Cinema Kings: Popular Culture and Jewish Identities in Buenos Aires, 1905–1930." PhD diss., Emory Univ. Atlanta.

Libermann, José. 1966. *Los judíos en la Argentina.* Buenos Aires: Editorial Libra.

Linder, Miguel Abruch. 1995. "Mexico: Old Antisemitism and New Situations." Paper presented at the 8th International Conference of Latin American Jewish Studies, Mexico.

Liwerant, Judit Bokser. 1991. "El movimiento nacional judío: el sionismo en México, 1922–1947." PhD diss., UNAM, Mexico City.

———, dir. 1992. *Imágenes de un encuentro: la presencia judía en México durante la primera mitad del siglo XX.* Mexico City: UNAM, Tribuna Israelita, Comité Central Israelita de México and Multibanco Mercantil Probursa.

Lockhart, Darrell B. 1997. "Growing Up Jewish in Mexico: Sabina Berman's *La bobe* and Rosa Nissán's *Novia que te vea.*" In *The Other Mirror: Women's Narrative in Mexico, 1980–1995,* edited by Kristine Ibsen, 159–73. Westport, CT: Greenwood Press.

Loker, Zvi. 1991. *Jews in the Caribbean: Evidence on the History of the Jews in the Caribbean Zone in Colonial Times.* Jerusalem: Misgav Yerushalayim.

Loyola, Beatriz. 2004. "Género, etnicidad y nación en la narrativa judío-mexicana de Angelina Muñiz-Huberman, Rosa Nissán y Sara Levi Calderón." PhD diss., Univ. of Colorado, Boulder.

Marcus, Simon. 1965. *The Judeo-Spanish Language.* Jerusalem: Kiryat Sepher.

Martelli, S. 1999. "Ni secularización ni resacralización, más bien desecularización. La teoría sociológica de la religión ante el cambio social." *Religiones y Sociedad* 7:153–67.

Martinez, Elizabeth Coonrod. 2004. "Rosa Nissán: Cultural Memory and the Mexican Sephardic Woman." *Mosaic: A Journal for the Interdisciplinary Study of Literature* 37, no. 1 (March): 101–17.

Matitiahu, Margalit. 1988. *Kurtijo Kemado/Hatser harukhah*. Tel Aviv: `Eked.

———. 1992. *Alegrika*. Tel Aviv: `Eked.

Matza, Diane. 1992. "Self-Perception among American Sephardim." *Melton Journal* (Autumn): 11.

———, ed. 1997. *Sephardic-American Voices: Two Hundred Years of a Literary Legacy*. Hanover: Univ. Press of New England.

Medina, Manuel. 2000. "Imagining a Space In Between: Writing the Gap Between Jewish and Mexican Identities in Rosa Nissán's Narrative." *Studies in the Literary Imagination* 33, no. 1 (Spring): 93–96.

Menachem, Nachum. 1990. "The Jews of Syria and Lebanon between Arabic Nationalism and the Zionist Movement" [in Hebrew]. PhD diss., Hebrew Univ. of Jerusalem.

Mennell, D. Jan. 2000. "Memoria, *Midrash* y Metamórfosis en *Novia que te vea* de Guita Schyfter: Un diálogo textual-visual." *Chasqui* 29, no. 1 (May): 50–63.

Milgram, Avraham, ed. 2003. *Entre la aceptación y el rechazo: América Latina y los refugiados judíos del nazismo*. Jerusalem: Yad Vashem.

Millon, A. 1989. "The Changing Size and Spatial Distribution of the Jewish Population of South Florida." MA thesis, Univ. of Miami.

Mirelman, Victor A. 1976. "The Zionist Activity in Argentina from the Balfour Declaration until 1930" [In Hebrew]. In *Pirkei Mechkar Betoldot Hazionut*, edited by Yehuda Bauer, Moshe Davis, and Israel Kolat, 188–223. Jerusalem: Hasifria Hatzionit.

———. 1982. "Early Zionist Activities Among Sephardim in Argentina." *American Jewish Archives* 34, no. 2 (November): 190–205.

———. 1987. "Sephardic Immigration prior to the Nazi Period." In *The Jewish Presence in Latin America*, edited by Judith Laikin Elkin and Gilbert W. Merks, 13–32. Boston: Allen and Unwin.

———. 1988. *En búsqueda de una identidad: los inmigrantes judíos en Buenos Aires, 1890–1930*. Buenos Aires: Editorial Milá.

———. 1990. *Jewish Buenos Aires: In Search of an Identity, 1890–1930*. Detroit: Wayne State Univ. Press.

———. 1992. "Sephardim in Latin America After Independence." *American Jewish Archives* 44, no. 1 (Spring–Summer): 235–65.

Mizrahi, Rachel. 2003. *Imigrantes Judeus do Oriente Médio em São Paulo e no Rio de Janeiro.* São Paulo: Ateliê Editorial.

Moghrabi, Alberto. 2001. *Pequenos contos de enredo indeterminado.* São Paulo: Editora e Livraria Sêfer.

Mohl, Raymond. 1990. *Searching for the Sunbelt.* Knoxville: Univ. of Tennessee Press.

Molho, Michael. 1960. *Literatura sefardita de Oriente.* Madrid/Barcelona: Instituto Arias Montano.

Monaco, C. S. 2005. *Moses Levy of Florida.* Baton Rouge: Louisiana State Univ.

Monasterio, Mónica. 1996. *A las orillas del Bir.* Solfavil, compact disc.

———. 1999. *Sefarad XXI: Cantares del avenir.* Solfavil, compact disc.

———. 2003. *Luvia.* Solfavil, compact disc.

———. 2005. *Almendrikas y piniones.* Solfavil, compact disc.

Montanaro, Pablo, and Ture. 1998. *Palabra de Gelman: en entrevistas y notas periodísticas.* Buenos Aires: Corregidor.

Moore, Deborah Dash. 1994. *To the Golden Cities: Pursuing the American Jewish Dream in Miami and L.A.* New York: Free Press.

Mörner, Magnus, and Harold Sims. 1977. *Adventurers and Proletarians: The Story of Migrants in Latin America.* UNESCO Paris: Univ. of Pittsburgh Press.

Mujaled, Emilio Mussali. 2000. *Memorias.* México: Noriega Editors.

Muñiz-Huberman, Angelina. 1989. *La lengua florida: antología sefardí.* Mexico City: UNAM.

Nes El (Arueste), Moshe. 1984. *Historia de la comunidad sefaradí de Chile.* Santiago: Editorial Nascimento.

Nicoïdski, Clarisse. 1978. *Lus ojus, las manus, la boca.* Translated by Kevin Power. Loubressac-Bretenoux, France: Braad Editions.

———. 2006. *Cara Boz i Locura.* Edited and translated by Avner Perez. Maaleh Adumim, Israel: Maaleh Adumim Institute.

Nissán, Rosa. 1992. *Novia que te vea.* Mexico City: Planeta.

———. 1996. *Hisho que te nazca.* Mexico City: Plaza y Janés Editores.

———. 2002. *Like a Bride / Like a Mother.* Translated by Dick Gerdes. Albuquerque: Univ. of New Mexico Press.

Nizri, Vicky. 2000. *Vida propia.* Mexico City: Miguel Angel Porrúa.

Papo, Joseph M. 1987. *Sephardim in Twentieth Century America: In Search of Unity.* San Jose and Berkeley, CA: Pele Yoetz Books and Judah L. Magnes Museum.

———. 1993. "Sephardim in North America in the Twentieth Century." In *Sephardim in the Americas: Studies in Culture and History,* edited by Martin A. Cohen and Abraham J. Peck, 274–76. Tuscaloosa and London: Univ. of Alabama Press.

Perera, Victor. 1995. *The Cross and the Pear Tree: A Sephardic Journey.* New York: Knopf.

Pérez, Lisandro. 1990. "The 1990s: Cuban Miami at the Crossroads." *Cuban Studies* 20:3–9.

Petriella, Angel. 1984. *Fusión y cambio organizacional en el cooperativismo de crédito.* Rosario: Idelcoop.

Pimienta, Gladys. 1982. "Las Kantes de Matesha." *Aki Yerushalayim* 4, no. 13:30–32.

Poniatowska, Elena.1997. "*Las tierras prometidas* de Rosa Nissán." *La Jornada* (30 March): 21–22.

Portes, Alejandro, and Robert L. Bach. 1985. *Latin Journey: Cuban and Mexican Immigrants in the United States.* Berkeley and Los Angeles: Univ. of California Press.

Portes, Alejandro, and Alex Stepick. 1993. *City on the Edge: The Transformation of Miami.* Berkeley, Los Angeles, and London: Univ. of California Press.

Porzecanski, Teresa. 1994. *Perfumes de Cartago.* Montevideo: Trílice.

Pulido, Angel. 1904. *Españoles sin patria y la raza sefardí.* Madrid: Estab. Tip. de E. Teodoro.

Rattner, Henrique. 1977. *Tradição e Mudança: A Comunidade Judaica em São Paulo.* São Paulo: Editora Atica.

Rein, Raanan, coord. 2008. *Árabes y judíos en Iberoamerica.* Sevilla: Fundación Tres Culturas.

———. 2009. "Un pacto de olvido: peronismo y las divisiones dentro de la colectividad judeoargentina." *Investigaciones y ensayos* 58: 429–68.

República de Cuba, Secretaría de Hacienda, Sección de Estadísticas. 1903–30. *Inmigración y movimiento de pasajeros.* Havana: República de Cuba, Secretaría de Hacienda, Sección de Estadisticas.

Ricupero, Rubens. 1997. Preface to *Imigrantes Judeus, Escritores Brasileiros*, by Regina Igel, xvii. São Paulo: Perspectiva.

Rieff, David. 1993. *The Exile: Cuba in the Heart of Miami.* New York: Touchstone.

Robinson, George. 2000a. "Holiday Music for Hanukah." KlezmerShack. December 6, 2010. http://www.klezmershack.com/articles/robinson/001206.hanuka.html.

———. 2000b. "Sephardic Survey." KlezmerShack. May 20. http://www.klezmershack.com/articles/robinson/0005.sounds.html.

Rodgers, Susana. 2005. *Los judíos de Alepo en Argentina.* Buenos Aires: Ediciones Nuevos Tiempos.

Roffé, Reina. 1987. *La rompiente.* Buenos Aires: Puntosur.

Romero, Elena. 1992. "Literary Creation in the Sephardi Diaspora." In *Moreshet Sepharad: The Sephardic Legacy*, vol. 2, edited by Haim Beinhart, 438–60. Jerusalem: Hebrew Univ., Magnes Press.

Rosenberg, Stuart E. 1970. *The Jewish Community in Canada.* Vol. 1, *A History.* Toronto/ Montreal: McLelland and Stewart.

Rot, Dina. 1970. *Cancionero tradicional sefaradí.* AYUI, compact disc.

———. 1999. *Una manu tumó l'otra.* Acqua Records, 2004, compact disc.

Rubel, Iaacov, ed. 1992. *Presencia sefaradí en Argentina.* Buenos Aires: Centro Sefaradí para Latinoamérica.

Sable, Martin H. 1978. *Latin American Jewry: A Research Guide.* Cincinnati: Hebrew Union College Press.

Salzman, Daniela Gleiser. 2000. *México frente a la inmigración de refugiados judíos: 1934–1940.* México: CONACULTA, INAH, Eduardo Cohen's Cultural Foundation.

Santa Puche, Salvador. 1999. *Antolojia de poetas sefaradis kontemporaneos.* Valencia, Spain: Edisiones Capitelum.

Sarna, Jonathan D. 2004. *American Judaism: A History.* New Haven, CT: Yale Univ. Press.

Schallman, Lázaro. 1971. "History of the Jewish Press in Argentina" [in Hebrew]. *Gesher* 68–69 (December): 200–12.

Schenkolewski-Kroll, Silvia. 1991. "The Influence of the Zionist Movement on the Organization of the Argentinean Jewish Community: The Case of the DAIA 1933–1946." *Studies in Zionism* 12, no. 1:17–28.

———. 1993. "La conquista de las comunidades: el movimiento sionista y la comunidad ashkenazí de Buenos Aires (1935–1949)." In *Judaica Latinoamericana: Estudios Histórico-Sociales,* vol. 2, edited by AMILAT 191–201. Jerusalem: Editorial Universitaria Magnes, Universidad Hebrea.

———. 1996a. *The Zionist Movement and the Zionist Parties in Argentina, 1935–1948* [in Hebrew]. Jerusalem: Magnes Press.

———. 1996b. "Zionist Political Parties in Argentina from the Revolution of 1943 to the Establishment of the State of Israel." In *The Jewish Diaspora in Latin America: New Studies on History and Literature,* edited by David Sheinin and Lois Baer Barr, 239–49. New York: Garland.

Schers, David. 1992. "Inmigrantes y política: los primeros pasos del Partido Sionista Socialista Poalei Sión en la Argentina, 1910–1916." *EIAL* 3, no. 2:75–88.

Schneider, Judith Morganroth. 1999. "Inscripciones de la otredad judeofemenina en las novelas de Alicia Steimberg y Rosa Nissán." In *Encuentro y alteridad: vida y cultura judía en América Latina,* edited by Judit Bokser Liwerant and Alicia Gojman de Backal, 582–92. Mexico City: Fondo de Cultura Económica.

———. 2001. "Rosa Nissán's Representation of Diasporic Consciousness: Reflections on Genealogy, Geography, and Gender in *Las tierras prometidas.*" *Modern Jewish Studies* 12, no. 4:65–83.

Schorsch, Jonathan. 2007. "Disappearing Origins: Sephardic Autobiography Today." *Prooftexts* 27, no. 1:82–150.

Scliar, Moacyr. 1987. *The Strange Nation of Rafael Mendes.* Translated by Eloah F. Giacomelli. New York: Harmony.

Scliar, Moacyr, and Márcio Souza. 2000. *Entre Moisés e Macunaíma: os judeus que descobriram o Brasil.* Rio de Janeiro: Garamond.

Scliar-Cabral, Leonor. 1990. *Romances e canções Sefarditas.* São Paulo: Massao Ohno Editor.

———. 1994. *Memórias de Sefarad.* Florianopolis: Livros de Athanor.

Scott, Renée. 1995. "*Novia que te vea y Sagrada memoria:* Dos infancias judías en Latinoamérica." *Revista Interamericana de Bibliografía* 45, no. 4:605–12.

———. 1998. "La experiencia sefardí en Latinoamérica: Tres novelas de Teresa Porzecanski y Rosa Nissán." *Sefarad* 58, no. 2:387–99.

Sefamí, Jacobo. 2002. "Memoria e identidad en la literatura sefardí y mizrahi en Latinoamérica." *Sefarad* 62:143–67.

———. 2004. *Los dolientes.* Mexico City: Plaza y Janés.

Segal, Ariel. 1999. *Jews of the Amazon: Self-Exile in Earthly Paradise.* Philadelphia: Jewish Publication Society.

Seligson, Silvia. 1973. "Los judíos en México: un estudio preliminar." BA diss., National Institute of Anthropology and History, Mexico City.

Senkman, Leonardo. 1983. "Gerchunoff y la legitimación hispánica." In *La identidad judía en la literatura argentina,* 39–57. Buenos Aires: Pardes.

Sephiha, Haim Vidal. 1977. "Clarisse Nicoïdski, la dernière poétesse judéo-espagnole." *Homenaje a Mathilde Pomès: estudio sobre la literatura del siglo XX,* 26:293–301. Madrid: Revista de la Universidad Complutense.

———. 1986. *Le Judéo-espagnol.* Paris: Entente.

———. 1997. "Le Judéo-espagnol de Sarajevo: Clarisse Nicoïdski, née Abinun, conteuse et poétesse judéo-espagnole." In *The Proceedings of the Tenth British Conference on Judeo-Spanish Studies,* edited by Annette Benaim, 53–64. London: Queen Mary and Westfield College, Univ. of London, Dept. of Hispanic Studies.

Seroussi, Edwin, and Susana Weich-Shahak. 1990–91. "Judeo-Spanish Contrafacts and Musical Adaptations, The Oral Tradition." *Orbis Musicae* 10:164–94.

Serruya, Abraham. 1989. Preface to *El Enigma de la Juventud,* by Aharón Barth, 1. Buenos Aires: Centro de Estudios de Torá Sucath David.

Setton, Shaul David. (1928) 1981. *Diber Shaul* (Responsa). Reproduction of the 1st edition. Jerusalem: Majon Haktav.

Shaw, Stanford J. 1991. *The Jews of the Ottoman Empire and the Turkish Republic.* New York: New York Univ. Press.

Sheskin, Ira M. 1982. *Population Study of the Greater Miami Jewish Community.* Prepared for Greater Miami Jewish Federation, Miami.

———. 1985. "The Migration of Jews to Sunbelt Cities." Paper presented at the Sunbelt Conference, Miami.

———, ed. 1989. "Thesis Completed on Changing Geographic Distribution on Jews in South Florida." In *Florida Jewish Demography* 3, no. 1 (December 1).

———. 2005a. "Ten Percent of American Jews." In *Jews of South Florida,* edited by Andrea Greenbaum. Waltham, MA: Brandeis Univ. Press.

———. 2005b. *The 2004 Greater Miami Jewish Community Study.* Miami: Greater Miami Jewish Federation.

———. 2006. *The 2005 South Palm Beach County Jewish Community Study.* Palm Beach, FL: South Palm Beach Federation.

Shokeid, Moshe. 1988. *Children of Circumstances: Israeli Emigrants in New York.* Ithaca, NY: Cornell Univ. Press.

Sidicaro, Luis. 1970. "La comunidad sefardí de habla española en Buenos Aires." In *Comunidades judías en Latino América.* Buenos Aires: Comité Judío Americano.

Sieskel, Dov. 1991. "A Zionist Newspaper in Arabic in Argentina" [in Hebrew]. *Kesher* 10:80–85.

Sklare, Marshall. 1971. *America's Jews.* New York: Random House.

Sofer, Eugene. 1982. *From Pale to Pampa: A Social History of the Jews of Buenos Aires.* New York: Holmes and Meier.

Statistics Canada. 2006. http://www.statcan.ca/english/Pgdb/demo02.htm. Accessed March 15, 2011.

Stavans, Ilan. 1999. "On Separate Ground." In *Passion, Memory, and Identity: Twentieth-Century Latin American Jewish Women Writers,* edited by Marjorie Agosín, 1–16. Albuquerque: Univ. of New Mexico Press.

———. 2002. Introduction to *Like a Bride / Like a Mother,* by Rosa Nissán, xi–xv. Translated by Dick Gerdes. Albuquerque: Univ. of New Mexico Press.

———, ed. 2005. *The Schocken Book of Modern Sephardic Literature.* New York: Schocken.

Stein, Sara Abrevaya. 2003. *Making Jews Modern.* Bloomington: Indiana Univ. Press.

Stillman, Norman A. 1991. *The Jews of Arab Lands in Modern Times.* Philadelphia and New York: Jewish Publication Society of America.

Stillman, Yedida, and Norman Stillman. 1999. *From Iberia to the Diaspora: Studies in Sephardic History and Culture.* Leiden, Boston, Cologne: Brill.

Sutton, Bella Attie, Sofia Betech Tawil, Gloria Carreño, and David Placencia Bogarían. 2005. *Estudio histórico demográfico de la migración judía a México 1900–1950.* México: Tribuna Israelita, Comunidad Ashkenazí de México, Centro de Documentación e Investigación de la Comunidad Ashkenazí, Maguén David y Archivo General de la Nación. DVD.

Sutton, Joseph A. D. 1979. *Aleppo in Flatbush.* Brooklyn, NY: Thayer-Jacoby.

———. 1988. *Aleppo Chronicles: The Story of the Unique Sepharadeem.* Brooklyn, NY: Thayer-Jacoby.

Suzy, and Margalit Matitiahu. 2005. *Aromas y memorias.* Primary Music, 2 compact discs.

Swetschinski, Daniel M. 2000. *Reluctant Cosmopolitans: The Portuguese Jews of Seventeenth-Century Amsterdam.* London and Portland, OR: Littman.

Teubal, Nissim. 1953. *El Inmigrante: De Alepo a Buenos Aires.* Buenos Aires: N. Teubal.

Trigano, Schmuel. 2004. "Forgotten Exodus." Speech at B'nai Sephardim Shaare Shalom of Hollywood, California.

———, ed. 2006. *Le monde sépharade.* 3 vols. Paris: Editions du Seuil.

Trochon, Yvette. 2006. *Las rutas de Eros: La trata de blancas en el Atlántico Sur. Argentina, Brasil, y Uruguay (1880–1932).* Montevideo: Editorial Santillan.

Tsur, Yaron. 2001. *A Torn Community: The Jews of Morocco, 1943–1954* [in Hebrew]. Tel Aviv: Am Oved Publishers.

Valdés, María Elena de. 1998. *The Shattered Mirror: Representations of Women in Mexican Literature.* Austin: Univ. of Texas Press.

Vilar, Juan Bautista. 1972. "Emigrantes judíos del norte de Marruecos a Hispanoamérica durante el siglo XX." *Maguen* 21 (February): 21.

Vincent, Isabel. 2005. *Bodies and Souls: The Tragic Plight of Three Jewish Women Forced into Prostitution in the Americas.* New York: William Morrow.

Voinot, Louis. 1948. *Pélérinages Judéo-Musulmans du Maroc.* Paris: Larose.

Wallace, A. 1956. "Revitalization Movements." *American Anthropologist* 58, no. 2:264–81.

Wartenberg, Hannah Schiller. 1994. "Cuban Jewish Women in Miami: A Triple Identity." In *Ethnic Women: A Multiple Status,* edited by Vasilieki Demos and Marcia Texler Segal, 186–99. Dix Hills, NY: General Hall.

Weisbrot, Robert. 1979. *The Jews of Argentina: From the Inquisition to Perón.* Philadelphia: Jewish Publication Society of America.

West, Rebecca. 1941. *Black Lamb and Grey Falcon.* New York: Viking.

Wiznitzer, Arnold. 1960. *Jews in Colonial Brazil.* New York: Columbia Univ. Press.

Zack de Govesensky, Bertha. 1993. *Religión: un legado de vida judía.* Vol. 4 of *Generaciones Judías en México: La Kehilá Ashkenazí (1922–1992),* edited by Alicia Gojman de Backal. México: Ashkenazi Community of Mexico.

Zadka, Pnina, Ira M. Sheskin, and Henry A. Green. 1989. "A Comparative Profile of Jewish Elderly in South Florida and Israel." In *Papers in Jewish Demography*, edited by U. O. Schmeltz and S. DellaPergola, 154–64. Jerusalem: Hebrew Univ.

Zadoff, Efraim. 2005. "La red de entidades financieras judías y su dirigencia en la vida comunitaria judía argentina en el Siglo XX." In *Judaica Latinoamericana: Estudios Histórico-Sociales 5*, edited by AMILAT, 129–44. Jerusalem: Magnes Press.

Zárate, Guadalupe. 1986. *México y la diáspora judía*. Mexico City: National Institute of Anthropology and History.

Zemer, Moshe. 1994. "Ambivalence in Proselytism." In *Conversion to Judaism in Jewish Law: Essays and Responsa*, edited by Walter Jacob and Moshe Zemer, 88–91. Tel Aviv and Pittsburgh: Freehof Institute of Progressive Halakha.

Zenner, Walter. 1987. "Middleman Minorities in the Syrian Mosaic." *Sociological Perspectives* 30, no. 4:400–21.

———. 2000. *A Global Community: The Jews from Aleppo, Syria*. Detroit: Wayne State Univ. Press.

Zimmels, H. J. 1976. *Ashkenazim and Sephardim*. Hoboken, NJ: Ktav.

Zohar, Zvi. 1993a. "Militant Conservatism—On the Socio-Religious Policy of Rabbis in Aleppo in Modern Times" [in Hebrew]. *Pe'amim* 55:57–78.

———. 1993b. *Tradition and Change* [in Hebrew]. Jerusalem: Ben Tzvi Institute.

———. 1996. "Sephardic Rabbinic Responses to Modernity: Some Central Characteristics." In *Jews Among Muslims: Communities in the Pre-Modern Colonial Middle East*, edited by Shlomo Deshen and Walter P. Zenner, 64–80. New York: Macmillan.

Index